Born and educated in England, Lieutenant-Colonel G.B. Courtney was commissioned in the Queen's Own Royal West Kent Regiment in October 1935. From 1946 to 1955 he was attached to the Foreign Service, during which time he travelled throughout the Middle East and East Africa. He is the youngest brother of Roger Courtney, who created and commanded Nos 1 and 2 Special Boat Sections between 1940 and 1944, and he himself served in the unit from April 1942 until the end of the war in the Far East. He now lives in Victoria, Australia.

G. B. COURTNEY MBE, MC

SBS in World War Two

The story of the original
Special Boat Section of the
Army Commandos

PANTHER
Granada Publishing

Panther Books
Granada Publishing Ltd
8 Grafton Street, London W1X 3LA

Published by Panther Books 1985

First published in Great Britain by
Robert Hale Limited 1983

ISBN 0 –586–06433–8

Printed and bound in Great Britain by
Anchor Brendon Ltd, Tiptree, Essex

Set in Times

Every man thinks meanly of himself for not having been a soldier, or not having been to sea.

Samuel Johnson

Contents

AUSTRALIA AND THE FAR EAST

Photographs

Foreword
by Admiral Jerauld Wright DSM
USN (Ret)

The Special Boat Section of Combined Operations was well placed under the overall command of Admiral Lord Mountbatten, a leader truly dedicated to the operations of all services, land, sea and air of all allied nations.

They were a specialized group of highly trained men recruited mostly from the British Army, but who operated independently of nation or service. Their activities took them to the most dangerous areas of the war, hostile landing beaches and into enemy territory beyond. They were generally brought to their objective areas by submarine carrying their flimsy 'folbots' later passed up through hatches and launched from deck, or by fast surface craft.

Once launched they were completely 'on their own', free of any support and dependent for success and for their lives on their flimsy boats, on their superb training, on their physical stamina, and above all on their courage and wits.

Their basic mission was to bring maximum damage to enemy forces with a minimum of expenditure of men and stores. In detail, their activities consisted of reconnaissance of landing beaches and offshore approaches, sabotage of enemy land and sea communications, transport of secret agents, and enemy deception. Their beach reconnaissances resulted in valuable information on approaches, gradients, runnels, wire, submerged obstacles and sand texture. Their intelligence formed the basis for plans of the amphibious landings of assault troops.

Inland from assault beaches their demolition of rail, communications, bridges and ammunition dumps paid big dividends of assistance to assaulting troops.

Their return involved finding their hidden 'folbots', launching them through the surf and locating the 'mother' submarine lurking in the darkness beyond. But frequently they were required to 'hole up under enemy noses' and await the advance of friendly troops.

Their activities were not limited to operations against the Germans and Italians of the European Theatre but extended beyond against Axis forces in the Middle East. Further east their skills were in high demand by Allied forces operating against the Japanese in Burma and Malaya, and beyond in the East Indies.

No job was beyond their willingness to undertake, regardless of location or of the risk of execution if captured and accused of spying.

Such were the men who comprised the Special Boat Section of Combined Operations. Any military commander, American or British, who benefited from their information will testify that their contribution to Allied success was out of all proportion to their meagre numbers and is well deserving of the recognition given to them in the following pages.

An unusual feature of these accounts is that most of the information therein comes directly, frequently in their own words, from the men who carried out the actual operations.

JERAULD WRIGHT, Ad, DSM, USN (Ret)
Commander-in-Chief, US Atlantic Fleet and
NATO Supreme Allied Commander, Atlantic 1954–60

Author's Preface

In early 1980 I began my research into the story of the Special Boat Section of the Army Commandos for personal reasons, but conscious that a book on this arcane subject would mainly be of interest to the student of military history and to those of my generation who had been involved in amphibious warfare in World War II. There had been a brief flare of publicity in Britain and America in late 1942 after the North African landings, but nothing more had been heard of the unit in the intervening forty years. Its continued existence in peacetime under the mantle of the Royal Marines was virtually unknown to the British public.

Then came the Falklands emergency, and the initials SBS began to appear in news bulletins with those of the well-known SAS (Special Air Service), both working in pre-invasion intelligence roles and frequently together. According to the July/August 1982 issue of *Globe and Laurel* (the journal of the Royal Marines), parties of SBS and SAS were landed in April on South Georgia to find out the location and strength of the Argentine forces on the island. Appalling weather, with scouring winds and glacier ice, which punctured the skins of the Gemini assault boats, foiled the first attempts of the SBS teams to land. They were withdrawn by helicopter and reinserted the next day, 24 April 1982, arriving in time for the Argentine surrender two days later.

Then from 1 May SBS and SAS reconnaissance patrols were inserted into the main islands of the Falklands group to carry out pre-invasion intelligence missions. According to Brian Hanrahan and Robert Fox of the BBC, they were told to keep away from the islanders and to stay up in the hills. Some of them remained up there for a month, living in that bleak countryside with no cover and having to remain completely out of sight. They gradually fed back information on their radio sets about the location and strength of the enemy units – information that was of great value to the Task Force Commander when planning his operation against San Carlos. The *Sunday Telegraph* of 17 October 1982 wrote that 'Even seasoned military observers were surprised by the SBS – exceptionally hard men and wild in appearance with long hair and motley uniform' – hardly surprising after a month on wintry hillsides with the sheep.

The invasion fleet entered San Carlos Water, later known as Bomb Alley, on 21 May to land No. 40 Marine Commando and a recce troop of the Blues and Royals at San Carlos Settlement itself. Simultaneously, SBS had the job of taking out an Argentine company already in position on Fanning Head covering the northern entrance. A fierce fight ensued, the enemy were driven off, and Forward Observation Officers from No. 148 Commando Battery Royal Artillery were installed in their place to direct and control naval gunfire in support of the landings at the San Carlos bridgehead.

Thereafter it appears that SBS were employed on aggressive patrolling in West Falkland as well as on the main island.

The Ministry of Defence has maintained strict silence about the techniques employed by the SBS during the Falklands campaign, which is entirely justified in view of the continuing tension in the area. The government of the United States of America did give some material and intelligence support to the British government during the conflict. In October 1982 I was given an opportunity to express our gratitude for this support, provided by them at the cost of much South American goodwill, to a very senior body of Americans at a Washington luncheon. There was a growl of approval round the table.

The modern SBS, the Special Boat Squadron Royal Marines, must certainly operate with techniques far in advance of the bow-and-arrow methods of their prede- cessors in World War II. Nevertheless they, as well as the general public, may now read the story of how it all began forty years ago with interest, some benefit, and even amusement.

I must make it quite clear that I am relating the ex- periences of officers and men of the Special Boat Sections of the Army Commandos, who were the pioneers among small boat men in World War II. The story begins in July 1940 and ends in October 1945. We were in no way connected with the Special Boat Squadron of the SAS formed in September 1942, nor with the Special Boat Squadron of the Royal Marines, established after the war, which is the lineal descendant of the wartime Royal Marine Boom Patrol Detachment (RMBPD).

I have written this story for three reasons: as a memorial to my eldest brother, Roger Courtney, its founder and inspiration; as a record of the exploits of the officers and men who served in it from 1941 to 1945; and as a reason- ably comprehensive history of a small but unique com- mando unit – of benefit, I hope, to future students of Special Operations.

Forty years after the event would seem to be a little late in the day for such a task but nobody else seems earlier to have been able to devote the necessary time to the amount of research involved, the magnitude of which became apparent as I went along. It has taken eighteen months of intensive correspondence and study of many books published since World War II to gather and compile enough factual material. This has not been made easier by the distance between Melbourne, where I live, and the United Kingdom, the source of most of the information.

Until SBS came under the control of the Small Operations Group in Ceylon in mid 1944, we were widely scattered on loan to various organizations in penny packets, and few operational records were maintained in SBS Headquarters itself. It was therefore difficult to know where to start, but a search in the Public Record Office in Kew and in the Royal Marine Museum in Eastney Barracks yielded a certain amount of basic information. This, combined with a short list of addresses kindly provided by Henry Brown of the Commando Association, and some help from the Royal Navy Submarine Museum at Gosport, gave sufficient leads for research and expansion.

I was determined to avoid fiction, or padding with imagined dialogue, and have used source material as near to the original as possible, or at least not more than one step removed from it. It soon became obvious that enough interesting material would not be forthcoming from official records, my own recollections or piecemeal from postwar books. Luckily, as the work progressed, the response from ex-officers and NCOs of SBS became so prolific that most of it has been done for me, and my role has finally become that of compiler of their articles and anecdotes in continuous narrative rather than the creator of my own version of events.

This book is therefore a co-operative effort, and credit has been given whenever possible in the text to individuals who have contributed. However, complete accuracy on all points cannot be guaranteed as our memories of events of forty years ago have dimmed in proportion to the hardening of our arteries and growing girth. The nominal roles shown in the Appendices have been compiled from piecemeal references in post-war books and from recollections of individuals. They are not from official records, and some names, regiments and decorations will have been omitted through ignorance – for which I can only apologize. However, when opinions are expressed, they are my own and I take responsibility for them.

Melbourne
January 1983

Acknowledgements

Grateful acknowledgement is made for permission to quote from or make use of copyright material in the following chapters (page numbers cited are those of the works used):

Commandos and Rangers of World War II by James Ladd, published by Jane's Publishing Company Limited, London, New York and Sydney, pages 58–61; in Chapter 1.

The Filibusters by John Lodwick, published by Methuen & Co. Ltd, 1947, pages 10, 14, 24–32; in Chapters 1 and 3.

Now It Can Be Told by James Gleeson, published by Paul Elek Ltd, 1951, pages 43–51; in Chapter 3.

Love and War in the Apennines by Eric Newby, published by Hodder & Stoughton Ltd, 1971; in Chapter 3.

The Green Beret by Hilary St George Saunders, published by Michael Joseph Ltd, 1949, Chapter IX; in Chapter 4.

The Ship with Two Captains by Terence Robertson, published by Evans Brothers, 1957, Chapter IV; in Chapter 4.

The Sea Our Shield by W.R. Fell, published by Cassell Ltd, 1966, pages 213, 224; in Chapter 13.

The World Within by Tom Harrisson, published by Cresset Press, 1959, pages 276–8; in Chapter 13.

Above Us the Waves by C.E.T. Warren and James Benson, published by George Harrap & Co. Ltd, 1953; in Chapter 8.

The Secret Invaders by Bill Strutton and Michael Pearson, published by Hodder and Stoughton Ltd, 1958; in Chapter 11.

SRD Official History Part II (Operations), Australian Archives, Canberra; in Chapter 13.

The author would also like to thank Eric Lunn and Alex McClair for their assistance in the final stages of preparation of this book, I.D. Crane for the Index, and the following for supplying pictures; Geoffrey Wood for providing the photographs of Sergeant Sandy Tough, Corporals Bill Merryweather and Sid Longhurst, and himself, in Ceylon and Burma, 1945; Sir Sam Falle for his picture of the ruined villa at Messelmoun, 1982; and the Imperial War Museum for their photo of a 'folbot' being stowed aboard a wartime S Class submarine.

Introduction

To the best of my knowledge no official history has ever been written of the Special Boat Section (SBS) of the Special Service Brigade of Combined Operations. Isolated descriptions of the work of some of its members have appeared in official and private publications in Great Britain since World War II, but only as an adjunct to the story of other, similar organizations or a part of a global war history. Proper credit has never been given to the founder of this particular unit, who was the pioneer of clandestine landings by canoe from submarines. His SBS was the precursor of several specialist canoeist 'private armies' which developed during the war.

SBS was founded by my eldest brother, Roger, in July 1940. He was an adventurous character twelve years my senior who had been a professional hunter and gold prospector in East Africa between the World Wars. He had finished up as a sergeant in the Palestine Police. In between he had paddled down the Nile with a sack of potatoes and an elephant spear, which was all that he owned at the time.

From this experience he realized that a small canoe could be ideal for carrying out secret landings on enemy coasts in wartime. After the fall of France he demonstrated his belief to Admiral Sir Roger Keyes, then chief of the newly formed Combined Operations Command. The demonstration took the form of a challenge by Brother Roger that he would be able to board the commando ship *Glengyle* unnoticed by night and depart again, leaving incontrovertible proof of his visit. The Navy pooh-poohed the idea but nevertheless kept strict watch. They woke up next morning to find several crosses chalked along the hull to simulate limpet mines, and three Oerlikon covers and two breech-blocks missing. Meanwhile, to prove his point, a dripping Roger in bathing-trunks had burst in without ceremony upon a high-level naval conference at the local hotel, at which the Captain of the *Glengyle* was present, and thrown down her after-pom-pom cover.

The Admiral, though impressed, was a careful man and ordered another test against the nearest submarine depot-ship. This time Roger and his companion succeeded again in approaching unobserved and in chalking crosses around the hull. They should have been content with that. Swarming up a tempting rope ladder, they were greeted at the top by the Master-at-Arms and two Marines with fixed bayonets who had been lying in wait, presumably forewarned by the previous victim.

Roger was promptly told to go and form the first special boat section of twelve men, known initially as the Folboat Troop, and train them on the Isle of Arran in western Scotland. He took them to Egypt in February 1941 and operated with the First Submarine Flotilla based at Alexandria in the Eastern Mediterranean. A year later he was ordered to form No. 2 SBS in Britain as part of No. 1 Special Service Brigade under Brigadier R.A. ('Bob') Laycock at Ardrossan-Saltcoats on the Ayrshire coast.

About that time I had finished a tour of duty in the (then) Gold Coast Regiment of the Royal West African Frontier Force and had been sent home unfit for infantry service. The rocky hills of pre-war Palestine and a tendency to be overweight had contributed to fallen arches. Route marches in West Africa had finished them

off. I was rescued from military oblivion in the Holding
Battalion of my British Regiment, the Queen's Own
Royal West Kent, by my brother. He reckoned that I
could fight the war on my bottom in a canoe irrespective
of the state of my feet. To him I shall ever be grateful.

He was a wild man and should have been an
Elizabethan freebooter. He was a tremendous leader of
men, with magnetism and cheerful courage, and
ambitious only for his SBS and for its reputation. He lived
hard and died early at the age of forty-seven, following his
philosophy of high living and low thinking (his own
words). He was no respecter of authority and suffered
much frustration from his superiors in rank. Mind you, his
outlook is illustrated by the motto composed at his request
by a classical don at Oxford University for his beloved
SBS:

'Excreta Tauri Astutos Frustrantur' ('Bullshit Baffles
Brains'), so perhaps his superiors suffered also.

The Sufi sage Omar Khayyám puts Roger's philosophy
in Stanza 54 of the *Rubáiyát*:

> Waste not your Hour, not in the vain pursuit
> Of This and That endeavour and dispute;
> Better be jocund with the fruitful Grape
> Than sadden after none, or bitter, fruit.

After four years of independent operation, SBS was
absorbed by the Royal Marines. Roger was conveniently
exiled as District Commissioner in a one-camel town
called Gardo in ex-Italian Somaliland. Gladly back in
Africa again, he never returned to England but transferred later to the Desert Locust Control.

He died in Hargeisa in British Somaliland on 14
February 1949, supported to the end by his indomitable
wife, Dorrise. His grave is in a dry watercourse (*wadi*)

outside Hargeisa under a thornbush, at his head a
Portuguese cannonball, which they had found together on
the beach at Malindi and kept as a good-luck charm.
Under the cannonball is one of those tin funnels used for
filling kerosene lamps. Every year, on the anniversary of
his death, the young men of the Locust Control would
hold a picnic on his grave, and sometimes raise the
cannonball to pour down a tot of gin for 'Old Roger'.
Some twenty-five years later I was visited in Dubai in the
Persian Gulf by a British officer who had served in
Hargeisa, and he told me the same story. By that time
nobody could remember who 'Old Roger' was but the
tradition had been handed down and still continued.

Roger was that sort of man.

The Mediterranean

1
No. 1 SBS in the Mediterranean, 1941

In February 1941 the Folboat Section sailed for Egypt from Arran in Scotland in the Landing Ship Infantry (Large) HMS *Glenroy* via the Cape of Good Hope. They were part of Layforce, composed of 7, 8 and 11 Commandos, under the command of Lieutenant-Colonel R.E. (Bob) Laycock (Royal Horse Guards), who was later to become Chief of Combined Operations. The Section consisted of Captain R.J.A. Courtney (King's Royal Rifle Corps), Lieutenant R. Wilson (Royal Artillery), Sergeant George Barnes (Grenadier Guards), Sergeant Allan (Royal Marines), Corporals J.B. Sherwood (Royal Army Service Corps), G.C. Bremner and J. White, and Marines W.G. Hughes and Miles.

After a period of training and acclimatization on the Bitter Lakes in Egypt, they were attached to the 1st Submarine Flotilla in HMS *Medway* in Alexandria harbour. This removed them effectively from Army control, and from the empire-building ambitions of some staff officers at GHQ, but only for the best part of twelve months. The party was renamed 'No. 1 Special Boat Section.'

During training on the Great Bitter Lake at Kabrit, Roger Courtney was introduced to Lieutenant-Commander Nigel Clogstoun-Willmott, Royal Navy, by Laycock and by Captain S. Raw, commanding the 1st Submarine Flotilla. Willmott was a trained navigator and was a member of a team planning a full-scale invasion of the island of Rhodes. He had been present at the raid on Narvik in Norway in 1940 and was becoming obsessed with the dangers of trying to land large numbers of troops on the hostile shores of Rhodes with plans based on inadequate charts and aerial reconnaissance alone.

The assault force was to consist of the three Layforce Commandos, a British division and a division from the Anzac Corps. Now Willmott had heard a fair amount about Gallipoli in his youth from his uncle, Captain H.O. Clogstoun (Royal Engineers), who founded one of the first field companies of the Royal Australian Engineers in 1911. He accompanied them through Gallipoli and France in World War I and was badly wounded. Willmott was determined that history should not be allowed to repeat itself. There can be little doubt that Uncle 'Cloggy's' reminiscences triggered his dedication to the crusade for thorough beach reconnaissances twenty-five years later. This crusade was to culminate in preparations for the most tremendous sea invasion in history, on the beaches of Normandy in June 1944.

Roger Courtney and Nigel Willmott formed an instant liking for each other which was to endure through four years of close co-operation and thereafter until Roger's death in 1949. Together they planned the first-ever beach reconnaissance by canoe from submarine and spent the next two weeks in intensive training and assembly of stores in HMS *Medway*. This is graphically described by James A. Ladd in his interesting book *Commandos and Rangers of World War II* (1978).

'The Army Captain taught the Commander the knack of hoisting himself aboard a canoe over the stern, and how to vault astride one steadied by a paddler already aboard. He learned then and in later practice how to jump into a bobbing canoe, letting his feet give under him without capsizing the frail Folboat. He became adept at launching himself over the canoe's side; first leaning back with legs outstretched athwart the cockpit, a quick flip of the body brought him face down towards the water before lowering himself into it. Although this may sound a simple piece of gymnastics it was no parlour trick at night with a sea running and the canoe's stability always in doubt.

'The first action using any new technique is usually one of the most interesting, for the simple principles can be seen without any complications of secondary purposes or complicated gear, and this is true of the first beach reconnaissance at Rhodes. The army captain and the naval navigator practised swimming ashore at night, taking turns to act the part of a sentry while the other stalked around the acting guard until this could be done without the swimmer being detected. A stone hurled at a raised arm splashing casually in the approach, or the noise of stones crunched underfoot, was sufficient reminder of more deadly missiles that would come the way of a careless visitor on an enemy beach. In these practice runs the characters of the two canoeists contrasted; Nigel Clogstoun-Willmott, tall, good-looking, and in his early thirties, meticulous over details with the mathematical approach of a navigator in facing the problems; Roger Courtney, as we have seen in training off Arran, a heavily built man, something of the adventurer with a flair for improvisation in a tight corner. For all their mutual confidence in each other and their shared patience – although one suspects from the records that the navigator had more of this essential quality than the adventurer – each brought his own special talents to this technique of beach reconnaissance. Nigel Clogstoun-Willmott has described it as an art "needing the patience of an animal", and undoubtedly there would be times when physical strength and endurance were the key to survival, for survive they must to make any contribution from their efforts. For men on beach reconnaissance had further to go than the saboteur or the raider bent on more disruptions; the reconnaissance report had to reach the main force.'

In March 1941 Courtney and Willmott sailed with Corporal J.B. Sherwood in HMS/M *Triumph* for the beaches of Rhodes on Operation Cordite. Returning to James Ladd's book:

'In March 1941, the drill was very simple, but in later years all manner of complexities were necessary. Nevertheless, landing in heavily greased jerseys and long-john underwear, with a revolver in a supposedly waterproof packet and carrying the waterproofed torch and compass, was difficult enough after several days in the confined quarters of submarine HMS *Triumph*, while she made a periscope survey of Rhodes' beaches, often having to dive below sixty feet, because in those clear waters a submarine at shallower depth is plainly seen from the air.

'On reconnaissance nights the submarine had to use precious hours of moonless darkness while she charged her batteries before trimming down in the water with her saddle tanks just awash, the slight swell breaking occasionally over the casing. Ratings now steadied the canoe as it was put over the side, lying on the hydroplanes. They took a soaking, no doubt relieved in an attitude of "rather you than me, mate" as they watched the canoeists jump and sit in one motion the way they had practised boarding. Already aboard were a tommy-gun, grenades, a thermos of coffee laced with brandy – they would need this – and the infra-red signalling gear. This RG equipment sent a beam of invisible infra-red light from an Aldis-type lamp, the signal being visible only when the beam was on a little black box-camera-sized receiver with a screen, which when the beam was intercepted, showed a green spot against the speckle of green pin-pricks of infra-red light from the stars.

'Once cast off from the submarine they began the steady rhythm of paddling which took them along their course with a mile and a half to the beach, their sweat-raising stroke giving 3 knots – equal to a steady marching pace. A hundred yards from the beach Nigel Clogstoun-Willmott followed the drill and went over the side. The sharp cold, after his warm exertions, took his breath away for a moment as he hung on the stern of the canoe, but as soon as he had recovered his breath the Commander struck out for the shore in a strong breaststroke that did not disturb the phosphorescence more than he could help, and barely ruffled the water. As his feet touched the bottom he was thinking of the tanks the Allies had intended to land on the rocky promontory before him; clearly this was not possible, for now in the starlight he could see its rock face was impassable.

'He swam back into the bay and along the coast for some hundred yards before swimming in again. The sand felt firm here under his feet and he dog-paddled while checking the depth before easing on shore to lie with his chin on pebbles at the water's edge, hearing the talk of sentries, and just able to make out two figures behind a wall beyond the beach. In the surge of each wave he slithered forward until, for a moment, he felt the sentries' eyes turned towards him; he froze clenching his teeth to stop them chattering. Several minutes rock still and the sentries no doubt mistook him for part of the shore over which the seas were gently breaking. The Italians moved off, and the Commander crossed the beach to a road. Making four landings in this way at different points along the shore, Nigel Clogstoun-Willmott discovered a number of things. There was a false beach fifteen yards from the shore, the water on the shore side deep enough to drown a tank. In the grounds of the hotel used as an Axis headquarters, he heard a sentry yawn but found no guns. Shingle samples were stuffed under the navigator's jersey. From these scientists could calculate whether a metal road was needed across the beach or if tanks could pass over it without help from engineers, and what size of wheeled vehicles could pass over the pebble bank. Next time he came on one of these recces he would bring a bag for these trophies, but the chinagraph pencil had worked well in noting on his slate the depths of water and the position of the false beach.

'Checking his watch he saw it was time to swim back to the canoe and his rendezvous with Roger Courtney, who had been paddling off-shore for the last few hours, keeping the canoe head or stern towards the beach so that it was less likely to be seen. The stimulus of the Commander's benzedrine tablets was wearing off as he swam out to sea after three hours' creeping and sliding around the beach, and now, his senses dulled by a chilling exhaustion, he felt the first pangs of doubt; would Roger Courtney see the flickering torch among the waves before an enemy patrol boat caught sight of it? He summoned all his willpower, forcing numbed fingers in his upstretched arm to flash again the morse "R". Out of the darkness came Roger Courtney with firm, fast paddle strokes bringing the canoe alongside the Commander. The Commander had been waiting with disciplined patience some 400 yards out. Every time he lifted the cap of his luminous watch the hand seemed to have barely moved, but now he hauled Nigel Clogstoun-Willmott into the canoe and passed him the flask of coffee.

'The swig merely pricked the swimmer's gums – beach

reconnaissance teams usually spoke of the "swimmer" as the man who went ashore and the "paddler" as the man who stayed with the canoe. A gulp from the coffee thermos, however, brought the first faint warmth to his bones as they paddled into a thickening mist. This cleared and the submarine picked up their infra-red signals, taking them back aboard before continuing her patrol.

'They made landings on each of the following two nights, the last, when Roger Courtney was the swimmer, being a near disaster. Gripped with cramp at the water's edge he could not move, and the furious barking of a dog drew Nigel Clogstoun-Willmott towards the shore, his tommy-gun cocked. The swimmer's great frame was contorted in agony, yet he struggled out to the canoe and with a supreme effort of will got aboard in a tortuous heave.

'As they returned from these reconnaissances with a good deal of useful information, authority was pleased. However, the invasion of Rhodes was cancelled when German troops came into the fighting in Greece.'

Nigel Clogstoun-Willmott went back to his planning duties, but most of his time was spent training young RNVR officers to find the right beaches at night in rough weather, when acting as landing-craft pilots. This was followed by a spell with the Long Range Desert Group as navigator, then in training navigators of the 22nd Armoured Brigade to take astro-sights – the army skills being necessary to find one's way in the desert as on the sea. Despite the success of Cordite in demonstrating that physical beach reconnaissance was essential before assault landings, barely sporadic interest seemed to be taken in the principle by planners.

It was a further twelve months before he was called upon at short notice to train beach-reconnaissance teams for Operation Torch – the Anglo-American invasion of

North Africa. For his work on Rhodes he was awarded the DSO (Distinguished Service Order).

Roger Courtney went back to the Special Boat Section and sabotage raids from submarines on targets on the coasts of the eastern Mediterranean. He was awarded the MC (Military Cross).

In February 1941 General Wavell had defeated the Italians in the Western Desert. Then on 30 March the arrival of Rommel and the Afrika Corps altered the whole position for the worse, and the picture of the war in the Mediterranean became very gloomy for the Allies. Rommel drove ahead against our weak advance guards at Mersa Brega and Benghazi, German forces invaded Greece and Yugoslavia, and the pick of Wavell's army was sent to Greece in a vain attempt to dislodge them.

At this time Laycock was ordered to mount a raid with his commandos on Bardia, with the object of harassing Rommel's line of communication and inflicting as much damage as possible. On the night of 21/22 April 1941, No. 7 Commando in HMS *Glengyle*, escorted by an anti-aircraft cruiser, HMS *Coventry*, and by three Australian destroyers, HMS *Stuart*, *Voyager* and *Waterhen*, raided the port.

Roger Courtney and Company Sergeant Major George Barnes, with Sherwood to help, were ordered to place a navigation light on an islet in the harbour as a guide for the landing-craft. However, their carrying submarine, again HMS/M *Triumph*, was late at the rendezvous after being bombed by British aircraft *en route*. The weather had deteriorated and the heavy swell smashed their canoe under the foreplanes during the launching. In effect, the whole raid was a fiasco, with landing-craft going to the wrong beaches and inexperienced troops hesitating when they should have pressed on. Many lessons were learned and the almost complete absence of enemy ashore in Bardia made the lessons comparatively inexpensive. However, as a consequence, the Germans did then withdraw the greater part of an armoured brigade from Sollum, on the border of Libya and Egypt, to guard their rear. So something was accomplished.

Among the Commandos, whose ranks he had contrived to join by some mysterious means, was the seventy-one-year-old Admiral Sir Walter Cowan KCB, DSO, MVO. He was admired as much for his command of language as for his bravery and was later captured in Tobruk attacking a tank single-handed with his revolver. It is said that he was handed back to the British with a polite note. Two years later he was observed scaling crags on the Dalmatian coast with No. 2 Commando.

During the rest of 1941 a series of special operations from submarines was carried out by members of 1 Special Boat Section.

On 7 June 1941 Roger Courtney and CSM Barnes landed from HMS/M *Taku* at Mersa Brega on the Gulf of Sirte to attack a fort and signal station. *Taku* was patrolling that part of the enemy-occupied coast in the hope of intercepting any south-bound convoy or of inflicting damage and disruption, at the discretion of the submarine's captain. The SBS team were carried as an extra weapon in *Taku*'s armoury to tackle any worthwhile and accessible targets ashore.

In 1943 Roger Courtney wrote an account of their adventures:

'There was plenty to interest us along this bit of coast. The RAF had recently reported furious activity on the part of enemy transport columns, and we spent most of the daylight hours with our eyes glued to the periscope.

We were only a couple of miles off shore, and the high-powered periscope brought objects on the land to within a few hundred yards of us as it were. It was an eerie sensation which I as yet have never got used to. Observing one's enemy from beneath the waves, so close does he seem that one imagines it must be impossible to remain unobserved. Until one realizes that all which is visible of our submarine from the land is two or three feet of slender rod, and a pin feather of spray as it slides through the water. Peering and turning for half a minute at a time, then swiftly withdrawing beneath the surface, to reappear after a similar cautious interval. A submarine's periscope, when seen on the surface, has an inexpressibly sinister and impersonal look as it cuts smoothly through the waves. But it would take the sharpest of sharp eyes on shore to spot such an object moving along two miles out to sea.

'It was obvious that no one was aware of our presence. The village and harbour of Mersa Brega lay shimmering and cooking under a blazing summer sun. It almost hurt the eye to look out through the periscope onto this airy, sunlit world, then to turn away from the eyepieces to the old familiar scenes of our dark little world below. The dim electric lights shining on the bodies of shipmates who lay or squatted in the various corners of our steel prison. Or the phosphorescent glow of the compass card reflected from the face of the peering steersman.

'"Port Four" comes the low voiced order, the wheel is "twiddled" over a few spokes, and the periscope above us cuts a wide arc through the water as it edges closer in towards the shore.

'Again, it is my turn to look through the periscope. This is damned interesting. The Italian troops are going to have a bathe. An enforced one, it would appear, for they are being marched down to the beach in the charge of NCOs,

who are ranging round like sheepdogs herding a lot of
depressed and apprehensive sheep. The results of our
observations are discussed over the wardroom table with
the captain. There is a signal station on shore with a
multitude of telegraph lines running from it. It looks easy
to sabotage. There is also a small fort on the top of the
hill, which appears to be unguarded. Fifty pounds of
guncotton stuffed through an embrasure could do it a lot
of no good is the general opinion. In spite of the fact that
it is a period of full moon, plans are laid for that very
night. On either side of Mersa Brega the coast appears to
be unwatched. The weather is calm, and in any case both
Barnes and I are browned off with our stuffy prison of the
last twelve days and are dying for a run around if it is only
for fresh air.

'Accordingly that night, of 7 June 1941, the submarine
surfaced in the bright moonlight about three miles
offshore. We set off in our little boat, Barnes and I, with
our tommy-guns and knives, and about fifty pounds of
explosive apiece. This was made up into pack loads which
had the fuses and detonators inserted all ready for action.

'We landed in the white sand-dune country to the west
of the village. It was nearly as light as day, and therefore
concealment was impossible in such bare country. So we
decided to bluff it out and march up towards the fort,
which was our first objective, in the hope that if any
person did spot us from a distance, they would take us for
"locals", arguing to themselves, no doubt, that no enemy
would have the cheek to wander about in such a brazen
fashion. Well, it worked . . . this which was the simplest
form of bluff possible, and we reached the fort in safety. I
have reason to believe from later evidence that we were
spotted and had not passed unremarked as I had hoped.
When we arrived at the fort, we found that we had made a

fruitless journey, for although the fort looked quite sound from the front, it had at some time been blown to smithereens. Whether by accident or design I have never yet found out. Our next objective was the signal station, which was situated just outside the village. This we decided to approach by re-embarking in the boat and pulling round the point to the edge of the harbour. We hoped the shadow of the low bluffs and our own scouting ability would get us through. If only we had stuck to the brazen bluff method instead of the cunning scout one on such a night, we might indeed have reached our objective. To the unseen watchers, however, our methods of approach were obviously suspicious. We had hardly landed on the point when we saw dark, armed shadowy figures creeping down through the rocks above us. It was a time for quick thinking. Those menacing figures were barely one hundred yards away, and I could see the hesitant movement as several rifles came up to the shoulder. They were still uncertain whether we were friend or foe. There was just time to get the bows of our boat turned out to sea again, before the first shot rang out and a bullet spat viciously into the sand at our feet.

'Thank goodness I have a retentive memory for seemingly unimportant things. I had been reading a book in the submarine's wardroom, which was about the Italian salvage ship *Artiglio*. It gave some of the agonized expressions of the crew in Italian when things were going wrong. It was this memory for trivialities which came to my aid now, and probably saved our lives.

'My voice rose in passionate protest until ending in a squeak, "*Basta . . . basta.*" This caused a sudden silence among the threatening figures above; they were obviously asking themselves whether they had nearly made a ghastly mistake. We were a hundred yards or so out to sea again before they awoke to the fact that they had been fooled.

Then came a perfect fusillade of shots, which continued until we were well out of range. How they managed to miss us I don't know, because I could have sworn that I felt the wind of those bullets fanning my neck. And so we did get away with it and we were lucky.

'After this misadventure we were two hours too early for the rendezvous, and hung about miserably waiting for the sound of Italian E-boats. Our friendly submarine arrived at the right place to pick us up, and on time. The Captain felt strongly that nobody should be allowed to get away with being beastly to his Pongos (soldiers), sailed close inshore and put a four-inch shell into the headquarters of the Italian patrol.'

After the fall of Crete Sergeant J.B. Sherwood and Corporal G.C. Bremner helped to evacuate many British soldiers in HMS/M *Torbay* in August 1941. During this trip TORBAY sank two large caiques full of German soldiers and torpedoed a U-Boat. Bremner was awarded the MM and recommended for a commission in the field, but after being commissioned he was sent to join the reinforcements at El Alamein and never returned to SBS. A similar evacuation was carried out by HMS/M *Triumph* with Corporal Durand and Private Edsall.

In September 1941 SBS acquired another role to add to its repertoire. This was the insertion and evacuation of secret agents and stores behind the enemy's lines. Roger Courtney sailed in HMS/M *Osiris* to pick up secret agents from a beach near Scutari in Albania. Close inspection through the periscope revealed that the operation had been compromised and the agents probably captured. Agents were also landed in Greece by Sergeant Barnes and Corporal Bremner from HMS/M *Triumph* later in 1941. The operation was abandoned.

Also in September 1941, Lieutenant J.B. Sherwood MM and Corporal I. Booth DCM had the job of landing eight Cretans in their home island from HMS/M *Thunderbolt*. This operation fully illustrated the difficulties encountered when persons with one interpretation of military discipline were responsible for those with quite another. Sherwood and Booth ferried a man each ashore in their canoes, instructing them to wait on the beach until the party was complete. By the third journey, however, all those previously ferried had disappeared, with Sherwood getting the blame for this from the new arrivals.

The Commandos of Layforce were thrown into the battle for Crete in a desperate effort to stem the German invasion, and by the late summer of 1941 the Force had virtually ceased to exist. It was disbanded but Colonel R.E. Laycock and fifty-three men remained as a raiding force attached to the 8th Army. He and his small force, which included Lieutenant-Colonel Geoffrey Keyes, son of Admiral Sir Roger Keyes, were given the job of eliminating General Rommel.

By that time Rommel had established a personal psychological ascendancy over his enemies. He was thought to be at a headquarters inland at Beda Littoria in Cyrenaica. The force embarked in HMS/MS *Torbay* and *Talisman* and arrived off the coast on the night of 13 November 1941. A week earlier a reception and guidance party led by Captain J.E. Haselden, an Arabic speaker, had been taken to within walking distance of the chosen landing beach by a patrol of the Long Range Desert Group from Siwa Oasis. During the evening of 14 November Lieutenant Ingles and Corporal Severn of the Special Boat Section paddled in from *Torbay* and made contact with Captain Haselden on the beach as a prelude to guiding in the assault parties. The weather was swiftly becoming worse, and the canoe and several rubber dingh were swamped, with the result that only thirty-six of the fifty-four all ranks were landed.

Ill luck continued: Keyes was killed in the attack on the headquarters building, and most of the force were captured by the Germans. Laycock and a Sergeant Terry succeeded in reaching the British lines on foot after an epic journey for thirty-six days through the desert.

John Lodwick, in his book *The Filibusters* (1947), tells the following story from the viewpoint of the two officers and two corporals of the SBS involved in the operation – Lieutenants Ingles and Langton and Corporals Severn and C. Feeberry DCM; I have summarized his version below:

'Four days later the submarines returned to the same beach for the pre-arranged pick-up. The agreed signal from the beach was seen and an attempt was made by Ingles and Severn to land. Their canoe was washed overboard while being launched. Meanwhile a report had been received from the beach, presumably by radio, that 22 survivors of the Keyes party were present. They had no idea what had happened to the others, and the rubber dinghies in which they had landed had disappeared. No further boats being available they were advised to swim off to the submarines at daybreak. This they declined to do, as some of them could not swim at all.

'Dawn was near, so the submarine submerged, departed, and returned on the following night. This time, no signal from the beach was seen. Langton and Feeberry went in to reconnoitre in their canoe. They found the beach deserted. Some distance away there was a light, of the correct colour as pre-arranged but not giving the correct signals. They returned to the canoe and paddled just outside the breakers towards the position of the light.

The glow of a cigarette could be seen beside it and this could only mean the enemy. Langton and Feeberry paddled out to their submarine through the rough sea and arrived in a sinking condition. Next day, through the periscope, they observed groups of German soldiers on the beach. They returned to Alexandria, unaware of the fate of the party ashore until Colonel Laycock turned up unexpectedly overland on Christmas Day.'

The irony of the whole business was that Rommel was in Italy on leave at the time. He never used the building at Beda Littoria as his headquarters in any case.

2

Major 'Tug' Wilson, DSO and Bar (Royal Artillery)

'Tug' Wilson, slim, slight of build, and no more than medium height, with fair hair, a neat military moustache, and gentle, expressive blue eyes, was the complete opposite of the commando of fiction, usually portrayed by post-war journalist-authors as rip-roaring, bloodthirsty thugs ever ready to slit a throat. He has been described as a 'splendidly offensive-spirited little cove'. He was Roger Courtney's second-in-command after the arrival of No. 1 SBS in Egypt in February 1941. He became a specialist in refined railway sabotage, and carried out six operations in canoes from submarines against Italian railways during 1941, of which four were very successful; the remaining two were foiled by patrols and sentries at the target. In addition, he twice landed secret agents in North Africa and twice penetrated enemy harbours in search of shipping to sink. During the second of these he was taken prisoner, and he spent the rest of the war escaping from prison-camps in Italy. The Germans got tired of this and locked him up securely in the Fatherland until the end. He was, without doubt, the most skilled and experienced railway saboteur in SBS, and his survival, against the law of averages, is as much a tribute to Brother Roger's training and inspiration as the result of his own courage and good judgement. He is now living quietly in retirement with his wife, Marjorie.

In December 1939 'Tug' volunteered for active service in France, and in early 1940 he found himself there with the Third Survey Regiment (Royal Artillery). After the fall of France he volunteered for the newly formed commandos and was sent to the Isle of Arran for training. There he met Roger Courtney, who was expounding his ideas on the use of canoes from submarines to attack enemy shipping in harbour with delayed-action explosive charges. They formed an instant liking for each other and, after passing Roger's character test with flying colours, he became his second-in-command in the Folboat Section, as it was then called.

As explained elsewhere, Roger liked to test a man's character by making him tiddly in the local pub and observing his behaviour. 'Tug' survived by discreetly pouring much of his share into various flowerpots and helped a stricken Roger back to his billet at the end of the evening.

In January 1941 the Section embarked in the commando ship *Glenroy* and sailed as part of Layforce to Egypt round the Cape of Good Hope. Layforce comprised three ten-thousand-ton twenty-knot vessels, *Glenroy*, *Glengyle* and *Glenearn*, flying the White Ensign. In Cape Town they were given shore leave and were greeted with tremendous hospitality. They gathered that the locals were a bit cautious when Australian convoys appeared, as the Aussies were notoriously boisterous. However, on one occasion they were not cautious enough. A quiet, orderly and unassuming lot of Australian soldiers wandered up the main street at eleven o'clock one morning. All the mothers of Cape Town were in the big stores having a quiet gossip over a cup of coffee; their babies were parked outside in their prams. The Diggers swapped babies from pram to pram all up and down the street and retreated quietly before the storm broke.

The convoy of troopships sailed north past Dar-es-Salaam and Mombasa, with their picturesque old

Arab towns and sailing-dhows down from the Red Sea and Persian Gulf, no longer trading in slaves but in cheap Indian cotton and other goods for the bazaar markets. Roger Courtney would have told many a good story to the young Commandos about big-game hunting on the Serengeti Plains, prospecting for gold in Masai country and poaching elephants in the Northern Territory.

Passing Aden and through the Red Sea, fortunately in the cool season, they arrived at last at Suez, to be greeted by news of the fall of Crete, and three days of blinding sandstorms. The Folboat Section remained for a while at Kabrit on the Egyptian Great Bitter Lakes, while Roger waged a bitter battle in GHQ to retain autonomy, with freedom to specialize in operations from submarines, for which he and his men had been trained. At this stage of the War soldiers in canoes were a novelty. They were viewed with some reserve by naval officers, who maintained that the duty of submarines was to sink ships and not to play around with special operations. Attitudes began to change after Roger and Lieutenant-Commander Nigel Clogstoun-Willmott RN carried out their first-ever beach reconnaissance by canoe from a submarine in March 1941 on the island of Rhodes. Roger and his men were then given sanctuary from military molestation by the 1st Submarine Flotilla in HM Submarine Depot Ship *Medway* in Alexandria harbour with gin at 2d a tot, whiskey 3d and fifty Players 1s 3d, and were renamed the 'Special Boat Section'.

On 24 April 1941 'Tug' was given his chance and sailed in HMS/M *Triumph* to attack shipping with limpet mines in Derna and Benghazi harbours on the North African coast. Bad weather aborted the operation, but on the way back they sighted an Italian two-masted copper-bottomed schooner named *Tugnin F* in the Gulf of Sidra. She was made to heave-to with a four-inch shell across the bows. 'Tug' and the submarine's navigating officer went on board and found her to be loaded with macaroni. They collected some samples, the ship's papers and pictures of Hitler and Mussolini. *Triumph* had submerged during the search so as not to be spotted by enemy aircraft, and 'Tug' induced her to surface and pick them up by holding up a picture of the Führer in front of the periscope. The crew was sent shorewards in the ship's lifeboat, the schooner was sunk by gunfire, and *Triumph* returned to Alexandria.

'Tug' then left for Malta in HMS/M *Cachalot* on 12 June 1941 with his canoe partner, Marine W.G. Hughes. They were to operate as a team until December of that year. 'Tug' describes Hughes as short, lean, tough and ready to tackle anything.

'Shrimp' Simpson, then Captain (S) of the 10th Submarine Flotilla in Malta, was still reluctant to accept the idea of SBS canoe teams as an extra weapon in the submarine's armoury but, after continual badgering, allowed them to sail in HMS/M *Urge*, just to get them out of his hair.

On 29 June 1941 they were cruising submerged off the Sicilian coast and examining through the periscope a railway tunnel lying between Taormina and Catania almost at the foot of Mount Etna. That night *Urge* surfaced four miles off the coast, and they lifted their canoe and explosives through the forehatch and onto the dripping deck. They completed the erection of the canoe by fixing the transverse frame into place, which had been previously removed to allow passage through the hatch. They then loaded their arms and explosives and sat in the canoe on top of the casing, firmly grasping their paddles. The submarine moved quietly in on her diesel engines to about two thousand yards from the coast, trimmed down, and the two men floated off.

On their way in to the beach, they had to make several detours to avoid Italian fishing vessels, but they reached it without incident. They unloaded the explosives and hid them under a rock. At the entrance to the tunnel they found to their delight that the railway was single tracked, which meant that they did not have to worry about which line would carry the first train. They collected the explosive from the shore and returned to the tunnel. A spot about thirty yards inside the tunnel was selected and, when the explosive was firmly in place, they packed a pressure switch under the rail and connected it up. They slipped down to the canoe and made their way back to *Urge* without difficulty and undetected. Not long afterwards the Captain called them up to the bridge on the conning-tower in time to see a train approaching the safe end of the tunnel. A few minutes later they heard the muffled boom of a large explosion. For two days *Urge* remained in the vicinity keeping watch on the tunnel. Breakdown gangs appeared but no traffic passed through it. There could be no doubt about the success of the first SBS sabotage operation in the Mediterranean.

As *Urge* patrolled her 'billet' a few miles south of the Straits of Messina, she met two ten-thousand-ton eight-inch Italian cruisers escorted by six destroyers. The Captain promptly fired a salvo of torpedoes at the cruiser *Gorizia*, which sank in a few minutes. Then they suffered a violent attack of more than one hundred depth-charges. 'Tug' recalls: 'The noise of the attack was appalling, as I tucked myself out of the way, I remembered Roger Courtney's illuminating instruction to SBS personnel which ran like this: "To SBS personnel – when you are privileged (?) to be on one of HM submarines during an enemy depth-charge attack, be calm, hide yourself away in a corner of the control-room, or anywhere else, out of everybody's way. Be seated, say nothing, hold an open book and look at it. It does not matter if it is upside down – they will not notice it.'"

With Malta in sight, the 'Jolly Roger' skull-and-crossbones flag was hoisted to show the submarine's successes. It carried a bar to denote the sinking of an enemy cruiser, and in a corner the bosun had embroidered a dagger to celebrate the first pinprick inflicted on the Italians by the SBS.

Captain (S) sent a signal to Alexandria asking permission for 'Tug' and Marine Hughes to remain under his command for operations, and this was readily granted.

Nearly a month after their first success near Mount Etna, 'Tug' and Marine Hughes were again at sea, this time in HMS/M *Utmost*, commanded by Lieutenant-Commander R. Cayley. On 24 July 1941 they successfully derailed a train in the Gulf of Sant' Eufemia on the instep of the foot at the southern end of the Italian mainland. They lay among the rocks to watch the results and saw the Italian guard-houses along the line erupt like anthills at the explosion, looking for blood. Some unfortunate Italian officers and their girlfriends were enjoying a nude bathing party in the half-moon light and were promptly hustled away to a guard-house as suspected swimmer-saboteurs.

Again, on 19 August, from HMS/M *Utmost*, and with Marine Hughes, 'Tug' attacked a large railway bridge over the River Seracino in the Gulf of Taranto. This bridge was vital to the transport of Italian war supplies as it was at the junction of two railway lines. It was camouflaged on the seaward side with brushwood and would obviously, from its size, need a fair amount of explosive. When darkness came, Wilson and Hughes were sitting in their canoe on the forward casing, loaded with four hundred pounds of explosives. *Utmost* went in close to the shore, trimmed down and floated them off. They paddled in to the beach and unloaded the stores. 'Tug' glanced at the submarine and noticed that she was close in and too visible for comfort. He paddled out and suggested to the Captain that he should clear off a bit further out.

Back on shore, he and Hughes made their way cautiously across the beach and up a fairly steep embankment, their tommy-guns at the ready. The bridge consisted of two steel spans on a central pin and, after three trips to fetch the explosives, 'Tug' mounted the steel web of the nearest span. When all the charges were securely lashed, he connected them up with 'Fuse Instantaneous Detonating' and then tied ten feet of safety fuse which was attached to a pull-push ignition switch. This would allow a certain time-delay in the explosion to enable the two men to make it to the beach. 'Tug' pulled the switch, and he and Hughes ran like hell along the track, crashed down through the bushes and flung themselves prone on the beach. A vivid orange flash lit the night sky, followed by a tremendous explosion. Pieces of debris plopped into the sand around them and splashed into the water. The canoe was luckily undamaged, and they rejoined *Utmost*.

It was too much to hope that the Italians would not by now be thoroughly aroused by these pinprick raids against their precious bridges and tunnels.

On their next trip in HMS/M *Utmost*, 'Tug' Wilson and Marine Hughes had planned to derail a train in a large tunnel on the west coast of Italy south of Naples. On 22 September 1941 they landed and went up to the tunnel but were detected by an Italian patrol and were fired on before they could place their charges. The next night they landed again and approached a three-span bridge just north of Sant' Eufemia. They were again challenged, this time by a sentry on the bridge, and had to make their escape back to the canoe under fire. *Utmost* was obliged to leave in a hurry and to ditch the canoe in the process.

On their return to Malta, 'Tug' was hauled before Captain (S) and was told that Higher Authority had ruled that his operations were too dangerous and that they must 'cease forthwith'. Ever persistent, 'Tug' refused to take 'No' for an answer. He explained that, while the Italians had obviously increased the sentries on bridges and tunnels as a result of their raids, there were still long stretches of unguarded railway line to be dealt with. He further explained that he had thought up a new technique. The explosive charge would be tailored for the job and made up beforehand, ready for placement at short notice when a train was approaching, with no patrol in sight. Previously he would have put the explosive in the right place, and then attached fuse, detonator, fuse wire and firing mechanism – a lengthy process exposing him and his device to danger of discovery.

Captain (S) gave him full backing, and he and Hughes sailed in HMS/M *Truant*. On the night of 27 October 1941 they successfully derailed a train on the electrified section of the main Brindisi to Milan line between Ancolia and Senegallia in the upper Adriatic. From his description, a fine display of fireworks, sparks and flashes was the result.

They got back to Alexandria on 17 November, and 'Tug' was congratulated by Roger Courtney on his promotion to Captain. When they had recovered from the subsequent party, they devised a new method of placing limpet mines on enemy ships, consisting of a frame holding three linked limpets which could be attached to the side of a vessel in one motion.

The limpet is a marine gasteropod mollusc which clings

to rocks with its sucker-like foot. The limpet which came into use about the middle of 1941 was a two-pound charge of plastic explosive which was held to a ship's side by six magnets. The delayed-action fuse was activated by tightening a butterfly nut at the end of the container. The limpet was placed by the canoeist on the ship's side below the waterline by means of a pole, and preferably outside the engine room. It could blow a six-foot-diameter hole in the plate of most merchant ships but was not thought to be really effective against naval vessels of any size. The first limpet operation against enemy shipping to be carried out by No. 1 SBS was on 21 July 1941. Sergeant Allan and Marine Miles entered Benghazi harbour from HMS/M *Taku* and sank a merchant ship with limpet mines. On their way out they holed their canoe on a jagged rock and were captured. Looking at it cold-bloodedly, the loss was worth it when compared to the damage caused to Rommel's supply line. Both men survived the war.

Four months after the achievement of Allan and Miles, 'Tug' and Marine Hughes lost no time in trying to put their new idea to the test, and they left on 9 December 1941 in HMS/M *Torbay*. Their target was to be enemy shipping in Navarino harbour on the west coast of the Greek Peloponnese. On arrival they slipped round the boom at the entrance but, after searching the harbour, could find no suitable target and paddled some twelve miles before they got back to the submarine. Five nights later they tried again, with 'Tug' intending to swim in from a position just outside the boom. The water was much too cold, and he was forced to give up and climb back into the canoe in a state of frozen exhaustion.

The Captain of *Torbay* was a notoriously strong-minded and short-tempered naval officer, and one not to be trifled with. On the way back to Alexandria, *Torbay* fired a torpedo at a destroyer. It developed gyro-failure and circled the submarine at forty knots, leaping lethally like a playful porpoise, but presumably it did not have the temerity to approach such a formidable officer too closely. (Incidentally, he finished the War with a Victoria Cross, a Distinguished Service Order and Bar, and a Distinguished Service Cross.)

'Tug' was told to take some leave in Britain, also re-joining Roger Courtney, who was in the process of forming No. 2 SBS, and then in January 1942 returned to the submarine flotilla in Malta, but this time without his experienced canoe partner, Marine Hughes.

His next two operations were somewhat less hair-raising and consisted of ferrying secret agents to the coast of Tunisia, railway sabotage being apparently out of favour with the Planners for the time being.

The first operation was carried out from HMS/M *Urge* on 12 January 1942. He and the agent capsized in the surf near the beach but no harm was done. It was raining hard and it did not matter that his passenger got a bit wet. Recovering his suitcase and radio, the agent donned his raincoat and set off to catch a train. On his return to Malta, 'Tug' was told that he had been awarded the Distinguished Service Order (DSO) and that he had also been Mentioned in Dispatches (MID).

The second operation was to land two agents in Tunisia near Carthage on 9 April 1942. This was successfully completed and 'Tug' transferred at sea from HMS/M *Upholder* to HMS/M *Unbeaten* on passage to Gibraltar. He then went on to the United Kingdom to join Roger Courtney with No. 2 SBS at Ardrossan-Saltcoats, Scotland.

Tragically *Upholder* was sunk with all hands later on the same patrol. 'Tug' has commented that he had decided to transfer to *Unbeaten*, commanded by Lieutenant-Commander E. Woodward RN, despite a bad sea running at the time. It was later described as a fateful decision, and without doubt he must be the only man to have sailed on a submarine's last mission and left her just before she was lost with all hands. Consequently he was the last living man to exchange words with the acknowledged ace submariner of the Second World War, Lieutenant-Commander M.D. Wanklyn VC, DSO and two Bars.

During the autumn of 1942 'Tug' was confronted with a new invention from the fertile brain of the late Sir Malcolm Campbell. This was a miniature torpedo, 21 inches long and powered by twin opposed screws, with a 1½-pound cavity charge in the nose. This worked wonderfully on the test bed, and 'Tug' was satisfied with it as a potentially improved method of sinking enemy shipping in harbour from a distance. Unfortunately it does not seem to have been thoroughly tested under operational conditions. 'Tug' was appointed guinea-pig to give the device its first operational test against Italian shipping in the Mediterranean.

He flew out to Malta in August 1942, via West Africa, with five torpedos under his care marked as auto spare parts or something equally innocuous. Then his luck ran out.

On 6 September 1942, with his new canoe partner, Bombardier Brittlebank, he sailed in HMS/M *Unbroken (P.42)* to try the torpedoes against merchant shipping in Crotone harbour, on the heel of the Calabrian coast in south-east Italy.

They slipped into the harbour through a gap in the breakwater with four mini-torpedoes but were challenged and escaped. They missed the rendezvous with *Unbroken* and were captured on shore late the following afternoon at the beginning of a 250-mile paddle back to Malta. Such epic journeys have sometimes been completed, but not in a badly damaged canoe, and the end was inevitable. It is interesting to note from 'Tug' Wilson's final report, written by him on 11 May 1945 after his return from prison-camp, that conditions for an operational test of the torpedoes could not have been better – flat calm inside the harbour and the range ideal. Nevertheless, despite his confidence that the torpedo was, when last seen, running true towards the centre of the target, it did not score a hit. This was confirmed in a book written after the War by the Captain of the *Unbroken*. One can only assume that it behaved in the same manner as the mini-torpedoes used two months later by SBS in the assault on Oran and did not steer straight. (By kind permission of the Public Record Office his post-war record on this last operation in SBS is reproduced in full in Appendix A.)

In retrospect it is interesting to read the story of 'Tug' Wilson's last operation from the point of view of the submarine's captain. This was published as part of a trilogy called *Three Great Sea Stories*, with the story of *Unbroken* by Alastair Mars. From this it is quite clear that the reason for the missed rendezvous was the presence of two E-boats fitted with Asdic. These hunted *Unbroken* in earnest, forcing her away from the first rendezvous position. *Unbroken* was able to elude them and circle round to the alternative rendezvous several miles off Crotone but was obliged to remain submerged and did not contact the canoe. At 0820 hours two anti-submarine schooners emerged from the harbour and began to comb the area with depth-charges. *Unbroken* reluctantly withdrew.

After capture and interrogation, 'Tug' was sent to prison-camp at Sulmona in Italy, where he found Bombardier Brittlebank very much alive in the Other

Ranks section of the camp. 'Tug' and a fellow officer swapped places with two of a daily fatigue party of which Brittlebank was in charge, and escaped. They were soon recaptured by *carabinieri* and sent to another camp, at Bologna. After the surrender of the Italian Government to the Allies a year later, the prisoners were loaded into cattle-trucks by the Germans for transport by train to Germany.

'Tug' escaped from the moving train and was befriended by an Italian railway worker, who fitted him out with a railwayman's hat and uniform and handed him over to Italian partisans. He travelled to Rome on a false identity card and was taken to a safe house where other British escapees were lodged. In Rome he enjoyed himself and was even taken with another officer one night to the opera *Il Trovatore* by two attractive Italian girls. He persuaded one of them to take his programme to the box occupied by Field-Marshal Kesselring and ask for his autograph. (To obtain funds to pay for this fairly carefree existence, he would write cheques on pieces of paper drawn on his account with Lloyd's Bank, Cox & King's Branch in London. These were all honoured in due course.) Tiring of the flesh-pots, he tried to seek sanctuary in the Vatican, disguised as a priest, but got thrown out by the Swiss Guards.

Shortly afterwards he was arrested by the Gestapo and finished up in Oflag 79, a prison-camp in Czechoslovakia, from which he was released by the American Army in early 1945.

In December 1945 he was awarded a Bar to his DSO. Bombardier Brittlebank was awarded the Distinguished Conduct Medal (DCM).

After the war, 'Tug' returned to regular soldiering and served in Palestine, Korea and Malta, finally as a

Commander of 37 HAA Regiment in the Royal Artillery. In Korea he was Mentioned in Dispatches for the second time. He retired on 1 April 1958, finding peacetime soldiering a little dull.

To my mind, one person who does deserve a Mention is his wife Marjorie, who married 'this splendidly offensive-spirited little cove' in November 1939 and spent most of the next twenty years waiting for him to come home.

3

No. 1 SBS in the Mediterranean, 1942

In December 1941 Roger Courtney returned to the United Kingdom from the Eastern Mediterranean to form No. 2 Special Boat Section. Behind him he left fifteen officers and forty-five other ranks under Major M.R.B. Kealy (Devonshire Regiment). After his departure the long battle of attrition for the independence of No. 1 SBS was lost, and it was attached to No. 1 Special Air Service (SAS), raised and commanded by the expansionist, influential but very effective Lieutenant-Colonel A.D. ('David') Stirling (Scots Guards) of desert raiding fame. The role of SBS was changed from beach reconnaissance and shoreside sabotage to small-scale assault raiding, with a consequent sharp increase in casualties.

However, before this change of role came about, No. 1 SBS suffered the tragic loss of Corporal Severn and Corporal Childs in HMS/M *Triumph*, which sailed with them for the Aegean in late December 1941 and failed to return from patrol. I have been unable to find details about their mission, but official records state that *Triumph* was probably mined in early January 1942 and that her loss may have been in connection with the special operation.

During 1942 No. 1 SBS carried out several operations in support of the 8th Army campaign in North Africa, and I am indebted to *The Filibusters* by John Lodwick for many of the details. These have been confirmed and amplified by members of No. 1 SBS from that period.

In early 1942, at the time when the forward limit of

Rommel's advance on Egypt was at Gazala in Cyrenaica, a detachment of No. 1 SBS under Major Mike Kealy was sent to Tobruk to work in conjunction with Royal Navy motor torpedo boats (MTBs). The enemy was using barges to bring supplies forward by night and was said to release them offshore to drift in to the beach. The role of SBS was to lob 'sticky bombs' into the barges from the MTB as it ran past them. Lieutenant Tommy Langton recalls that they practised this on one occasion but that it was an almost impossible task as the MTB jumped all over the place and the 'sticky bomb', once its cover was removed, stuck mostly to themselves. Anyhow, no barges were sighted as far as he knew. They also acted as volunteer anti-aircraft gunners on the MTBs.

When it was reported that a German plane had crashed on an island near Gazala Point, Captain Grant-Watson (Scots Guards) with Sergeant J.B. Sherwood (RASC), Lieutenant T.R. Langton (Irish Guards) and Sergeant C. Dunbar, left in an MTB with two canoes to capture him. It was fairly rough, and the skipper of the MTB had difficulty in locating the island. They launched the canoes, supposedly off the island, but both capsized in the surf when trying to land. Langton was sent back to the MTB to fetch a rubber dinghy but, on return, could not find Grant-Watson or Sherwood. He and his companion were then surrounded by an armed patrol apparently speaking in a foreign language. Before shooting could start, one of them uttered a good English swear word, and Langton quickly surrendered to what turned out to be members of the 1st South African Division. He had completely missed the island and had reached the mainland instead.

Shortly afterwards Langton heard a cry from the sea, went out in the dinghy and found Sherwood clinging grimly to the body of Grant-Watson, who was not a strong swimmer and who had drowned.

Meanwhile, the remainder of the SBS was back at Kabrit, south of the Great Bitter Lakes, training to attack enemy shipping in harbour with limpet mines. On 17 January 1942 Captain G.I.A. Duncan (Black Watch) and Corporal E. Barr (HLI) were lent to a party of No. 1 SAS and were transported overland to attack enemy shipping in Bureat harbour in the Gulf of Sirte. The journey by lorry over the desert caused much damage to their canoe, and they had to be content with blowing up a radio mast on shore.

For the next four months No. 1 SBS seems to have been virtually unemployed. There were various reasons for this. The authorities did not really know how to use them; the submariners were too busy trying to interrupt sea-borne supplies flowing to Rommel across the Mediterranean, and SBS was a trifle too 'exotic' for Staff acceptance, being composed of a hotch-potch from different regiments. They might have been taken more seriously if they had all agreed to transfer to the Royal Marines, which at one time was suggested, and they did not attain respectability until the remnants had been absorbed into Major Lord Jellicoe's Special Boat Squadron at the end of 1942. However, above all, the driving force of their founder, Roger Courtney, had disappeared when he was ordered back to the United Kingdom in December 1941 to form No. 2 SBS.

Then, on 22 May 1942, Captain R.K.B. Allott (Middlesex Regiment) and Lieutenant Duncan Ritchie of the Royal Navy left Tobruk in an MTB to reconnoitre the coast between Cape Ras-Al-Tin (Cyrenaica) and Gazala Inlet – a distance of over a hundred miles. They were dropped with their canoe and stores and lay up in a low sandhill about fifty yards from the beach. A few of the stunted bushes peculiar to Cyrenaica crowned the sandhill. During the morning nothing much happened except that Ritchie made himself thirsty by eating too much chocolate. At noon a German staff car drove up. Three officers got out and bathed in the sea in front of their position without seeing the marks left on the sand by the canoe. Allott and Ritchie were having a quiet laugh about this when the sound of singing was heard, and no less than a hundred German soldiers arrived at the beach. They bathed, performed strenuous physical drill and ended up with a game of hide-and-seek among the sandhills. They did not leave until six o'clock, miraculously unaware of the intruders.

At the end of May 1942, the massive German thrusts towards the Caucasus began and by 25 August had reached Mozdok, more than halfway down towards the Persian and Turkish borders.

In late June Captain Montgomerie, Lieutenants D.G.R. Sutherland (Black Watch), Eric Newby (Black Watch) and T.R. Langton (Irish Guards), Sergeant J.B. Sherwood and one other NCO were ordered to report to Lattakia in northern Syria to survey the coast from there to Haifa in Palestine. This operation, named 'Aluite', was a precaution in case the Germans should come south from the Caucasus through Turkey or Persia to the Mediterranean – the other half of the pincer movement to support Rommel and the Afrika Corps in their drive to capture Egypt. The British plan was to hold a line eastward from Haifa, and it was therefore essential to know the coastline to the north so as to be able to land raiding-parties behind the German lines. Newby, Sherwood and Langton eventually settled themselves near a monastery in the mountains above Beirut for about two months and worked from there, drawing maps and marking caves and caches for stay-behind stores. In a burst of invention, probably fathered by Major Jasper Maskelyne, the famous magician, who was on the Staff for magical purposes at the time, GHQ Cairo had arranged for the manufacture of papier-mâché rocks, under which the stores were to be concealed.

Meanwhile, Rommel attacked the Eighth Army position at Gazala on 26 May, captured Tobruk on 20 June and came to a standstill before Alamein by the end of July, preparing for the final assault on Egypt. The key to his continued success would lie in the ability of the Germans and Italians to maintain an adequate supply of food, munitions and, above all, petrol to their forces in North Africa. British submarines based in Malta were taking a heavy toll of merchant shipping in the Mediterranean, and an all-out effort was made by the Axis to neutralize the island by air attack as a prelude to invasion.

The destruction of Axis aircraft was of paramount importance. The various small-scale raiding forces, such as the Long Range Desert Group (LRDG) and the SAS were therefore to be employed during the rest of 1942 in attacking airfields behind the enemy's lines. No. 1 SBS was also used in this new role but under the directional control of No. 1 SAS. Because of its specialized training and experience in amphibious operations, SBS was used mainly to attack airfields which could be approached only from the sea, such as those on the islands of Crete, Sicily and Rhodes.

On the night 6/7 June 1942, a party from SBS landed near Cape Trikala in Crete to destroy aircraft and installations on Kastelli, Timbaki and Maleme airfields. Captain Duncan, Lieutenant Barnes and Corporal Barr succeeded in destroying seven aircraft, petrol, oil and bomb dumps and motor transport on Kastelli. Lieutenant

Sutherland and Corporal Riley found that Timbaki had been abandoned, and Major Kealy, Captain Allott and Sergeant Feeberry were unable to attack Maleme as it was too heavily defended. They brought out with them eight New Zealanders.

By August 1942 Malta was in desperate straits, and on the 9th a large British fleet entered the Mediterranean at Gibraltar to escort fourteen fast merchant vessels for the supply and relief of the island. This convoy included the American tanker *Ohio*, whose cargo was vital. The enemy had meanwhile strengthened his air forces in Sardinia and Sicily.

On 11 August 'M' Section of the SBS, consisting of Captains Duncan and Buchanan, Lieutenant Newby, Sergeant Dunbar, and Corporals Booth, Butler and Duffy, was landed in Sicily from HMS/M *Una* to attack a German bomber base threatening the convoy (Operation Whynot). An account of this raid, based on *Love and War in the Apennines* by Eric Newby (1971), is here given.

'M Section of SBS were landed from the submarine HMS *Una* with little time for proper rehearsal on the afternoon of 11 August 1942. Their purpose was to disrupt a German bomber base in range of a relief convoy sailing for Malta. The available information was meagre – sketchy might be more apt – before they prepared to launch their canoes when the submarine surfaced about 2100 hours. After 36 hours in artificial light, the night seemed terribly black but, once the canoeists were accustomed to it, it seemed very light indeed. One canoe was holed in launching and had to be left behind: the other three got away in arrow-head formation with a strong wind at their backs raising a nasty swell. Bombers thundered a few feet over their heads.

'Eric Newby and Cpl H.H. Butler felt very lonely when

they reached the beach, for 50 feet away was a wire entanglement some 20 feet wide. They carried the canoe to the wire, set the fuses in their thermite bombs – "big black conkers" on white cordtex lines of fuse – concocted with plastic explosive. They buried the canoe and retraced their steps to the water's edge, so they could remove all their own footmarks, before cutting a path through the wire midway between two blockhouses 150 yards apart. Avoiding the more obvious anti-personnel mines, they were through the wire an hour after leaving the submarine, but they were behind schedule. This was a quick in-and-out job, and the submarine would lie off the coast until an hour after midnight. They hurried on, down a deserted track, hearing the appalling sound of marching men which turned out to be only the champ of a horse's teeth as it chewed grass; they crossed a high wall and blundered into a farm, but its barking dogs roused no-one. Half a mile further on they were in the workshop area of the aerodrome among buildings frighteningly bright with lights. Here they left some bombs on crates of new engines – it seemed a terrible waste of explosives when they intended to prevent bombers taking off next day.

'They were just about to split up and place their charges when a squad of Italians came up, George Duncan's "Camerati Tedeschi" did not sound very convincing: an Italian took a shot at these "German Comrades". Yet all might have been well had not one of the raiders fired back. Immediately floodlights lit the airstrip, lorries started up. Very lights were fired. In the confusion Eric Newby was about to shoot a German shouting loudly when the figure growled in lowland Scots "Don't shoot, you stupid bastard, it's me." The raiders dodged into the shadows of the workshop buildings, thankful there were no guard dogs as reported from Cretan airfields.

'"What we ought to do," said George Duncan, "is . . ."
"Eff off" answered an NCO. "Eff off while there's still
time." This experienced raider's advice was taken, and the
parked JU88's were left in their many ranks as the men
headed back for the beach. They dropped their bombs at
the base of a pylon which could be repaired in a couple of
days or less, and were moving south-east when a lone
R.A.F. Wellington bomber came in, a planned diversion
which put out all the airfield lights by its presence, not its
bombs. By now it was 2230 and they were among the
coastal batteries and apparently empty trenches when Sgt.
Dunbar, bringing up the rear, stepped on what he took to
be ordinary ground. He fell through the groundsheet
cover of an Italian defence post and was wounded before
being captured. Fortunately for "M" Section, though, this
outpost apparently had no telephone contact with its company headquarters.

'Coming through some wire they were equally lucky
when twelve Italians saw them, but, instead of starting a
fuss, they pushed off, and the commandos continued their
scurry towards the canoes. But which way were these?
North or south of where they now came through the wire?
Rather than follow the Italian patrol, they turned left and
came to the gap they had cut in the wire some two hours
previously. One canoe was unusable and they launched
the other two, one with three men up, in a rising wind.
Offshore they flashed their hooded torch but no submarine appeared and they had no infra-red RG. By 0300
both canoes were waterlogged, and when Eric Newby's
sank they clustered round their last canoe, pushing it
towards the shore opposite the rendezvous for the next
night. They never reached it. The sun was rising on a
beautiful morning, Mount Etna's smoke plume "like the
quill of a pen" away to the north above the haze, when

some friendly fishermen pulled them out of the water about breakfast time.

'HMS/M *Una* came in three nights running, but "M" Section were all prisoners.'

This was a sad finish for Corporal Booth, who had been awarded the Distinguished Conduct Medal (DCM) for good work as spare machine-gunner aboard HMS/M *Torbay*, whose commanding officer was notoriously difficult to impress if one was a soldier.

The same month Captain Montgomerie, Lieutenant Michael Alexander, WO George Barnes, Sergeant Sherwood MM and Corporal Gurney landed from an MTB at Daba behind Alamein with orders to destroy a transport dump. Daba, location of a forward fighter aerodrome and staging point, was close behind the Alamein front line. To reach their targets the raiders had to pass lines of tents, a German mobile cinema and canteen full of happy soldiery drinking Pilsener beer. Delayed-action charges were laid on tents, trucks and fuel dumps. Alexander and Gurney were missing when the party returned to the beach. Gurney was wounded, and both had been taken prisoner but not, according to later reports, before causing considerable confusion behind the enemy lines.

On 31 August Rommel launched his last attempt to break through to Cairo but was defeated at the Battle of Alam Halfa. His assault had been expected and every effort was being made to hamper the build-up of his supplies. On the same day a detachment of No. 1 SBS embarked in the Greek submarine *Papanikolis* from Beirut to attack and destroy enemy aircraft on Marizza and Calato airports on the island of Rhodes. From these airfields, German Junker and Italian Savoia-Marchetti bombers were harassing our Mediterranean convoys.

The SBS party consisted of Captain R.K.B. Allott

(Middlesex Regiment), Lieutenant D.G.R. Sutherland (Black Watch), Sergeant Moss (Devonshire Regiment), Corporal Mackenzie (HLI), Private Blake (Hampshire Regiment) and Marines Duggan, Barrow and Harris.

A graphic description of this operation is reproduced below from *The Filibusters* by John Lodwick.

'The party left Beirut in the Greek submarine *Papanikolis* on the last day of August 1942. The voyage of four days was passed in cramped boredom and in language difficulties. On 4 September a periscope reconnaissance was made, the landing-beach verified, and that same night the patrol put ashore in conditions of flat calm from three Carley floats and a folboat.

'The usual under-estimates of time taken to cover distance now made themselves felt. When looking at a map in conditions of comfort at base, wishful thinking, however sternly abjured, is inevitable. A fifty-pound pack, a dark night, a mountain with a razor edge, which was but a contour until two hours ago, make up the difference. Hercules himself would lag behind his schedule.

'On the first night the party covered only three miles, on the second five, and on the third, five again. They did, however, reach a cave which they considered a suitable rendezvous before splitting up; Allott being about to continue north to Marizza, Sutherland moving down to Calato. One reason for this slow progress was the incompetence of the guides, who at first maintained that they knew the way, but later openly confessed that they were ignorant of their surroundings. "One can hardly blame them," wrote Sutherland, "since they volunteered to come on the operation at great risk to themselves. No guide, however, is better than a bad one."

'On the night of 7 September Allott's party moved off towards Marizza. Sergeant Moss, normally David

Sutherland's "mucker" and strong-arm man, accompanied them, since only he knew sufficient Italian to converse with the guide. Sutherland himself moved off a little later. He had time to spare: the attacks were not due to take place until 12 September, the rendezvous with Allott was not due until the 16th. Two days later, he was lying-up on the mountainside, overlooking the aerodrome and the entire valley in which it lay. Water was now the main problem, and the carriage of it involved contact with the civilian population. The guide, however, was reassuring: he could barely tell a goat-track from a secondary road, but he seemed either to know or to be related to everyone in the area. Much useful information about the enemy defences was forthcoming, and meals of fruit, cheese, and bread were provided. At night the party, who numbered six, slept in groups of three. The position of "centre" man was much coveted, for it was very cold.

'On the target night the party was further split up, Marines Barrow and Harris being allocated to Lieutenant Calambakidis, the Greek officer, and Marine Duggan accompanying David Sutherland. The guide was instructed to withdraw to the rendezvous with all spare stores. The two sections separated on the dry bed of a river close to the aerodrome. "From that moment," wrote Sutherland, "I never saw any of 'B' party again."

'It was now very dark, with pelting rain: ideal for concealment, if not for comfort. Sutherland had thoroughly pin-pointed his targets from the mountainside, and now had only to approach them. By the side of the first, a Savoia-Marchetti bomber, a sentry was standing. Sutherland waited. At midnight that sentry obligingly moved off, and Sutherland laid bombs on this aircraft and on two other bombers alongside of it. Crossing some wire and an anti-tank ditch, he walked down a path between buildings and the main landing ground. A sentry stepped forward, challenging and shouting. Duggan nudged Sutherland and they withdrew into the obscurity. To be discovered at this early stage might compromise the other party.

'Investigating cautiously, Sutherland found a petrol dump. He adorned it with bombs, adding some more to the aircraft which he had already attacked, and withdrew. By the time he was back in the river-bed three bombs were exploding followed shortly afterwards by those of the other party. From this moment onwards explosions were frequent. A red glow spread over the rainy sky and fifteen separate fires were visible. These fires spread. Ammunition, bombs, and materials of all kinds in the vicinity of the planes caught alight. From the runway the wailing of enraged Italians could be plainly heard. Search-lights swept the bay and the foothills. Panic-stricken though they were, the enemy seemed to realize that this had been a ground attack. The very considerable garrison spread out in all directions. At about three in the morning Sutherland heard the sound of automatic fire from the north-west, to which a Thompson gun was replying.

'"B" party were in the bag – or dead.

'Sutherland's guide now began to give trouble. The searchlight beams were worrying him and he would not move. Since the man could easily pass as a civilian, Sutherland decided to leave him. Sutherland made his way back to the rendezvous. Here he contacted Captain Tsoucas, the second of the Greek officers. Together, at first light, they observed the damage done to the airfield. The wreckage of burnt-out aircraft and fuel dumps lay everywhere. At 0900 hours, a large aeroplane landed, and was immediately surrounded by ground staff running from all sides of the field. A general had arrived to tot up his losses.

'Sutherland now moved to a position above the beach selected for the re-embarkation. He had seen signs of intense enemy activity in the plain, and wished to head off Ken Allott before he ran into the danger zone. Allott, however, was not to arrive: he had penetrated the very stiff defences of Marizza and done his job, but was to be captured with all his men as they reached the beach. Early in the afternoon of the following day, Marine Duggan spotted twenty-four soldiers advancing in the direction of the lying-up area. They were accompanied by civilians. The three meh seized what kit they could carry and ran over the crest of their hill, eventually arriving on a small sloping ledge fairly high up the mountain, with a well behind it. They had not even had time to conceal them-selves here before a number of small parties appeared round the foot of the mountain.

'The second arm of the pincers had arrived and was closing in.

'Sutherland lay with his two comrades in the open, not daring to move. It was now obvious that one at least of the guides had been captured and forced to reveal the point of landing and embarkation. This was afterwards verified. The information was obtained by torture. The Italian search-parties moved slowly, combing the bare slope. One group passed not more than ten or fifteen feet below the crouching fugitives. The enthusiasm of the enemy was evident, but their reasoning was at fault. Unaware of the height which a man with liberty at stake can climb in five minutes, they presently resumed their fruitless patrolling of the lower slopes.

'An hour or two later, Sutherland observed a boat coming down the coast from the direction of Lindos. He identified her as a motor torpedo-boat of the Baglietto class. On the fo'c'sle a small group of soldiers were standing, evidently a landing-party. Disappearing behind a cliff, the MTB cut off her engines. Presently, she emerged towing three black objects which were only too easily recognizable as the British party's Carley floats.

'Sutherland and Duggan were now in a dreadful position. They were, and had been for three days, without food. They were without any means of re-embarkation and, with the beach compromised and the hunt at its hottest, it would be very difficult for the submarine to put in for them at all. Sutherland decided that his only chance was to go down to the beach, where some Mae Wests and signalling torches had been hidden in a cave.

'Tsoucas was left with the haversacks by the well. At nightfall Sutherland and Duggan moved off. They succeeded in slipping past the enemy sentries, recovered a torch and lifebelts from the cave and made their way back. Meanwhile a very large enemy party had moved into position between themselves and Tsoucas, with the evident intention of waylaying Ken Allott and his party when they should attempt to reach the sea.

'The area in which Sutherland and Duggan could move freely was now small indeed. They crouched under an overhanging rock, and at dawn observed about fifty enemy soldiers not far away, who were talking and shaking out their greatcoats preparatory to moving off. These men again searched the whole neighbourhood, and one sat for five minutes on the rock under which Sutherland was lying. The sun was now very hot, and both men were enduring agonies from thirst and from the cramped nature of their hiding-places. Shortly after midday, they heard the sound of shots from the direction of the cave. Much shouting followed, and all the troops in the area seemed to converge towards the beach. Sutherland and Duggan lay low until dusk, when they moved on promptly with the intention of reaching the shore before the night patrol took up its position.

'They were successful: no enemy were to be seen, but Tsoucas, who should have joined them, did not arrive and had obviously been captured. At 2130 hours, Sutherland sent out his first group of recognition signals. Duggan said that he thought that he had seen a faint reply, but could not be sure of this . . . actually the reply had been flashed through the periscope of the submarine, which was still submerged. At 2200 hours Sutherland at last received a positive acknowledgement and replied with the words: "Swimming . . . come in."

'Note: This was the night of 17/18 September, 1942.

'The pair inflated their Mae Wests, entered the water and swam for about an hour in the direction of the signals, Duggan occasionally replying to them with his own torch. The sea was very calm, "But," wrote Sutherland, "our physical condition for such a swim was hardly adequate" – a statement which is scarcely surprising when one considers that neither man had eaten for five days nor drunk any water for two.

'They swam one and a half miles. Eventually they heard the sound of engines, but when these died away they were very near to abandoning all hope. "However," wrote Sutherland, "we encouraged each other to continue, for we would not, in any case, have had the strength to return." Numb, haggard, starved, and utterly exhausted, they were discovered by the submarine about five minutes later and helped on board. They were taken below and the submarine submerged, to be immediately depth-charged severely by the Italian destroyer which was hovering in the vicinity and the source of the "engine noise" which the swimmers had heard.

'Next morning they reached Beirut, where Sutherland

was found to be dangerously ill. It had not been my intention to intersperse this book with gratuitous comment, but of this operation, I can only say that it is a privilege to write of it. Further, the devotion to duty shown by all ranks in HM Submarine *Traveller* in standing by for over two hours in dangerous waters cannot be too highly praised.'

According to *The Special Air Service* by Philip Warner (1971), 'the Marizza and Calato airfields which they had attacked were severely damaged and partly put out of action for several weeks. Mediterranean convoys benefited considerably from the consequent easing of pressure.'

On 14 September 1942 the 11th Battalion Royal Marines raided Tobruk harbour on Operation Agreement to demolish the port installations and to deny use of the harbour as a supply point for the Germans during their advance on Egypt. Bad weather halved the strength of the force actually landed, and only seventeen of those who made it to the shore were able to return. Enemy reaction was swift and effective, and the destroyer HMS *Sikh* was sunk by gunfire from shore batteries. The anti-aircraft cruiser HMS *Coventry* and the destroyer HMS *Zulu* were sunk by enemy aircraft on their way back to Alexandria. Tommy Langton was the only member of the SBS on this operation, and his role was supposed to be that of guiding MTBs in from shore. The story is told by John Lodwick in *The Filibusters*:

'Tommy Langton, with that fragment of SBS not in Syria under Sutherland, was now called upon to take part in the great autumn raid of 1942 upon Tobruk harbour. This was a very ambitious operation indeed, involving the offshore co-operation of the destroyers *Sikh* and *Zulu* and the landing of parties from motor torpedo-boats at various points.

'On 22 August 1942, a squadron of the Special Air

Service left Cairo in seven three-ton lorries for Kufra Oasis. They were accompanied by detachments of Royal Engineers, Coastal Defence, Signals, and anti-aircraft units, and were later joined by a patrol of the Long Range Desert Group under Captain Lloyd Owen. The intention was to drive into Tobruk in three of these lorries, disguised as British prisoners-of-war, with a guard made up from members of the party dressed in German uniforms.

'The lorries were intended to drive along the south side of Tobruk harbour, then to halt in a secluded wadi, where the troops would de-bus and divide in two parties . . . Lieutenant-Colonel Haselden (commanding the group) was then to attack positions on the west side of the bay; Major Campbell, his aide, to capture the positions on the east. Meanwhile, Langton was responsible for signalling in the MTBs and meeting the landing-parties as they came ashore.

'The entrance went on smoothly. No check posts were encountered. After de-bussing and sorting their stores, the German uniforms were hidden and the two parties set out. Langton, with a section under a Lieutenant Roberts, had not gone far before a rifle shot was heard, evidently a warning. Roberts took his section round the back of the hill and discovered a number of Germans about to man a machine-gun. He killed them. At the same time, the success signal, a Very light, was fired by Lieutenant-Colonel Haselden's party. Langton and his men now became intrigued by a small building which they judged, correctly, to be a wireless station. This was destroyed and the personnel inside it dispatched, again largely by Lieutenant Roberts.

'Langton now went down to the beach alone and began to signal to the MTBs. There was no definite reply. While thus occupied, he had left his haversack and tommy-gun upon a rock and, on returning, found them missing. A moment later he almost walked into two well-armed Germans. "I hit them," he said, "with my revolver." The Germans ran away.

'Farther down the coast Langton found two MTBs which had succeeded in getting inshore. They were already unloading. He borrowed another tommy-gun and resumed his signalling. The alarm, however, had now been given, and searchlights were sweeping not only the harbour, but also the shore. Langton found the lingering inquisitive beams definitely unpleasant, but he was in a happier position than the MTBs still at sea. "I could see the tracer positively BOUNCING off them," he said.

'Dawn was now breaking. In the growing light, in this devastated town 800 miles behind the front line, Langton spotted one of the MTBs ashore some distance away. He hailed her but received no reply. Thinking it time to contact the main party he made his way up the hillside. A platoon of Germans lay blocking his retreat some three hundred yards away. Prudently, Langton returned to the water-bottle and made a breakfast of bully and biscuits. While he was munching, Lieutenants Russell and Sillito and Privates Hillman and Watler came on board. A conference was held, and it was decided to put the ship's guns to some practical use. Accordingly, Lieutenant Russell opened up with the twin Lewis-guns for'ard against the now more aggressive Germans on top of the hill. The Germans disappeared.

'Private Watler, a mechanic, now made an attempt to start the ship's engines, but this was quickly seen to be a hopeless task. By no means discouraged, the five men embarked in one of the assault craft lying alongside the ship and paddled sedately round the bay pursued by heavy but inaccurate small-arms fire from the astonished enemy.

Parties both of Germans and British could be seen playing hide-and-seek in the rocks and caves of the harbour. From one point the smoke of heavy explosions was rising. Far out to sea, HMS *Zulu*, with HMS *Sikh* in tow, was limping home under shell-fire. The position was confusing.

'After he had put what seemed to be a reasonable distance between himself and the enemy, Langton beached his assault craft and, leading his party, crossed a couple of minefields and discovered about twenty survivors of the raid in a deep wadi. From there he was able to obtain some idea of the sequence of events: the action led by Lieutenant-Colonel Haselden had gone remarkably well. A number of strong-points had been captured and the enemy manning them exterminated, with the unfortunate exception of four Italians, who had run off towards the town shouting the alarm.

'Germans are always reluctant to move by night, but at dawn they had effectively counter-attacked with a force of not less than a battalion. Lieutenant-Colonel Haselden's party had taken to their trucks and attempted to escape, but were ambushed and halted, with the exception of Lieutenant Barlow, who drove straight through the road-block, dismounted and brought his two Lewis-guns into play from the flank with terrible effect. Many men were now wounded or dead. Lieutenant-Colonel Haselden, therefore, shouted to those who were left to charge the enemy. He led the charge himself and was killed by a grenade a few yards from a party of screaming Italians, who did not live to boast of their exploit. Lieutenant Barlow rallied the now tiny force and withdrew with them under heavy enemy fire. Farther to the left, Lieutenant Roberts and his section had been left behind to deal with some concrete gun-emplacements. That they dealt with them there can be no doubt; no man was to return to base from this detachment, but in one night's work they had accomplished more than many people in the entire course of the war.

'The survivors in the wadi now split up in the interests of safety. They made for the Tobruk perimeter. Twenty-five strong then they set out on their march, only three men were to reach safety. These three were Langton and Privates Watler and Hillman. For the first few days they followed the desert road, dodging German camps, being fired upon frequently by patrols, sleeping at night in caves. Finally, desperate from hunger and thirst, they reached an Arab village, where they were hospitably received, fed and given water.

'The next stage in their journey was less arduous. The Arabs passed them from village to village, informed them in good time of the approach of enemy patrols and reconnoitred the ground ahead. One night, when they were lying up close to the sea, a boat put in, and a voice shouted, "Any British here?" Langton and his companions, who had already observed a large *carabinieri* post close to this point, were not deceived.

'After three weeks, Sergeant Evans, who had accompanied the party and marched gallantly despite acute dysentery, became too ill to go any farther. He was carried to the road at night and left to be picked up by the enemy in the morning. One of the two Fusiliers Leslie, who were twins, suffered the same fate a night or two later; his brother elected to go with him into captivity. That left only Langton, Hillman, and Watler, who, with ten water-bottles, some bully-beef and some goat meat, started on the last long lap on 26th October.

'Three nights later they crossed the frontier wire between Cyrenaica and Egypt. On 13th November they were picked up at Himeimat, 400 miles to the west of

Tobruk. They had been marching for seventy-eight days, the greater part of the time with bare feet. The only comment made by Langton when congratulated upon his great feat was that he wished he had been better supplied with world news. Had he known that Montgomery was about to break through at El Alamein he would have attended the Eighth Army in comfort among the Arabs. A party was held in his honour, at Kabrit, towards the end of which Major Mayne drove a jeep through the mess. Casualties were slight.'

For his feat of courage and endurance Lieutenant T.R. Langton was granted the Military Cross (MC).

A much depleted No. 1 Special Boat Section was then finally absorbed into No. 1 SAS and became part of the Special Boat Squadron under the command of Major the Earl Jellicoe with Langton and David Sutherland as commanders of its two Sections. This unit operated with great distinction in the Aegean, mainly in caiques (small Levantine sailing coasters) after the capture of Colonel Stirling in January 1943. From 11 November 1943 it came under the co-ordinating umbrella of Raiding Forces Middle East, and it continued to operate in the Aegean and then in the Adriatic. But by the end of 1942 it had ceased to have any connection with the original Commando Special Boat Section. This similarity of names, and the identical initials (SBS) has caused some confusion to researchers investigating the history of the units.

4
SBS in the Invasion of North Africa, 1942

Although we did not know it at the time, the training of No. 2 SBS was leading up to the Anglo-American landings in North Africa which were being planned for the autumn of 1942. Morocco and Algeria were controlled by Vichy France under German influence, and many senior American and some British commanders had misgivings over the proposed landings, codenamed Torch, for if the French resisted with German support, the Allies would be caught up in a conflict that could give little help to Russia. Yet Stalin wanted proof of the Western Allies' intention to fight the Germans on more than the British Eighth Army's desert front in Egypt. Also success in North Africa could open the way to landings in southern Europe and offer the prize of French fleets in the North African ports.

SBS took part in four separate subsidiary operations before and during Torch: Flagpole – the secret mission of the US staff officers to Algeria before the main invasion; Kingpin – the evacuation of General Giraud from the South of France at the eleventh hour; Torch itself – COPP/SBS marker guides for the Allied landing; and Reservist – the assault on Oran harbour.

The SBS contribution to the success of Torch was considerable considering the small size of the unit and the comparatively few men involved. A contingent left by sea for Gibraltar at the end of September 1942 to join the nucleus of COPP (Combined Operations Pilotage Party) under Lieutenant-Commander Nigel Clogstoun-Willmott, Roger's old friend. He had been hurriedly brought back from the Middle East in June and given the impossible task of training a sufficient number of naval officers in the art of beach reconnaissance and pilotage to carry out the vital pre-invasion tasks before Torch itself.

We in SBS had to make up COPP numbers with paddlers and, in addition, provide the canoes, some of the arms and gear, and help with the canoe training of COPPists. On 13 October we all collected in Gibraltar in HMS *Maidstone*, the depot ship of the 8th Submarine Flotilla, and started serious training. Someone with a wry sense of humour, who must have known Willmott, had allotted the covername 'Inhuman' to the COPP/SBS party. We were woken at 0530, given cocoa and a ship's biscuit at 0600 and made to run up the Rock (altitude twelve hundred feet) before breakfast. Being portly and short of breath, I did not take too kindly to this over-enthusiasm by our clean-living Naval Commander and was happy to disappear on Operation Flagpole inside HMS/M *Seraph* a week later.

1. Operation Flagpole

Flagpole has been described as a *Boy's Own Paper* adventure story, and it received some publicity in America and Great Britain soon after Torch. It was hailed as the first operation of its kind involving close partnership between British naval, army and air units with our American allies and, in the opinion of Captain G.B.H. Fawkes, then commanding the 8th Submarine Flotilla, was a happy augury for the future. It also saved a lot of lives.

The unit of the British Army was our Special Boat Section, represented by Captain G.B. Courtney (Royal West Kent Regiment) and Lieutenants R.P. Livingstone (Royal Ulster Rifles) and J.P. Foot (Dorsets). We had with us in the submarine five members of the US General Staff; Major General Mark Wayne Clark, head of mission and deputy of General Eisenhower, Brigadier General Lyman Lemnitzer, principal US planner on Eisenhower's staff, Colonel Arch Hamblen, logistics expert, Colonel Julius C. Holmes, formerly of the State Department and a specialist in French government, all of the US Army, and Captain Jerauld Wright, of the US Navy, whose over-riding interest was in the fate of the French fleet.

Our orders were to put these officers safely ashore at a spot where a white light would be shining from a large house with white walls and a red tiled roof at a small place called Messelmoun about sixty miles west of Algiers. The house was said to sit on a large hill about halfway between the shore and the coast road, with a path leading up to it and, down by the beach, a small grove of olive trees. When safely ashore, the Americans expected to meet General Mast, the commander of the French forces in the Algiers district. He would be accompanied by Robert Murphy, President Roosevelt's diplomatic representative in North Africa, and Consul-General in Algiers, and Ridgway Knight, US Consul at Oran. They hoped to persuade Mast to co-operate in making the imminent landings peaceful and unopposed by the forces under his command. They would emphasize that the whole Torch operation would be under American control because of the deep hostility felt by many Vichy French towards the British. Meanwhile we were to look after the Americans ashore and bring them safely and secretly back to the submarine.

During the evening of 20 October 1942, we instructed our charges in the art of boarding the frail and unstable canvas and rubber canoes, which would be used to take them ashore and bring them back again. Then at 0400 hours next morning, 21 October, *Seraph* closed to within half a mile of the shore onto a light shining from a house which exactly fitted the description of the rendezvous. This was a fine piece of accurate navigation by the Captain of *Seraph*, Lieutenant N.L.A. Jewell RN, and his navigator. *Seraph* then proceeded out to sea and submerged for the day, cruising up and down the coast while 'Dickie' Livingstone drew panorama sketches of the landing beach and background through the periscope. At dusk we surfaced and closed the beach again to wait for the light from the house. This did not appear until shortly before midnight, and we and the passengers made haste to get away.

Holmes, who knew some of the men ashore, went first with Livingstone. Lemnitzer and Jimmy Foot were next, then Wright and Hamblen. General Clark and I were to embark next but, as I stepped into the canoe, a wave overturned it, and it drifted under the foreplanes of the submarine, with some damage to the frame. I recalled Wright's boat, and Hamblen gave up his place to Clark. Although my boat was cracked in several places, Hamblen and I decided to risk it, and we were able to catch up with the rest of the party before they hit the beach.

In the words of 'Dickie' Livingstone, recorded in *The Green Beret – The Story of the Commandos* by Hilary St George Saunders (1949):

'Stopping at intervals to scan with our glasses the silent shore, seemingly empty in the bright moonlight, we slipped quietly through the calming water while the signal light shone high above us, now the only sign of any human agency to be seen.

'We touched the beach amid the soft wash of ripples, leaped out, and with the unease of all special boatmen on an open shore, prepared to get the boat up into the black shadows among the bushes at the foot of the bluff, when a man appeared out of the bushes to our left. Instantly we covered him as he crunched across the sand, but the Colonel recognized him as an old friend, and as several more figures appeared they were slapping each other on the back and asking after mutual friends. It was several minutes before I could get them to move the boat into cover. The General held a brief conference with the shore party and decided that the conversations could not be finished during the night and that we must stay over the day and come off the next night. Jumbo (Courtney) got in touch with the submarine by radio, identifying himself as arranged by referring to obscure and discreditable incidents in the past history of her crew, and gave them the news. After this everyone lent a hand to carry the boats and kit up to the house where we were all to be concealed during the coming day.

'Carrying our dripping canoes, we stumbled up a steep ravine through the aromatic bushes. There was a momentary alarm as we suddenly noticed a silent figure looking down on us from above. Then someone called softly: "C'est vous, René?" "C'est moi", was the quiet answer; it was a friendly picket watching the main road. The trees rustled softly, throwing a confused pattern of shadows on the moonlit ground as we staggered up the narrow, twisting path, the boats by now seeming to weigh tons. Then we came out to an open patch shaded by a huge twisted olive tree in front of the house, passed through a big green gate set in a white wall, and found ourselves in the courtyard of a villa. After some difficulty a place large enough to take them was found for the boats, and they were manhandled inside and locked in. Then we adjourned to a small brightly lit room where glasses of whisky were forced upon us – not much force was required – and we were able to take stock of our fellow conspirators. Introductions in a mixture of languages were made and everyone began to explain exactly how sure they had been that everything would be all right, in spite of everyone else's pessimism. The French were clearly on edge, but if the Americans were they didn't show it. When we heard that the coastwatchers had been removed and coastwise traffic stopped on our stretch of road, and that practically all local authority except the police and Navy were in the plot, we felt a good deal more secure than if we had been on an exercise with a lot of hair-trigger home guards on the watch . . .

'After resting we were awakened by the caretaker of the house with cups of splendid coffee (milkless) and rolls of rye bread. The generals had already been up two hours and were at work conferring in the courtyard. We had been told to be very careful not to show ourselves, and as there was nothing to do all day we were in no hurry to get up. The sun was shining brightly outside; there was a lovely tiled balcony to bask on, but we were not even allowed to open the shutters . . .

'The Frenchmen were very uneasy and it was decided that we should leave as soon as it was dark – about 2000 hours. All the important people had left and the conference was over, so there was nothing to do but wait. A strong northerly breeze had sprung up and there was more surf on the open beach than we cared for, though it was difficult to gauge its height from above. We hoped that the shore wind at dark would damp it down a bit.

'Soon after 2000 hours on the 22nd we began to get the boats out. Three of them were already in the courtyard when the caretaker, a dark nervous little Frenchman with horn-rimmed spectacles, came rushing in with the news that the police were arriving. At first we thought of making a dash for it, but second thoughts prevailed and the boats were bundled back again. After a few staccato exchanges between Colonel Holmes and the French representatives, we were ordered to the wine cellar (empty unfortunately), and descended a crumbling ladder into a dark and cobwebby pit, leaving the caretaker to cope with the police. . . . We were anxious to avoid fighting if possible, because it would have given the game away and would have also involved us in slaughtering a lot of half-armed and comparatively innocent gendarmes in order to cover the General's retreat . . . however, knowing that money talks, we had come liberally supplied . . . between us we had enough money to corrupt every policeman in North Africa.

'The trapdoor lowered upon us, barrels were rolled on top, and some artist scattered dust over the boards which percolated through and caused someone to sneeze devastatingly at intervals for some time, in spite of his efforts to suppress it. We sat silently in that pestilent cellar in pitch darkness, getting more and more cramped, for two hours, listening to the carefree whistling and cheerful shouts of the people upstairs, who were giving a fine performance as honest citizens with nothing to conceal, certainly not a cargo of contraband generals in the wine cellar. At one point General Clark could be heard tinkering with his carbine, clicking the mechanism up and down and muttering "How does this thing work?" This was far from reassuring to those on either side of him, as we knew it was loaded, and someone whispered fiercely "For heaven's sake put it down" in a tone no-one should use to a general.

'Eventually, a trundling sound was heard overhead and we cocked our guns in case we might have to shoot our way out, but it turned out to be our friends. They told us that we had three hours to get away in. We hauled out the boats and everyone lent a hand to hurry them down to the shore.

'From the shore, the surf, though lower, was still a nasty proposition, curling thunderously on the steep-to beach in a most unattractive way. . . After a few minutes the submarine appeared, accurately on the pre-arranged bearing to a hair, and the General and I prepared to make the first attempt. We floated the boat waist deep, waited for a lull with the undertow tearing at our legs, and at a favourable moment made a dash for it; but just as we were almost clear an extra large wave turned up. The boat reared up almost vertically; the crest of the wave crashed down on top of us, she rolled over, and in an instant we were struggling to free ourselves in a boiling turmoil of foam . . . just as the backwash relaxed enough to let me move forward, another wave crashed down and buried me. However, the others had now come to our assistance and everything was eventually rescued, including the all important paddles. The General swears he heard someone say: "Never mind the General, for heaven's sake get the paddles".

'After a further consultation it was decided to make one last attempt. Remembering the practice of the natives on the Gold Coast when launching their canoes, Courtney had decided on a new method. He enlisted the shore party, who had peeled off their clothes, and carried the boat out beyond the first line of surf, which was the worst. The General and Captain Wright watched their opportunity and scrambled in while the shore party heaved the boat up as each wave came in. Paddling furiously they surmounted by the skin of their teeth a series of waves, while the rest of us watched. Twice they swerved, then they were through, rising and falling on the smoother waves beyond. Jimmy (Foot) and Hamblen went next and were overwhelmed at once. We dragged them out and tried again. This time they got away. Then Courtney and Lemnitzer tried and also came to grief but the shore party, working like Trojans in the surf, hauled them out, shook the water out of them and launched them once more; this time they, too, got off. Colonel Holmes and I had our boat ready and rushed in close on their heels, taking advantage of the same lull. For a moment or two it was touch and go, but by furious paddling we won through with very little water inside. Just ahead we could see the others and soon, too, were able to pick up the submarine's conning-tower . . . There were lights on the coast road.

'One by one we came alongside, handed up our kit and scrambled out on to the casing. . . . As I scrambled up the conning-tower I looked toward the shore. The advancing headlights from Algiers were stationary in front of the house . . . the police had turned up after all. Thankfully we went below to change as *Seraph* turned seaward. The General brought glasses of whisky forward to us as we dried ourselves in the communications mess where we lived, a characteristically graceful action.

'Next morning a Catalina came over from Gibraltar, settling down on the sea close to the submarine. We ferried the generals and their luggage over to her, leaving them with mutually cordial farewells, and the promise of future meetings.'

I can add a few sidelights to Livingstone's description of our adventure. The sneezes in the cellar, which could have given us away, were in fact a series of smothered coughs, which finally ceased after General Clark had given me his personal piece of well-used chewing-gum to masticate. Following our flight from the villa and after the first abortive attempt by Clark and Livingstone to get back to the submarine, I well remember sitting disconsolately on the beach by myself watching the waves, while the others had concealed themselves in the bushes at the foot of the hill.

Jimmy Foot, as junior officer, gave his trousers to General Lemnitzer, who had already given his own to General Clark, who was soaking wet and shivering. It was an anxious half hour before I remembered the African boatmen on the beaches at Accra in the (then) Gold Coast. This finally got us off, and only just in time.

Forty years later, on the anniversary of our return to Gibraltar, Admiral Wright told me that the cover-story given to the Vichy police by Bob Murphy had hinted at wine, women and song and a naughty week-end. He was dressed for the part in khaki pants, a turtleneck sweater and sneakers, looking suitably dissolute, like a defrocked diplomat rather than President Roosevelt's personal representative. However, Monsieur Tessier, the owner of the villa, had previously banished his Arab servants for the occasion, and these, knowing that the place had been a centre for local smugglers, had reported to the police in the hope of a reward. Hence the police were still suspicious and said they would return with reinforcements.

The canoe in which Holmes and Livingstone returned to *Seraph* capsized and sank alongside, and Bill Jewell dared not wait to recover it. In it was a weighted bag containing letters and 2,000 US dollars in gold, intended for emergency use. We never learned that it was recovered, which is not surprising.

In 1956 I received a letter from Julius Holmes enclosing photographs taken the previous year of a memorial to our adventure put up by the French after the war near the villa in which we had been hidden. This included a marble plaque on which the names of the American, British and French participants were inscribed – presumably from memory if the spelling is any guide. Forty years after our landing, I was able to arrange for a relative to visit the site. In the intervening period the memorial had been badly damaged by gunfire, and the villa had become a complete ruin – casualties of the bitter strife between the French and the Algerians between 1956 and 1962.

2. Operation Kingpin: The Escape of General Giraud from France

Terence Robertson relates events in *The Ship with Two Captains* (1957).

The key principle in the concept of Torch had been the hope that a Frenchman could be found of such political integrity, patriotism and military renown that the varying factions in North Africa would rally to him and on the side of the Allies. 'At the house with the red tiled roof' on the coast, General Mast had been able to guarantee the loyalty of only the Algerian garrison he commanded. In his opinion, the forces at Oran and Casablanca were strongly pro-Vichy and would follow the orders of Pétain. Only one man could change their loyalty in a call to arms for a revival of France's military glory and weld all Frenchmen in North Africa under his standard to the Allied cause – General Henri Honoré Giraud, the very tall, spare and gaunt-faced hero of Wassigny on the

Belgian frontier. Giraud, a prisoner of war in Germany for two years, had escaped some six months before and was now sitting uneasily in Vichy France while Pétain and Laval planned to hand him back to the Germans in exchange for further concessions from Hitler. The Allied need for him out of France had already been communicated to Mast by Robert Murphy, and this had been relayed by secret courier to Lyons, where Giraud was living with his wife and family. The General had replied that he was willing to be smuggled from France to North Africa only if the Allies pledged to him a command in keeping with his rank and reputation.

'Now, on 25 October 1942, the day when HMS/M *Seraph* and the three SBS officers returned to Gibraltar after saying goodbye to General Mark Clark and his party, the Torch planners gave the green light for the invasion forces to gather. Later that day a signal was sent to Gibraltar formally requesting that *Seraph* be placed under the command of an American naval officer and held ready for immediate operations; this was because Giraud had refused to be picked up by a British submarine. No American submarine was available, and it was decided that *Seraph* would ostensibly be put under command of an officer in the American Navy, who would greet Giraud on deck and usher him swiftly below before he could catch on.

'In London Eisenhower and Clark told Captain Jerauld Wright to fly out to Gibraltar next morning. Julius Holmes was too much involved in Torch planning to be spared from London, so Colonel Bradley Gaylord of the 12th US Army Airforce was recruited by Wright from his office in Gibraltar. He spoke fluent French and was a cheerful character who could mix a mean martini. That evening he joined the "North African Canoe Club" – that

exclusive circle of American officers who sailed in *Seraph*
to carry out the "crazy stunts" which an official history has
since called "the two special operations which did more to
rejuvenate the fighting spirit of France and bring about
the downfall of Mussolini than the actual landings themselves".

'*Seraph* left HMS *Maidstone* at 2100 hours on 27 October
to proceed to the Gulf of Lions, from which any point on
the southern coast of France could be reached easily, and
to return with Giraud along a clearly defined path to
Gibraltar. On successive days a Catalina aircraft would fly
along that line at a certain time to act as escort or, if it
proved necessary, to facilitate the arrival of Giraud in
North Africa.

'Captain Barney Fawkes, commanding 8th Submarine
Flotilla, was preparing another of his flotilla to follow and
take over the operation should the enemy interfere and
cause *Seraph* to miss the rendezvous. Giraud was too
important to the Allies at that particular moment for all
the eggs to be carried in one basket. HMS/M *Sybil*, commanded by Lieutenant E.J.D. Turner RN sailed next
morning to take her place if necessary.

'On the 30th *Seraph* was clear of friendly shores, and
any aircraft or surface vessel could safely be assumed to be
an enemy. *Seraph* submerged until dark, when she
surfaced again for fresh air and breakfast. Then we repeated the parlour game of the previous mission by in-
sisting that Wright and Gaylord practise boarding a
folboat canoe off the wardroom table. This was mainly for
the airforce officer's benefit as Wright had shown on the
previous trip how expert he was at handling these boats.
Gaylord entered into the fun and soon managed to satisfy
the perfectionist, Foot. Of them all that evening, only
Livingstone, recently nicknamed "Doc" for his habit of

reading the classics in Greek, seemed very unhappy about the whole affair. He was a demolition and sabotage expert and only wanted to create big bangs.

'The next night Wright and Jewell were persuaded to let us carry out a proper run with the canoes. They were brought up through the forehatch and laid alongside, and Gaylord practised getting in and out with *Seraph* rolling unexpectedly and mischievously each time he had one foot in mid-air. Then Jimmy Foot and I took one away into the night to test the walkie-talkie set and the infra-red signal lamps. These proved to be working, so we returned and stowed away the canoes, and *Seraph* continued on her way, thankful that the enemy could be expected to sleep at that time of night.

'No news giving the time and place of the rendezvous with Giraud had been received by 4 November, only four days before the date of the landings in North Africa. Wright and Jewell decided that, once clear of the French coast after the mission had been accomplished, they would signal Gibraltar to take off the General. *Seraph* surfaced as usual at dusk. Suddenly, at 8 P.M. the radio operator poked his head out of his office and announced the receipt of a message in code.

'"Kingpin" [codename for General Giraud] with three others will be ready to embark in shoreboat at La Fosette 1000 yards east of Le Lavandou tomorrow Thursday night November 5th . . . if weather permits Catalina aircraft will subsequently rendezvous with you to take off passengers . . .'

'*Seraph* picked up speed and remained on the surface throughout the night, and at dawn the crew turned in for a brief rest until action stations were sounded a few minutes before the coastline came into view through the periscope. She approached to within five hundred yards, and Jewell handed over the periscope to the commandos, who took turns in making themselves familiar with the shore and its various distinguishing points in case we would have to land that night.

'At the same time *Seraph*'s sister, *Sybil*, was approaching the same coast, about thirty miles out, in accordance with a signal sent by Captain Fawkes to Lieutenant Turner. Giraud's rendezvous arrangement called for two pick-ups – he had divided his party to make sure that at least some got through – and his officers were to embark the following night.

'After dark on the 5th, *Seraph* surfaced to find a rough sea running. Rendezvous-time came and passed, and she was forced to dive hurriedly to escape a fleet of trawlers making for the fishing grounds. Meanwhile, weather reports indicated that two hours of the present roughness could be expected, after which it would become worse. The foredeck reception party changed into bathing-trunks and plimsolls. Odd flickering lights were coming from a large house ashore overlooking the front. On *Seraph*'s bridge a signalman read the flashes from the house ashore: "O-N-E-H-O-U-R". It was then midnight. Suddenly a look-out sighted a darkened ship out to sea about three miles away.

'Binoculars swung around and hearts stopped beating as an E-boat was seen cutting through the sea on her patrol. Jewell's immediate reaction was to dive; but he remembered in time that to dive now would probably mean failure to contact Giraud, and a miserable end to the whole operation. Wright read his thoughts, tapped him on the shoulder and shook his head. Jewell nodded, and they watched the enemy draw closer. *Seraph* presented a small silhouette, but it seemed impossible for her to escape detection. Fervent silent prayers were offered that Giraud would not start signalling and attract the enemy's attention. The minutes dragged and the enemy seemed to be slowing down. All movement in the submarine stopped and the engines were silenced. Five minutes of eternity ticked before the E-boat vanished into the shadows, the faint sound of her powerful motors subsiding until there was only the slap of the angry sea at *Seraph*'s sides.

'Her engines were started again and she was pointed at the beach, the conning-tower crew relaxing with deep sighs of relief. It had been too close, and there was no further stomach for jest and banter.

'Time seemed to stand still until the last look-outs, upon whom a submarine relies for safety, reported something moving at a jetty ashore. It was nearly one o'clock when they both reported again that a boat was pulling from the jetty. A cross-wind was blowing up and, now that zero hour was approaching, not much time would be left before the weather made embarkation impossible. All the bridge personnel could now see the boat. It was painted white and at about one hundred yards from the shore began signalling with a dim light. This was the correct recognition signal, but *Seraph* was reluctant to reply, hoping she would be seen without having to disclose her position not only to the Giraud party but also to any watchers ashore. Then it became obvious that the boat was heading in the wrong direction and would miss her unless something was done to attract her attention. There was no room in the narrow, rock-strewn water to manoeuvre across and intercept. With some misgivings, Wright ordered the reply to be given on a dimmed lamp. It was seen immediately, and the small white boat swung round. Spray was flying round the foredeck from the choppy sea as Wright, Gaylord and Bolton, the gunnery officer, left the conning-tower to join the embarkation party on the deck casing. Only a few inches below the surface were the big bulges of the ballast tanks. The five members of the crew tied lifelines round the Americans in case of accidents. Then the white rowing-boat came out of the shadows and was clearly revealed in the moonlight.

'The *Seraph*'s crew threw a line across to the boat and began to pull it alongside, but the sea was too strong, and Wright and Gaylord had to add their weight before the boat swung round abreast of the submarine and drifted closer. Gaylord saw that it was about to bump against the casing and yelled for everyone to stop heaving. If anyone was caught between the two vessels as they hit, a nasty mess would be the only result.

'As the boat hit the submarine, Giraud stood up, put one foot on the gunwale of the fishing-boat and made a great leap as the two vessels rebounded apart after the bump. He missed the *Seraph*'s deck and went down between the fishing-boat and the submarine. Luckily he landed on the ballast tanks just below the surface, and those within reaching-distance grabbed him. He was dragged safely onto the casing just before the fishing-boat came crashing alongside for the second time.

'When Giraud stood up, he seemed quite unconcerned and shook hands formally with Captain Wright who, with Gaylord interpreting, welcomed him aboard the USS *Seraph*. The ropes were let go, and the fisherman waved and pulled his brave little boat into the heavy sea to disappear into the night.

'With Giraud were his son Léon, his Chief of Staff, Captain André Beaufré, and an aide, Lieutenant Viret of the French Navy. Jewell gave his orders softly from the bridge, and *Seraph* turned about to move into the heavy sea to the safety of the wide open spaces. She had been confined for too long in dangerous shallow waters under the eyes and ears of the enemy.

'She was to head for Gibraltar along an agreed line above which the aircraft would fly at night. Above all, she was to stay submerged by day as, at this critical moment in the planning of Torch, all Allied aircraft had been ordered to bomb submarines on sight. *Seraph* surfaced at dusk, the usual rush of fresh air cleaned out smells, and the cook began to prepare breakfast.

'At 10 P.M. Jewell ordered the wireless operator to start sending his report to Gibraltar. This would be the first news of Giraud's escape. A few minutes later the wireless operator returned to the bridge to say that the transmitter had broken down. By dawn the cantankerous transmitter still refused to work, and the position began to look black. The landings were due to take place the next night. If Giraud had to stay aboard *Seraph*, he would not get to Gibraltar before the 11th – too late to be of much use to the Allies. Even worse was the thought that, as from the next day, the western Mediterranean would be filled with warships, convoys, anti-submarine patrols and aircraft. All would be searching for submarines who could not give the correct identification signals by radio and would therefore be legitimate targets.

'Jewell, Wright and Gaylord stood on the conning-tower bridge watching dawn rise on Friday 7 November. In a few minutes it would be time to dive unless they invited trouble by staying on the surface – and with Giraud on board this might spell disaster. In his patrol report Jewell wrote: "I decided to remain on the surface despite all orders to the contrary, because it seemed important to me to get Kingpin or a message through to Gibraltar as quickly as possible. If we failed to sight the Catalina, we might get through to a passing

Allied plane which could then inform Gibraltar of our predicament." At 8.50 A.M. a look-out shouted, "Aircraft on the port quarter, up sun, elevation thirty degrees." All eyes went round to gaze intently towards the yellow ball of the rising sun. There it was, just a tiny black speck. The next few minutes were filled with anxiety as the speck came closer but refused to alter course. Suddenly it was recognizable as a Catalina and, by its position, could only be the one sent out by Fawkes to look for them.

'Suddenly the aircraft dipped its wings in a right-hand turn and came towards *Seraph*, one of the airmen signalling the challenge of the day. The Catalina came low and circled the submarine while a message was sent, asking him to land and pick up passengers. He was also told to inform Gibraltar by radio of *Seraph*'s faulty transmitter. By the time he got down and headed into the wind about four hundred yards away, the commandos had the canoes ready to make the transfer. Giraud and his party were brought up on deck and stood on the foredeck waiting for Wright and Gaylord to say goodbye to Jewell. Suddenly there was a shout from another look-out: "Aircraft dead astern coming this way. Elevation ten degrees, distance about eight thousand yards." It was coming in low – about two hundred feet – and fast. The look-out shouted again, "Looks like a JU88, sir."

'They presented a perfect target – a Catalina squatting like a fat duck on the surface with a submarine almost alongside it. The plane was almost near enough to drop its bombs when, without explanation, it swerved, and Jewell, still half through the "lid", saw the twin split tails of a Hudson. He climbed back to the conning-tower with the crew and passengers while the Hudson went into a wide-circling patrol round them. The whole operation of trans-ferring the passengers to the Catalina would have been greatly helped had the aircraft stopped engines in the first place. *Seraph* had to turn to the wind and sea to create a lee for launching the canoes, but the aircraft proceeded at about one knot into the wind, slowly widening the gap between aircraft and submarine. Furthermore, the draught caused by the propellers of the aircraft made it most difficult for the canoes to approach it. Then, when the aircraft did stop its engines eventually, a sea anchor would have been of the greatest assistance in the operation. With engines stopped, the aircraft drifted to leeward nearly as fast as the canoes could proceed through the water, so that they could get no closer despite strenuous efforts.

'However, after frantic signals and shouting between *Seraph*, the aircraft and the canoes, all arrived safely and vanished into the Catalina's bulging belly. The commandos brought back the canoes and gathered around Jewell on the bridge to join him in waving at the aircraft, which had begun to surge along the surface.'

Thirty-nine years later Jimmy Foot recalls that he had been given the job of taking General Giraud over to the Catalina and that he had been threatened with court-martial if Giraud fell in the drink. Giraud was long-legged, lean and dignified and refused to sit down in the canoe in the approved fashion but perched himself on the stern with his legs inside the rear cockpit. The result was a very top-heavy canoe, difficult to paddle and liable to capsize. Thinking that the General spoke no English, Jimmy advised the reception committee, when coming alongside the Catalina, that his passenger was a silly old bastard and that they were welcome to him, or words to that effect. Once aboard the aircraft, Giraud turned round and thanked him in good English for a very pleasant trip and apologized for having caused so much difficulty on the way over. According to Giraud's son Léon, whom Jimmy Foot met at a submarine reunion after the War, his father used to tell the story with great amusement.

Meanwhile, their sister-ship, *Sybil*, was approaching the rendezvous point off La Fosette to meet the shoreboat with the ten members of Giraud's staff. With *Seraph*'s radio silent, Lieutenant Turner was uncertain of her whereabouts and kept an extra look-out for fear of ramming or interfering with the other operation.

'In his report Turner wrote, "At 0200 a small boat was seen pulling off from the shore and as it approached the submarine we could see it was painted white. Codeword for the operation has been given as 'Neptune', so after exchanging letters 'K' on dimmed lamps, I hailed the boat with 'Neptune ahoy'. I was surprised to receive a reply in a female voice saying softly through the darkness:

> 'They seek him here, they seek him there,
> Those Frenchies seek him everywhere,
> Is he in Heaven? Is he in hell?
> That demned elusive Pimpernel'."

The owner of the voice appeared from the shadows to reveal herself as an attractive young Englishwoman, married to Captain Beaufré, who introduced her three companions as members of Giraud's staff. She then asked Turner to wait while the fishing-boat returned to the beach to pick up three more passengers and their baggage. Half an hour later the remainder of the party was aboard, and *Sybil* headed out to sea. Three of the original party were missing and thought to be in the hands of the police at Marseilles.

'*Seraph* entered Gibraltar harbour on 10 November 1942 and tied up alongside HMS *Maidstone* while *Sybil* landed her passengers at Algiers on the 11th.'

3. The Invasion (Operation Torch)

On 8 November 1942 the Anglo-American forces landed on the North African coast at Algiers, Oran and Casablanca. To assist the assault some periscope beach reconnaissances were made from submarines during October by COPP (Combined Operations Pilotage Party). Unfortunately some senior planner had been over-cautious and refused to sanction normal COPP beach reconnaissances from canoes for fear of compromising the assault landings. The penalty was paid on Y beach near Oran, where the landing-craft ran foul of an undetected false beach just offshore, many being damaged or, broaching to, drowning their vehicles. For the actual assault, canoes and five submarines were prepositioned to act as markers and as guides to the beaches. The canoes were mostly manned by COPP naval officers but supplemented by Army officers and NCOs from No. 2 SBS, who had been busy training with them at Gibraltar. These were: Lieutenants B.N. Eckhard and P.A. Ayton, Sergeant S. Weatherall and Corporals N. Thompson, J. Gilmour, A. Le M. Salisbury and J. Hutchinson. SBS also provided canoes, some arms and equipment, and canoe training.

Stan Weatherall has written an account of his experiences:

'On Sunday 1 November 1942 Sub-Lieutenant I.H. ('Peter') Harris RNVR of COPP and I boarded the HMS/M *Ursula*, commanded by Lieutenant R.B. Lakin RN, with two canoes, one slung above the forward messdeck, and the spare one in the place of a torpedo. We set sail, and on 4 November we reached the Bay of Arzeu in Algeria and began to do periscope recces by day, and one or two panorama sketches at night. On Saturday 7th *Ursula*

surfaced and we found the sea very choppy as we launched
the canoe over the starboard ballast tanks and shipped a
fair amount of water. Once clear of the submarine we had
to start baling out; the baler had been swilled forward and
Peter couldn't find it, so I baled out with my boot whilst
he paddled and kept us on course. The dolphins were a
nuisance; they headed for us like torpedoes, making a
phosphorescent wake, then veering off, causing us to ship
more water, and made the canoe bob up and down like a
cork. However, we made good headway as the wind was
in our favour and reached "Z" beach at 9.15 P.M. We
dropped the kedges which anchored us about two hundred
yards from the edge of the beach, and sat there to await
the time to begin signalling. *Ursula* went out to sea after
discharging us to act as beacon for the main convoy.

'At 12.15 A.M. on Sunday 8 November we began to
flash "Z" in morse by the RG gear, the beam could only
be seen by an RG monocular on the assault craft. We
could pick up the craft's signals by the same method. The
assault craft carrying the US Rangers arrived and beached
on our starboard side at 1.15 A.M. ten minutes late. More
assault craft came towards our signals, then veered off left
and right to the beach; they were the second and third
flights. On land all was quiet for about an hour, when we
heard a few shots fired and saw Very lights. The last flight
to be guided in was tank- and jeep-carriers at 4.15 A.M.

'With approaching daylight our job was finished, so we
paddled up to the coast towards the White beach, but on
Red beach several craft were really stuck and so we gave
them a hand in getting free by carrying their kedges in the
canoe to deeper water. After that we went further up and
made a landing on White beach and were held up at gun-
point by five US Rangers who asked us if we were a
"human torpedo". We were amazed to see such a vast

amount of shipping in the bay, when only the previous night there were only five canoes along the beach.'

A few days before the assault a final rehearsal was held by the canoe teams so that each navigator could show the paddlers their canoe's position as navigational marks to guide in the assault waves on D-Day. During this rehearsal a sudden storm caught those on the eastern sector, and Lieutenant G.F. (nicknamed 'Thin Red') Lyne RN and his paddler, both of COPP, were in its teeth.

There is a most graphic description of the dangers to canoeists in the Mediterranean from sudden storms in *Commandos and Rangers of World War II* by James A. Ladd:

'They strove to keep the canoe's bows heading into steep seas while they baled with tin mugs whenever there was a moment's let-up in the fury. They had an hour to get back to the submarine when the storm strengthened, tossing them high on one wave before they slithered off its back to meet the next great sea, all the time in danger of broaching to across the waves that could then roll them over. One great comber filled the canoe before she shook free from the cascading crests; now they could not expect to make much headway and had to fight even harder to avoid broaching to . . . Two miles offshore they were seen by a French trawler and were taken aboard, not before Geoff Lyne had time to slit the airbags, sinking the canoe with its telltale gear.'

Lieutenant N.P.C. ('Nick') Hastings RNVR of COPP, with Corporal N. Thompson of SBS tried to slip through the Vichy French lines on a motor bike to reconnoitre beaches to the eastward of Algiers. On a bend in a mountain road they ran into what they thought was a tank but which turned out to be a camel. When it was all over, Thompson gave Hastings a snappy salute and said he would recommend a ride with him for any girlfriend of his in the family way who wanted to get out of it.

Meanwhile, Lieutenant D.H. Sidders of SBS was sent to Gibraltar to help local forces spike Spanish guns, should General Franco declare war – which, of course, he did not.

Lieutenant Basil Eckhard, who was left in charge of training with party Inhuman in Gibraltar after Livingstone, Foot and I had left on Operations Flagpole and Kingpin, earned a well-deserved King's Commendation for picking up and throwing away a live hand-grenade dropped in a trench by a sailor during training. He was later Mentioned in Dispatches for his work in Torch.

4. Operation Reservist

The Vichy French Navy were known to be bitter over the destruction of their fleet by the British in 1940 at Mers-el-kebir after the fall of France. To prevent them from sabotaging port installations at Oran, two former American coastguard cutters, now renamed HMS *Hartland* and HMS *Walney* were loaded with American troops and charged the boom at fifteen knots in the early hours of the morning on 8 November 1942. They were fired on and burst into flames and blew up – with heavy casualties. In the *Walney* No. 2 SBS was represented by Captain H.V. Holden-White (Royal Sussex Regiment) and Corporal D.C. Ellis (King's Shropshire Light Infantry) with two other SBS canoe pairs – Corporals Sidlow and Wright, and Blewett and Loasby. Each canoe was equipped with two miniature torpedoes with which to prevent Vichy naval vessels from escaping from the harbour. Also on the

Walney was Company Sergeant Major J. Embelin, whose job was to cut the boom with explosives if the *Walney* should fail to break it.

Embelin was killed by a shell from a French destroyer, and Holden-White and Ellis were captured and spent a few uncomfortable days ashore in prison. They were later awarded the Military Cross and the Military Medal respectively. Sidlow and Wright were also captured and later Mentioned in Dispatches.

On the *Hartland* No. 2 SBS was represented by Lieutenants J.C.C. Pagnam and E.J.A. Lunn (Royal Artillery), Sergeant A. Milne and Corporal L. Bates. They also were armed with mini-torpedoes but were unable to use them as their canoes were damaged by gunfire. They jumped into a Carley float with several Americans and came under heavy machine-gun fire, which killed half the latter. The survivors were taken prisoner and locked up in a fort until released by the arrival of American troops with a tank.

The SBS survivors were ordered to make their own way back to the United Kingdom as soon as possible, and the party then consisted of Pagnam, Bates, Ellis, Blewitt, Sidlow, Milne, Loasby and Wright. They all took passage in the troopship, *Ettrick*, which was torpedoed next morning, and were taken back to Gibraltar. Colin Pagnam and seven NCOs were flown back to the United Kingdom in a US Army Liberator through the good offices of Colonel Bradley Gaylord of the US Army Airforce, last met by SBS as a member of Operation Kingpin – a friend in need.

Jimmy Foot and I flew back to England in an American Flying Fortress which was short of crew, and we each manned a .5 calibre machine-gun. The pilot mistook France for Britain and wanted to land there. He also tried to fly through a balloon barrage. According to Jimmy, at a later stage in the War he dropped an atomic bomb on Japan, which he seems to have found without help from the SBS.

The mini-torpedoes were invented by Sir Donald Campbell, of land- and water-speed record fame, and were powered by a windscreen-wiper engine. They were twenty-one inches long with twin opposed screws and a 1½ pound cavity charge in the nose. While they were an excellent idea and very powerful, they seemed to have worked better in quiet water at home than under rougher operational conditions. Harry Holden-White has commented that SBS did not receive sufficient instruction before Operation Reservist (Oran harbour) on how to assemble and handle them. As an example of this, he and his partner, Corporal Ellis, fired at a destroyer and a submarine at a range of about 100 to 120 yards, only to learn afterwards that the maximum effective range was fifty yards. He thinks he hit the destroyer but bagged a small lighthouse with his second torpedo, much to the fury and amazement of the keeper, who popped out to curse them. Eric Lunn recalls that they were supposed to sink of their own accord when the engine cut out but that he had been horrified to see one afloat near the Oran quay while he was being marched away by the French marines before being thrown into a filthy prison.

After dark they were again marched through the streets and were handed over to the French Army where the officer in charge welcomed them as '*Mes amis*' and told them that they would shortly be liberated by American troops.

Lunn and Holden-White were immediately ordered back to England to give an account of the raid to Lord Mountbatten, the Chief of Combined Operations. Lunn also was awarded the Military Cross for this operation.

5. Rail Sabotage by Captain R.P. ('Dickie') Livingstone and CSM Stamford ('Stan') Weatherall

When Torch was over, the SBS contingent was sent back to Hillhead for rest and re-equipment, with the exception of Captain R.P. ('Dickie') Livingstone and CSM Stamford ('Stan') Weatherall.

Stan Weatherall has written an account of their next operation:

'On Friday 20 November 1942 Captain Livingstone and I boarded the submarine *Ursula*, commanded by Lieutenant R.B. Lakin RN, with one canoe, slung above the for'ard mess deck. When the canoe was being put down the hatch, I asked one of the crew how long we were going for; he said for a twenty-one day patrol. The previous trip on this vessel was plenty long enough for me, but twenty-one days cooped up again I thought would just about drive me round the bend, but I was wrong. I actually enjoyed it, more so because I was a good sailor inasmuch as I was never troubled by seasickness. At 11.30 A.M. the sub left the harbour, and as soon as we were clear of it, the spine-chilling klaxon was sounded, and then we dived to periscope depth. The next five days were spent travelling up the coast of Spain and then into the Gulf of Lions, where the sea became extremely rough. The sub rolled and scooped up water with the conning-tower, rode over the high rollers and dived into the deep troughs with a helluva thud; there was a lot of water in the control room. A few of the crew were seasick so I volunteered to do lookout on the bridge, which wasn't very pleasant in those seas. Poor old Dickie lay on his bunk as sick as a dog; poor chap wasn't a good sailor and we all felt sorry for him.

'One of the engine bearings gave up the ghost, filling the sub with smoke, and several of the crew made a dive for DSEA (Davis Submarine Escape Apparatus) sets, but they were not needed. The Asdic, the Sperry and the radio transmitter gave up too, so Lakin took the sub down to 125 feet; the waters were somewhat rough at that depth, causing the sub to roll. The two ERAs (Engine Room Artificers) got to work on the engine; they made and fitted new bearings and with continuous work without sleep got the engine in working order again. The other things which had gone wrong were put to rights. The sub reached the outer limits of the Gulf of Genoa on the 28th.

'We were north of the Ligurian Sea, and Dickie and I did periscope recces of the area where we were to make a landing. The authorities thought it a better idea to send the SBS on a routine patrol as they could probably make a better job [of railway sabotage] than a bomber, and less costly. On the night of Sunday 29th the sub surfaced and with the aid of depth soundings the skipper took us to within twelve hundred yards of the beach edge. We slipped the canoe at 8 P.M. and paddled to the beach, picked up the canoe and carried it up the beach to a four-foot dirt sea wall skirting the coast road right on the V of a Y-shaped road junction. One road followed the coast and the other went through the village, which was west of Savona. In the V of the Y stood a very large house with lots of shrubbery in the grounds. Two large iron gates directly opposite us were fastened with wire. Two people came down the road who turned out to be a courting couple; they held us up for quite some time at least over half an hour, as they stood necking at the gates. After they left and were some distance up the road, Dickie nipped across and cut the gate wire and opened one of the gates sufficiently to get the boat through. We then carried the canoe across the road and into the garden and hid it amongst the bushes. We then crossed the other road into an orchard, which I think was an olive grove on the side of a steepish hill. There was a high wall at the top of the tunnel, and a sheer drop down to the rail track on the other side. It was our intention to derail a train in the tunnel, which would make things more difficult for the enemy. We went back down the hillside to the road and walked up it a good way through the village; we left it to wend our way through an alley with houses on either side and could hear some of the occupants talking. We came to more houses and behind them were garden allotments. We came to the track, which was on a twenty-foot embankment, and proceeded towards the tunnel.

'We came to a building at the side of the track and went on the verandah. Inside some people were talking, when suddenly a man came out to make water, talking over his shoulder as he did so. He was only a matter of four feet away from us, not knowing that two knives were at the ready; but having come into the darkness from a lit-up room, we knew his eyes would not be adjusted to the darkness, which usually takes several minutes. This building was a guard room for the sentries guarding the tunnel mouth and was less than a hundred yards from it. There was a sentry at the top of the tunnel, and one beside the track at the bottom, who called to one another at intervals, and so we could not place the charges in it.

'However, Dickie had been given instructions to let the Eyeties know we had been there, so we then clambered down the embankment and crawled some distance away from the guardhouse. We had to lie down for a while as we heard some movement on the other side of the hedge – could have been cattle grazing. We then continued along the ditch, until well clear of the guardhouse, then climbed up onto the track and walked a little further on, where we found the track curving ideally. We placed charges on the track sufficient to blow a six-foot gap at least, also on the iron standards which carried the power cables for the electric engines, and electric cables which we surmised fed the villages along the line. These were linked in a ring main by FID (Fuse Instantaneous Detonating) to be activated by a pressure switch under the outside rail. Whilst we were laying the charges, a very long train passed by, travelling east, which would have been an excellent target.

'It was now about 11 P.M. so we had no time to lose before getting back to the sub before the moon rose, otherwise we would have to find a hiding-place until the next night. We got back to the village road but had to cut a hole in some wire netting. We walked at a brisk pace down the road and passed a group of soldiers talking. Dickie whistled a tune from some Italian classic, we were not challenged. Further down we passed another group of people talking under a tree on our right, then a lone figure came towards us who proved to be a soldier the worse for drink; he stopped to look at us then carried on, much to our relief. We got the canoe, then ran down to the beach with it, and paddled out to the sub, which we had no difficulty in finding. About midnight the lookouts on the bridge of the sub saw a brilliant flash and heard an explosion. It was published in the Gibraltar *Chronicle* that the line was blocked for some days.'

Livingstone and Weatherall returned to Algiers in *Ursula* on 10 December, flew to Gibraltar and sailed for Plymouth in the mine-laying cruiser HMS *Adventure*, arriving finally back at SBS headquarters at Hillhead on 27 December 1942.

There is nothing new under the sun. The first recorded

sabotage raid on an enemy railway from a submarine occurred in 1915. This was carried out by Lieutenant D'Oyly Hughes DSO, RN, by swimming from HMS/M E–11 to mine a culvert on a Turkish railway line by the Sea of Marmara. Oddly enough, Roger Keyes had been Commodore (Submarines) before World War I and was serving in the Aegean Sea at this time as Chief of Staff. Perhaps this was why he was so receptive to Roger Courtney's ideas in July 1940 when Chief of Combined Operations.

5
'Z' SBS in the Mediterranean, 1943–4

In early March 1943 a special sub-division of No. 2 SBS was formed at Hillhead for attachment to the 8th Submarine Flotilla in HMS *Maidstone* at Algiers. It was named 'Z' Special Boat Section and consisted of five canoe pairs: myself (as officer commanding) and Sergeant N. Thompson, Lieutenant E.J.A. Lunn and Sergeant J. Gilmour, Lieutenant N.G. Kennard and Sergeant F. Preece DCM, Lieutenant A.R. McClair and Sergeant R. Sidlow, and Lieutenant J.P. Foot and Sergeant Newsome.

We installed ourselves comfortably in our depot ship alongside Algiers wharf. We officers became honorary members of the wardroom, while our sergeants were looked after by the petty officers' mess. We spent our days strengthening our canoes, camouflaging them and the paddles with light khaki or grey dope, sprinkling them with sand to prevent shine, and checking our magnetic compasses inside the canoes to detect errors. In our spare time we sought out black-market restaurants, drank happily of the excellent white wines of La Trappe – merry monks they must have been indeed – admired the nubile but unapproachable daughters of the French 'Colons' on the beach at Sidi Feruch and prepared ourselves for the days of wrath to come.

One of the less traumatic duties which SBS was called upon to carry out was to ferry secret agents to and from enemy shores. During the first two weeks of April 1943 my second-in-command, Eric ('Sally') Lunn, and I were told to take a resistance leader and his party in HMS/M *Trident* to the east coast of Corsica and evacuate his predecessor, who was on the run. The story is told in Chapter 6, which was written by me in 1951, when my recollections of the frightening submarine patrol which followed were still uncomfortably vivid.

On 6 May Lunn returned again in *Trident* to Corsica on a similar mission, taking with him my Sergeant Thompson and a Corporal Watt of the SAS as spare man. There were two operations planned for them, the first to land agents and stores in the same place as before, and the second to land more stores further down the coast. The first operation was abandoned owing to bad weather, and the second failed because there was no reception committee waiting when they landed on 10 May after a postponement of twenty-four hours. Lunn left the boats a few yards offshore and went to look for the reception committee. After half an hour there was no sign of anybody, so they had to paddle back to the submarine with the loads. The rubber dinghy which he was towing full of stores sprang a bad leak on the way back and was a dead weight behind him.

In late June 1943 'Sally' Lunn and Sergeant 'Jock' Gilmour left Algiers in HMS/M *Sportsman* to land agents in northern Italy. After this they tried some railway sabotage but were landed in the wrong place. They vented their disappointment on a couple of fishing-boats. With the collapse of the Axis armies in Tunisia in May 1943, the planners in Allied Force Headquarters in Algiers were preparing for the assaults on Sicily and the Italian mainland. Nigel Clogstoun-Willmott's beach-reconnaissance teams of naval navigators and army engineers were under intensive training in the south of England. These specialists were to carry out the vital inspections of the

Sicilian beaches. SBS was employed on simulating beach reconnaissance in Sardinia, as a small part of elaborate and widespread deception planned to mislead the Axis about the target of the next major Allied amphibious assault.

On 26 May 1943 Sergeants Thompson and Gilmour and Loasby and I sailed from Algiers in HMS/M *Safari*. The operation, named 'Marigold', was in two parts. Part I was to simulate a reconnaissance of a beach on the east coast of Sardinia and was carried out by Thompson and myself. The story, which I wrote in 1951 when memory was green, is told in the next chapter. Part II was to accompany as boat-handlers a party of one officer and seven other ranks of No. 2 Special Air Service (SAS) on a cutting-out raid ashore to capture a prisoner. On reaching the rocky shore, someone slipped and dropped his tommy-gun. We were ambushed and beat a hasty and undignified retreat to the submarine. Sergeant Loasby was taken prisoner.

There was a short interlude when, in the absence of our usual forms of employment, SBS was used to help SAS with boat-handling from submarines, rather to keep us busy than for any really useful function we could perform.

At the end of June 1943 I was sent by myself as dispatcher in HMS/M *Severn* with a party from No. 1 Special Air Service who were to land on the west coast of Sardinia and raid enemy airfields inland.

In official records this operation was named 'Hawthorn', but to the participants it was known as 'Operation Swann', in deference to the literary taste of the party leader, who is an admirer of Marcel Proust. My job was to serve as boating guide, philosopher and friend and to see them safely away in their inflatable rubber dinghies, but not to accompany them ashore.

Due to sickness, bad luck and mechanical breakdown in

the submarine, only two of the three assault parties were landed. The third returned with us to Algiers for insertion by parachute in time for the imminent invasion of Sicily by Anglo-American forces. In the event, the operation was only partially successful, and all were captured after blowing up a few aircraft.

On the way back to Algiers, *Severn* proceeded to dive out of control until we nearly reached crushing-depth. We then popped up like a cork at an acute angle to break surface in broad daylight thirty miles off the Sardinian coast. We were not amused.

The party leader was John Verney, in peacetime an artist and writer, who has written a most entertaining account of his wartime career entitled *Going to the Wars*. In some post-war books by author/journalists about special operations there is a convention that commandos must be large, loud, bloodthirsty, galumphing oafs, to be used for comic relief. I am particularly attached to Verney as, in his book, he wrote of me as a 'cheerful fawn-like person who played a penny-whistle . . . strange pipe music that Pan might play, a watery tune without beginning or end, a merry brook-like tune entering my sub-conscious from another world . . . it could have been introduced into "L'Après-midi d'un Faune" without Debussy himself noticing the difference.'

SBS took part in another operation with No. 2 Special Air Service during June 1943. It was a raid on Lampedusa Island, which was also a failure. 'Sally' Lunn was accompanied by Sergeant ('Ginger') Milne of the SBS and two men on loan from SAS named Watt and Sinclair. They were launched in their canoes from an MTB but, on approaching the coast, could not find the beach. They split up to look for it, and the assault craft were coming along in behind them. All hell broke loose from the shore defences (non-existent according to Intelligence), and the assault craft turned back. Milne and Sinclair, who were together in one canoe, did not return to the MTB and were 'missing presumed killed'.

Later, in July, Alex McClair, Jimmy Foot and Sergeant Sidlow went in HMS/M *Severn* with Major the Earl Jellicoe to pick up the Hawthorn SAS party from the west coast of Sardinia after their raids on inland airfields to destroy German bombers. On 27 July, the prearranged date for the rendezvous, *Severn* observed a light flashing from the hills, following which beach lights were switched on. The SAS party had been captured entire and the rendezvous obviously compromised. On the way back to Algiers, *Severn* again suffered from acute engine trouble and limped along at about eight knots, lucky not to be detected and depth-charged.

It is worthy of remark that joint operations mounted in 1943 in which SBS were called upon to work with the Special Air Service, were not a success. Also expensive and not always profitable were those carried out in 1942 by No. 1 SBS on behalf of SAS after Roger Courtney's departure for the United Kingdom, as can be read in Chapter 3.

I believe that the basic cause of this failure lay in the fundamental differences between the roles of the two organizations, which called for a different type of man, trained differently and with different operational priorities.

SBS men were trained to work in pairs and to slip in and out secretly by canoe in the course of a single night, so as to minimize the danger of ambush to the submarine. Not only was the safety of the submarine of overriding importance, but overall strategic security demanded that SBS men should not be detected or captured on shore, particu-

larly while carrying out pre-invasion beach reconnaissances or ferrying agents.

The SBS were trained to be cautious, and discretion was
the better part of valour, even to the point of abandoning
or postponing an operation if it was judged too risky.
They were individualists and loners. SAS men, on the
other hand, were chosen and trained to act as amphibious
and airborne troops, fighting in company, with the simple
object of destruction by *coup de main*. This required a
high degree of aggressive team-work, with mayhem at the
target the primary object, and planning for escape the
secondary consideration; safe return was rather a toss-up,
though naturally desirable.

Generally speaking, during the early days of SAS in
1941 and 1942, it was, according to *The Special Air Service*
by Philip Warner, led by 'Scottish aristocrats, Etonians,
brilliant athletes . . . an eminent film actor, famous
riders . . . public schoolboys who had led lives of bizarre
adventure all over the world'. This basically feudal
background provided admirable and imaginative
leadership for small-scale *coup de main* raiding, and the
leaders were followed faithfully by the modern equivalent
of the yeoman archers of Agincourt.

But Roger Courtney, whose background was free-lance
big game hunting in East Africa, tended to favour the
village poacher in the non-commissioned rank for SBS
work, and the officer of equivalent mentality.

One of SBS's most experienced operatives had described his own feelings when on a raid as those of his pre-
war poaching days: 'Creep in, set the traps, hang about,
collect the spoils, and get away without being caught. If,
on one or two occasions, a few shots were loosed off at
one, well, didn't the gamekeepers do just the same, where
was the difference? The golden rule was "don't make any

slip-ups" and have your lines of retreat well thought out beforehand.'

Metaphorically speaking, SAS liked to burst in gallantly through the front door, while SBS preferred to slip in at the back through the bathroom window. These differing philosophies did not make for an efficient combination in practice.

After the successful occupation of Sicily (Operation Husky), plans were made by Allied Forces Headquarters for a major landing on the west coast of Italy at Salerno, south of Naples, known as 'Operation Avalanche'. COPP had suffered heavy casualties in Sicily, so SBS was called upon to help with pre-invasion beach reconnaissances. Captain E.J.A. ('Sally') Lunn, Sergeants Thompson and Gilmour, and I, together with a team from COPP, sailed in HMS/M *Shakespeare* in late August 1943. We were to carry out offshore reconnaissance of the beaches selected for assault landings by units of the American 5th Army. On the morning of the assault, on 8 September 1943, we acted as guiding beacons in our canoes for the waves of landing-craft carrying the 6th US Corps. A full account of the part played by *Shakespeare* and the canoeists is given in Chapter 6. It is interesting to read *Survey by Starlight* by R. Neville (1949) for the COPP point of view.

SBS went back to ferrying agents, and Captain Alex McClair and Sergeant Norman Thompson (nicknamed 'Tommo') sailed from Algiers at the end of August for northern Italy in HMS/M *Seraph*, still commanded by Bill Jewell, our old friend from Torch days. They were accompanied by Captain Andrew Croft of the Inshore Special Service Unit (ISSU6) with a supply of arms, radios and explosives for Italian partisans. These were duly buried on a beach near Portofino, between Genoa and La Spezia.

The party returned to Algiers on 9 September after a hectic patrol which included a near-fatal depth-charging. A graphic description of the voyage is given in Chapter 13 of *The Ship with Two Captains* by Terence Robertson.

A month later Sergeants Ron Sidlow and Charlie Blewitt landed agents in northern Italy from HMS/M *Sickle*. On their return from the beach, small-arms fire was heard and it was feared that their passengers had run into trouble. Shortly afterwards most of 'Z' SBS were sent back to England on leave and to prepare for a move to the Far East. However, a small contingent was left behind to help COPP with beach reconnaissance before the Allied assault on Anzio, some thirty miles south of Rome.

During November and December 1943 three reconnaissances of beaches off Anzio and Nettuno were carried out, two from Italian MAS boats under the command of Lieutenant Simpson-Jones RNVR of SOE and the third from an American PT Boat. The canoeists from COPP ME2 were Sub/ Lt K.G. Patterson RANVR with A/B G.D. Lockhead RN, and from SBS Captain A.R. McClair with Sergeant R. Sidlow, and Captain W.G. Davis with Sergeant J. Galloway. On the night of 28/29 November 1943 the three teams, under Patterson's command, carried out the first recce, of the Nettuno beaches, without incident. The second took place on the night of 2/3 December 1943 with the same teams. McClair relates that he was dropped in the wrong place, of which he was later able to produce convincing proof, and was obliged to paddle four miles to the right one. Offshore he found two false beaches, one fifty yards out with two feet of water over it, and the other 150 yards out with a fathom, which he thought could be crossed by small landing craft but not by heavy ones carrying tanks. By this time they were long overdue and it was nearly dawn, but the MAS boat was still waiting despite the risk involved.

Patterson and Lockhead were not so fortunate. They paddled towards the shore and found a sandbank close in, but worse, that there was a bad one some distance out, with a nasty gutter in between. They were late returning, inexplicably missed the rendezvous and, after all day at sea in a rising wind, decided to make for the coast and try to walk home. They were given food and shelter in a sheep hut by local peasants and remained there for a month so that the assault in Anzio should not be compromised if they were caught. They then moved south to try and get through to the 5th Army but with less than one kilometre to go they were discovered and rounded up by German soldiers on 3 February 1944. Patterson was liberated from Germany on 28 April 1945 and was repatriated to Australia. Lockhead also survived and emigrated there after the War.

The vital information from McClair revealing the existence of the two false beaches was believed by the British Admiral Morse, but the American commander preferred to rely on the evidence of local fishermen. The result was that many tank landing craft ran aground just offshore during the assault, with many casualties. It was tragic that Patterson had not returned as he would have been able to confirm McClair's information.

The third recce, on the night of 29/30 December 1943, was to end in tragedy. Bill Davis of SBS was in command with three Ensigns of the Scout and Reconnaissance Unit of the US Atlantic Fleet in two canoes. Ensigns K.E. Howe and C.F. Pirro were detected and were believed to have been killed on their beach, while Ensign J.C. Donnell, who was with Davis, was killed on shore later. Davis was to receive a letter of congratulation in due course from the Chief of Combined Operations on the excellent work done by SBS.

On 22 January 1944 the British 1st Division and the American 3rd Division, together with British commandos and US Rangers, landed at Anzio in an attempt to out-flank the Gustav Line. They had little success and suffered many casualties.

Meanwhile, 'Z' SBS was regrouping in Ceylon in HMS *Adamant* in preparation for the war against the Japanese. We had no immediate operational employment, and I spent an enjoyable period exploring that beautiful island, sailing small boats in Trincomalee harbour and pursuing a 'tiddly' Wren ('tiddly' when applied to a Wren means 'smart' and not 'sloshed').

No sooner had they arrived than Lunn, Kennard, McClair and their Sergeants Gilmour, Newsome and Sidlow were rushed back to Malta by air to carry out simulated beach reconnaissances for strategic deception purposes in the islands of the Greek Peloponnese.

During March 1944 McClair and Sidlow sailed in HMS/M *Unruly* to land on a beach in the island of Zante. The beach selected turned out to be too rocky, and the surf too heavy for landing. McClair relates that the captain of the submarine ordered him to break up their canoe and equipment and ditch it over the side, in the hope that the wreckage would be washed up on the beach. For security reasons, in case someone should talk indiscreetly on re-turn to port, this was not revealed to the crew, who accused McClair and Sidlow of funking the job and faking an excuse to get out of it.

At the same time Lunn and Gilmour, and Kennard and Newsome, sailed in HMS/M *Sybil* for the island of Cephalonia for the same purpose. Kennard and Newsome landed on the north coast of Cephalonia, left traces of their visit and regained the submarine without incident.

Lunn and Gilmour landed on the south coast on the

night of 23 March 1944. The weather on the approach run had been rough, but on surfacing it seemed that the on-shore wind had abated and it was decided to carry out the operation. 'Sally' Lunn tells the story of their adventures in his own words:

'The landfall was achieved without trouble, and half an hour was spent walking over the beach and leaving evidence of a recce. Meanwhile the wind had increased and the surf on the beach was heavy. The first two attempts to launch the canoe failed and at the third try it was flooded with sand and water and broke its back, thus rendering it useless. We had no option but to make our way inland and head for the "escape refuge" which I had been given in Malta. It was bitterly cold and we were drenched from the sea. Passing through a small village, we met a sentry who challenged and thrust a gun at my chest. He was quickly overpowered but not before his shouts brought others from a hut, shooting as they ran. We dived for cover and, in so doing, became separated; we were not to meet again for some days.

'I climbed up the mountain and kept moving in the rough direction of the village where I hoped to find refuge. The next day, avoiding villages because of enemy activity and my own villainous appearance, I found the place where I hoped to find the "safe house".

'The owner was a Greek dentist married to an Englishwoman, and although deeply suspicious they took me in. The next day I was interrogated by a woman who knew London far better than I did. After four days of anxiety for my hosts, I was handed on to the local Resistance group who moved me to their headquarters. There to my relief I found Gilmour, who had had a hard time establishing his identity. We were told that our folboat had been found and that the Germans suspected the presence of British "agents" on the island, so we were to be moved to the mainland as soon as possible. As an added complication, a mysterious caique was said to have been driven ashore about the same time as our own landing and about twenty-one men of various nationalities had been captured. There must have been some truth in this story as, later, when Jock Gilmour and I were waiting to be taken by boat to the mainland, we were joined by a Russian said to have escaped from the shipwreck, but nobody was willing to say anything when we asked for details. This Russian stayed with us until we were evacuated and it was amusing to note that, each time we stopped in a village for the night during our "trek" towards the British Mission, the Russian was hustled away to confer with the local Communists while we were in ELAS territory; the two British merely got dirty looks until it was found that I was carrying the money-bag!

'As soon as Jock and I had been taken in charge by the Partisans, life became more difficult and frustrating. First of all we were taken over a high mountain to a village on the east coast where, we were told, we would be taken by boat to the mainland. After a two-day march we arrived at another headquarters where we had a hostile reception and much interrogation by an officer who spoke French and made it clear to me that we were not welcome. He added that before we could be moved to the mainland he would have to get authority from his superiors. As a result of this and then some stormy weather, we remained in a cold building under guard for five days before the decision to move to the coast was finally taken; during this time our diet consisted entirely of maize bread, and goat's cheese supplemented by olive oil – even the latter did not prevent us from becoming constipated, because we were denied any form of exercise!

'The first part of the sea journey was by sailing-boat at night to the island of Ithaka, where we got a decent meal for a change. The next night we crossed by motor caique to the coast near Patras, where we had a great welcome from the local population. This was not to the liking of our Partisan guides, who did, however, allow me to be shaved before we were hustled away to start our long march to the British Mission. I should add that I'd learned while "under guard" that our canoe had been found by the Germans and the hunt for "two Englishmen" was on – this did not make us any more popular with our hosts. The march to the Mission which was in the charge of a Major Ramseyer, seemed interminable due to the inefficiency and slowness of the guides who, as I discovered later, took us miles out of our direct route.

'The journey took six days and at the end my felt-soled boots were in tatters and my feet quite raw. We stayed at the Mission for three days to enjoy some good food for a change and for my feet to recover; however, the new boots I was given only made matters worse and I continued to suffer with sore feet for some time. The next stage, which led to the main Mission headquarters up in the mountains nearer the coast, took us only three days instead of the five-day march forecast by Ramseyer, and this was achieved, I'm afraid, by some brutal bullying of our incompetent guides. It was on this stage of our journey that we left ELAS (Communist) territory despite the obstacles put in our way by "higher authority" and entered EDES-land. The boundary was a fast-running river which we had to cross in a small, leaking boat which did not inspire confidence, especially as the boatman was a boy of about ten years; I thought we could have used him in the SBS as he coped very well.

'Our arrival at the main British HQ was on the morning

of the Greek Easter Sunday, and the Mission personnel were all suffering from hangovers from the previous night's celebrations.

'My feet were giving me hell and I was not in the best of moods as it soon became obvious that our arrival was not at all popular with the local braves. Nevertheless we did not hesitate to join in the feasting and I consumed more meat that Easter Day than I had seen in the past month. The next day we were moved to a staging camp, of which I was put in charge, where we were joined by a dozen Russians who were also due for evacuation. I had been given plenty of money so we enjoyed a few days of ease and good living until we were moved to the coast near Preveza for embarkation in a landing-craft which was bringing in stores for the Resistance. We finally left Greece and landed at Minopoli in Italy. From there we went to Bari and were then flown back to Malta after a gap of thirty-seven days since we had sailed from there in HMS/M *Sybil*.'

Captain E.J.A. Lunn was subsequently awarded a Bar to his MC and Sergeant Jock Gilmour a bar to his MM. They returned to Ceylon to join the rest of 'Z' SBS in operations against the Japanese with Force 136.

So ended an eventful twelve months for 'Z' SBS as the 'private army' of the submarine flotillas in the Mediterranean. During that period the Section went on eighteen operations and suffered only two casualties.

6

Three Typical SBS
Operations, 1943

1. Agents to Corsica (Operation Etna)

HMS/M *Trident*, commanded by Lieutenant P.E. Newstead
RN, left Algiers harbour during the later afternoon of an
April day in 1943. She was one of the earlier 'T' class
launched before September 1939 and one of the few lucky
enough to survive for nearly four years. She was a tough old
lady and a veteran of much depth-charging. Although
slightly battered in consequence, she possessed a reserve of
resilience for which her passengers would be thankful.

The passengers consisted of a team from 'Z' Special Boat
Section and a party of Frenchmen and Corsicans and their
British Conducting Officer – a bearded ex-smuggler from a
highly secret organization. For this operation the SBS team
had been chosen from those who claimed to be French
speakers and was headed by me with a weird patois picked
up in Algerian nightclubs. A certain fluency in French was
considered necessary because of the type of operation in
which we were engaged.

My second-in-command was a long, lean, piratical gentleman who spoke fluent French acquired on the Côte d'Azur
before the War. According to him, he had been engaged in
persuading old ladies to invest their money to the advantage
of his bank. His surname was Lunn, inevitably nicknamed
'Sally' after the North Country teacake. (Also, in the British
army all Millers are 'Dusty' and Clarks are 'Nobby', which
does make introductions easier.)

The leader of the French Resistance movement on the island of Corsica, Commandant de Saule, was on the run, and his organization had broken up or gone to ground. It was planned to evacuate him, so that he might live to fight another day, and to land a party to take his place and build up the organization afresh. This party was the one with which we were involved and was headed by Captain Colonna Distria.

After so many years I cannot clearly remember any of them except one of the Corsicans. He was a professional murderer. His speciality was assassination in public places, and his methods were simple: he would approach his victim through the crowd with a lump of lead concealed in the palm of his hand, smite him on the temple and be far away before it was discovered that the man had not just fainted. He had reptilian eyes, and I always felt uncomfortable in his presence.

I will not describe the operation which followed in any great detail. It was comparatively simple, and treachery ashore and an accidental meeting with a beach patrol were the only dangers likely to be met.

On a pre-arranged night of quarter moon, the party paddled towards the shore in an inflatable rubber dinghy guided by 'Sally' and myself in a folboat canoe. Our task was to keep the party on the right compass bearing for the mouth of a small river. The rendezvous had already been fixed by radio with the reception group ashore. Following the successful disembarkation of our charges, we were to ferry the escaping Resistance leader back to the submarine in the rubber dinghy, towing him behind our canoe. The approach to the shore was carried out in silence and without incident. The aromatic smell of the maquis grew stronger and heavier on the wind as we slid near to the beach over the swell. The whiteness of the sand at the mouth of the river first appeared as a long, grey, horizontal smudge that was broken with the dark shapes of bushes.

On the shore, restraint completely deserted our party and they clustered on the sand talking at the tops of their voices. The noise increased when they were joined by the reception group appearing out of the shadows. 'Sally' and I, having shushed in vain, became impatient to get away. We were told that a beautiful maquisard had been waiting on the beach to embrace the brave British commandos. She had, however, gone home about an hour before our arrival.

'Sally' was upset, as he had counted on his superior command of idiomatic French to give the advantage over me in the encounter.

The escaping Resistance leader was shepherded into the rubber dinghy. Towed by us in the canoe, it made its unwieldy way, swaying across the crests of the rollers, to the safety of the submarine. *Trident* turned northward with an air of getting on with more serious business and set off for the Corsican port of Bastia, the terminus of one of the new sizeable Axis merchant ships left afloat in those waters.

On the second day the officer of the watch sighted the vessel, a five-thousand-ton merchantman, and the crew went to action stations. The captain gave the order to fire two torpedoes, and we waited for the hammerstroke of the explosion which would announce a hit. Following the Asdic screen, the CO suddenly realized that the track of only one torpedo was showing. Turning swiftly to his First Lieutenant, he sensed the same unspoken anxiety that the torpedo, running amok through some mechanical fault, might be circling crazily in our vicinity, unpredicted and unpredictable, like some mad underseadog. The rest of us, happily unaware, counted the seconds and made mental calculations of time and space and speed.

Trident moved slowly on, and as it became obvious to the most optimistic that no hit would be scored, the tension in the boat relaxed, in relief on the part of the two naval officers that it would not be scored on us, and disappointment on the part of the unworried remainder.

Knowing that the alarm would have been raised in Bastia by his recent abortive attack, the Captain of the *Trident* decided to continue to the northern limit of his patrol area. This was in the waters off the Ligurian coast to the west of Genoa. By this stage in the war, British submarine flotillas had established an ascendancy over enemy shipping so that the only targets to be found there were small coastal vessels which travelled hugging the shallows. Like Chuchundra, the musk-rat in Kipling's tale, they preferred not to venture into the middle of the room. The villages along the coast looked inviting when seen through the periscope. They appeared peaceful, clean and colourful in the afternoon sun, in marked contrast to the conditions within the submarine. Two weeks of patrolling, submerged by day through warm summer waters, had produced a bouquet which could only be fully appreciated after tasting the fresh air above.

Among the naval officers aboard there was a gunnery officer. He was young and enthusiastic and possessed a gun and several sailors to fire it. Hitherto his only target had been towed behind a British tug during trials, and he was anxious lest yet another patrol should pass without an engagement. It was not that he was in any way bloodthirsty. His attitude of sporting detachment was typical of that of many naval officers who never saw the actual faces of the enemy.

While the gunnery officer was on watch during the

afternoon of the second day, his interest was quickened by the sight of the mast and funnel of a small ship which was entering his arc of vision. He identified the vessel as a coastal tanker of a few hundred tons displacement and then called for the Captain.

The tanker was too small to justify a torpedo but was big enough to give good practice to the gunnery officer and his team. Even if it were not actually sunk, it would probably be forced to run ashore. The CO gave the orders to surface and for gun action. Reserve ammunition was passed up through a hatch situated in the wardroom, and 'Sally' and I moved up to one end of a settee to give the ammunition rating room to move freely. Through the open hatch we could see the blue sky and hear the shouted orders and the closely followed report of the gun.

Suddenly and unexpectedly the klaxon roared for a crash dive, and the gun's crew scrambled down through the hatch, which was slammed by the last man and then secured. The tanker, which should have run itself ashore in an obliging manner, had turned instead towards the submarine. In place of the leisurely ripple of water at its bows there appeared a high, creaming wave, and guns were visible where none had been before. An attractively presented piece of cheese had lured the mouse from its hole and had promptly turned into a cat. The mouse made a dive for it.

'Sally' went softly to his bunk so as to get out of the way. I swung myself into the hammock which was secured just under the deckhead of the wardroom passage. The curved steel of the hull was only a foot above my nose, and I composed myself with well-founded expectation of trouble to come. *Trident* dived steeply and swiftly with a twisting plunge into the depths where concealment and escape might be found. But the Italian decoy vessel had been too near, its speed too great for effective evasion, and it ploughed through the swirl of waters still bubbling to the surface from our hurried descent.

Lying in my bunk with my hands crossed over my stomach, I heard the thud of the screw as it passed overhead and the whispering patter of the Asdic echo along the hull above me. I knew that the hunters had located us and braced myself. After a few seconds of suspense, the steel of the hull whipped in and out as an exploding depth-charge split the water outside. Three times more the submarine was smitten as the pattern was completed and, in the wardroom, one of two lights went out. Again the thud of the screw was heard and again the agony of waiting ended in the rolling, echoing crash and shudder of exploding depth-charges. And again and again to a total of sixty-six as the hunters crisscrossed above us.

In the control room the Captain sat quietly in a camp chair and watched the dials and instruments about him. So close to shore, he had only half a circle in which to manoeuvre and less depth of water than he would have liked. He did not dare to make a dash for it as the beat of his screws would have been audible to the hydrophones of the hunter.

Towards twilight the shock of the explosions became less and seemed to drop slowly astern. By some lucky chance we must have passed over a wreck or some other object solid enough to give an echo which had misled the hunter. The latter released a few more charges above the apparently crippled quarry and, grateful for dusk and silence, we crept slowly away.

We had hoped that nightfall would see the end of our troubles, but the Italian Navy, knowing the weak points of submarines and wishing to confirm the kill, stationed armed motor launches on the strip of ocean where we would eventually emerge if still capable of movement. It was near midnight before the CO found a space 'upstairs' in which there might be a chance of escaping detection. By then we must surface to charge our electric batteries, and he gave the order to blow tanks.

Trident slid silently into the fresh night air, and the CO opened the conning-tower hatch and climbed onto the bridge. Below, passengers and crew waited anxiously for him to give the signal to start the main diesel engines. This would mean that all was clear above and that there would be some respite, for the hours of darkness at least, for our thread-bare nerves. To our consternation the roar of engines was heard above, and the scream of the klaxon and the clatter of the CO falling into the control room heralded a frantic dive to get away. *Trident* plunged downwards at a steep angle until the top of the conning-tower was swallowed in a flurry of foam. One of the steel bars securing the upper hatch had jammed; the lid was only partly closed and the sea poured into the conning-tower. The lower hatch, unseated and warped by the crushing force of the depth-charges, offered no obstacle, and an irresistible jet of water under high pressure shot into the body of the submarine.

There was no choice. On the one hand certain death by drowning if we remained below the surface; on the other hand a chance of survival if we could get the gun into action before shell, torpedo or depth-charge smashed the pressure-hull. The CO ordered the tanks to be blown, and the gun's crew crouched below the wardroom hatch, ready to fling themselves out and onto the gun with the speed of desperation. The water in the conning-tower drained away as the hull emerged and the CO scrambled onto the bridge. He arrived just in time to hear the roar of aircraft engines fading eastward as British bomber squadrons attacked the docks at Genoa.

After a quiet morning of recuperation on the way back to Algiers, the CO decided to check the hull and hydroplanes for damage. Searching the sea and sky through the periscope, he decided that it was safe to come to the surface. The main diesel engines rumbled into life, and the down-draught through the conning-tower sent a welcome breeze into every corner of the boat.

The CO and the First Lieutenant entered the wardroom and sat down to a cup of tea. They were thoughtful and their manner was anxious, so I asked them what was the matter. They told me that a torpedo was protruding from one of the forward tubes and that it was impossible, at sea, to move it one way or the other. This was the second torpedo fired off Bastia, the one which had failed to appear on the Asdic screen for the very good reason that it had never left the tube. Nobody could tell whether the nose was far enough out for the fuse to have armed itself. Even the failure of the warhead to explode under the shock of sixty-six depth-charges could not be taken as proof positive that the fuse was not still armed.

When feeling upset, submariners are happier below the surface, and the Captain decided to submerge and to travel onward and homeward at periscope depth. He would thus be able to keep an eye on what was happening upstairs without the risk of running into driftwood floating on the surface. He was a sincerely religious man and called for Divine Service in the control room after breakfast. We were glad to join in out of respect for the cool competence he had shown during a voyage which had been nerve-racking even by submariner's standards. *Trident* rose to the surface during the afternoon and came in cautiously through the clear sea to the safety of Algiers harbour and the comforts of the Depot Ship.

2. Strategic Deception (Operation Marigold I)

Hitler thought that the Allies were more likely to land in Sardinia (or in Greece) than in Sicily, as Sardinia would provide an easy stepping-stone into Corsica and a well-placed springboard for a jump on to either the French or the Italian mainland.

These ideas were fostered by receiving from Nazi agents in Spain copies of documents found on a 'British officer' whose body had been washed ashore on the Spanish coast. Besides identity papers and personal correspondence, the documents included a private letter – of which the dead man had been the bearer – written by Lieutenant-General Sir Archibald Nye, the vice-Chief of the Imperial General Staff, to General Alexander. This letter referred to recent official telegrams about forthcoming operations, and its supplementary comments indicated that the Allies were intending to land in Sardinia and Greece while aiming by their cover plan to convince the enemy that Sicily was their objective.

The corpse and the letter were part of the ingenious deception advised by a section of the British Intelligence Service. This was so well worked out that the heads of the German Intelligence Service were convinced of its genuineness. Although it did not alter the view of the Italian Chiefs and Kesselring that Sicily would be the Allies' next objective, it appears to have made a strong impression on Hitler.

In our small way we were part of the same deception plan. I was summoned in late May 1943 to a comfortable villa near Algiers and was told that the Planners required a simulated reconnaissance on a certain beach on the east coast of Sardinia. This was to be done in a way that would persuade the Italian General Staff that an assault landing was about to take place. Aerial photographs showed the beach to be defended, and gun emplacements and pillboxes were visible. It was not known whether the defences were manned or what system of patrolling, if any, was in force.

That was all the information available. This was usual in operations of the kind in which we were engaged. We would have liked to have been given more but there was some compensation in the complete absence of instructions on how the task was to be carried out. As specialists we preferred to stand or fall by our own efforts and not by somebody else's mistakes.

I returned to the Submarine Depot Ship HMS *Maidstone* which lay in the harbour below. During the next few days I conferred with the Staff Officer (Operations) and with the Captain of HMS/M *Safari* commanded by Lieutenant R.B. Lakin DSO, RN, who was to take us on the mission. Meanwhile my Sergeant Thompson was busy with preparing the canoe and testing the gear required. Sergeants Gilmour and Loasby of SBS were also with us to act as boat-handlers for a party of SAS on a snatch raid planned for later in the patrol.

Thompson was a wiry, stocky little man who hailed from Newcastle. Before the War he had been variously employed, sometimes as a coalminer and at others as a fiddler at country fairs. By nature he was a cheerful and philosophic fellow and took the world very much as it came. He was a great lover of women. His aptitude for dodging husbands was allied with determination, generally successful, to carry a thing through once he had started it. The combination of these two attributes made him admirably suited to the business of tip-and-run raids on enemy coasts.

Seven days before the period of no moon, *Safari* slipped her moorings and left the side of the Depot Ship. Little fuss was made over her departure, and our presence on board was accepted as nothing unusual. Indeed, owing partly to the lack of enemy shipping in the central Mediterranean and partly to the fact that a special operation was counted to the credit of the submarine, we rarely failed to receive a wholehearted welcome.

The sergeant settled down in the petty officers' mess and felt that probably it was just as well that he would be away from Algiers for a few weeks. I examined the contents of the wardroom library and noticed that the chaplain of the Flotilla, who supplied the books, had a pleasantly secular taste in literature.

Safari passed through a gap in the harbour boom and set off at her best surface speed so as to take advantage of the remaining hours of daylight and of the darkness to follow. Although her mean course was calculated to get her to the east coast of Sardinia, she travelled in a series of long zigzags so as to confuse the aim of any enemy submarine that might lie in wait across her path. The CO was alert for signs of aircraft, even in the vicinity of Algiers harbour, and recognition signals were kept handy. At that time it was not unknown for enthusiastic Allied fighter-pilots to dive happily upon British submarines and spray them with cannon shells. The CO thought he already had enough to contend with without having to dodge his own side.

A few days later we were cruising back and forth at periscope depth parallel to the beach selected for the operation. This beach was good for holiday canoeing because of its length and wide expanse of flat sand, but for these very reasons was not suited to clandestine landings. Like General Wolfe at Quebec, the Special Boat Section teams preferred to land on rockier and less comfortable shores where they would be comparatively inconspicuous. It was assumed that enemy beach patrols, being human and therefore idle, would tread the easier paths across the nice firm sand rather than clamber painfully over cold, hard, slippery rocks. In this case, however, the time factor made it necessary that the landing should take place on the centre and most exposed portion. I drew a panorama sketch of the beach and its background through the periscope. It was clear from the silhouette that there were no features sufficiently prominent to give reasonable guidance by night. There was therefore no alternative to paddling in the general direction of the centre and trusting to luck.

Thompson and I gathered together our torches, compasses and pistols and went on deck at about 10 P.M. The night air was pleasantly fresh after the stuffiness of the day spent below. We savoured its cool, salt scent as *Safari* slid slowly towards the loom of the land. Our canoe, with its sides greased to ensure easy passage through the hole, was passed up through the forward torpedo hatch and laid gently upon the forecasting. At about three miles from the shore the forward motion of the submarine became barely perceptible. The engines were put in reverse, the faint swirl of the waters caused by the backward tug of the screws moved along the hull, and she lay motionless in the calm sea. The canoe was lowered over the side. Held against the hull by two sailors, it seemed frail in comparison. We sat down in it carefully and paddled slowly away.

A faint offshore breeze carried the smell of aromatic shrubs from the mountainside intermingled with a thread of woodsmoke. On shore we could see the scattered lights of cottages set beyond the sand dunes. The beach itself was not clearly visible, owing to haze lying low on the

water. The splash of the waves smothered the small
sounds of our landing, and we concealed the canoe in the
shallow dip between the water and the dry sand. Some
yards inland a beaten track ran along the beach parallel to
the water and we crossed it swiftly and in silence.
Reaching the shelter of the scrub among the sand dunes,
we halted for a moment's deliberation.

During the afternoon I had been busy with the preparations of an Army field notebook which, it was hoped,
would eventually find its way into the hands of the Italian
General Staff Intelligence. I had torn out several top
pages, written down some harmless notes of a military
nature and then torn out the page upon which I had just
written. A faint imprint was left, which I hoped would
serve to confuse the issue. On the next two pages I had
drawn a rough sketch map of the beach and its defences as
viewed through a periscope and had added such queries
as, 'Calibre of guns?' 'Any underwater obstacles?' and
'Wop or Hun?'. My intention was to drop the notebook,
as if by accident, on some part of the beach where it
should attract attention and be picked up.

Leaving Sergeant Thompson to guard my rear and to
watch for beach patrols, I threaded my way between the
sand dunes towards the nearest gun emplacement. My
eyes and ears alert for any signs of movement, I crept with
increasing care as I came nearer to the objective. The gun
emplacement lay dark, squat and menacing before me.
For long minutes I watched and listened until sure that it
was empty of life. The sound of voices raised in discussion
from a hut further inland seemed to offer no immediate
danger, and I moved forward into the open. Two well-
worn tracks came together near the emplacement. I lay
down in the soft sand near the track junction so as to leave
a clear imprint of my body and allowed the notebook to

slip from my haversack. The cover flew open as it fell and the whiteness of the inner page was clearly visible against the dull grey of the sand.

Meanwhile, Thompson was fast becoming bored with bushes. He was debating whether to go and see what was happening in the huts behind us when he saw two men approaching on a path that would come close to his hiding-place. He shrank back hurriedly into the shadows, and the men strolled by him on the beach. He had a moment of anxiety as they lingered near the spot where the canoe was hidden but relaxed when they disappeared into the night. He went cautiously back to his original post to await my return.

Like shadows merging into the greyness, we met in brief, whispered consultation and broke apart to cross the beach towards the canoe. We pushed it a few yards out to sea, clambered aboard in silence and paddled swiftly away from shore. In the faint glimmer of the false dawn we could see the dim outline of the submarine which, anxious to be away before daylight, had edged inshore to meet us.

I never learned whether our work had produced any reaction or even if the notebook had reached the hands for which it was intended. For all we know, it may have been used by some illiterate peasant for cigarette paper or, unnoticed, lie to this day under a film of wind-blown sand, only a single thread in a complex web.

Nevertheless, on Hitler's orders the newly formed 90th Panzer-grenadier Division reinforced the four Italian divisions in Sardinia. As an additional insurance, Hitler moved General Student's 11th Air Corps (of two parachute divisions) down to the South of France, ready to deliver an airborne counter-attack against any allied landing in Sardinia.

3. Assault at Salerno (Operation Avalanche)

HMS/M *Shakespeare*, commanded by Lieutenant Michael Ainslie RN, left Algiers and HMS *Maidstone* on a late August day in 1943. She was a submarine of medium tonnage and a handy size for inshore operations in the central Mediterranean. She was capable of working in shallow waters and of submerging quickly. Passing through the boom at the entrance of the harbour, she turned north-east and settled down to a steady speed through the long, unruffled swell.

We were six extra passengers, tucked away in various corners of the wardroom and the petty officers' mess so as to avoid the bustle of the crew as the ship settled down to sea-going routine. Myself, 'Sally' Lunn and Sergeants Thompson and Gilmour of 'Z' SBS, Captain P.D. Matterson (later MC), a Sapper officer, and Lieutenant (N) R. Stanbury RN (later DSC) who, as a specialist navigator in COPP, was in charge of the whole operation. We expected the voyage which lay ahead to be longer than usual, and we took it in turn to clamber up on to the bridge of the submarine for a last glimpse of the sunlit world. To us the worst part of an operation was the long approach to the objective. The submariners had their duties and routine to keep them occupied but, for passengers, the gap between one meal and the next could only be filled by reading, sleeping and playing complicated games with dice. After a few days we would become doped with sleep, bad air and no exercise.

For almost a week *Shakespeare* pounded onward by night and passed quietly beneath the surface by day, until the heat-hazy mountains of western Italy rose up and the

Bay of Salerno opened out to fill the horizon. The art of amphibious assault landing was by then highly developed, and *Shakespeare* was going to act as a secret submersible beacon to guide the British and American assault flotillas to the bay some fourteen days later.

An equally vital reason led to our presence on board. Aerial photographs had revealed the shadow of a sandbar a hundred yards off the beaches inside the bay. They did not show with any certainty whether the depth of water above it was sufficient to allow the passage of assault landing-craft at speed. This was of great interest to the Planners, and to the soldiers who would hope to reach the beaches alive. We five soldiers and the naval lieutenant were there to answer the question. To make sure that we would be careful to answer it correctly, our next duty would be to station ourselves above the same sandbank to act as guiding beacons for the waves of landing-craft during the actual assault. That evening we considered the problem. To give the reconnaissance teams time to get back to the submarine by dawn, the canoes must be launched not more than three miles from shore. On the other hand, it had been reported that a minefield lay some five miles out from the beaches. It was not known how far it extended on either side towards the horns of the bay.

At this point we fell silent and looked at the Captain. Examining the chart, he weighed one risk against the other and decided to hug the rocks on the southern wing of the bay. He hoped that the Italians, while laying the minefield with due regard to the safety of their own ships, would not have done the same.

Next morning, submerged at thirty feet and slow, we edged through the gap. The Asdic showed mines to the left and rocks to the right. At long last the order was given to turn north, and a silent lessening of tension could be felt when we realized that the immediate danger had passed.

During the day COPP 5 studied the shoreline through the periscope, noting prominent landmarks, and drew a panorama silhouette at which Stanbury was an expert, to give some idea of how it would look at night. He checked the compass course which the canoes should take, and we checked and rechecked our weapons and gear. *Shakespeare* settled gently on the sandy bottom of the bay, and the ship's company slept until evening. That night COPP 5 carried out a successful reconnaissance of their sector of the beaches and returned safely despite bad weather.

The next evening *Shakespeare* rose again to the surface when the after-glow of the day had faded, and the Captain opened the lower conning-tower hatch. The air pressure inside the hull was so strong that it threatened to thrust him through the hole, and a rating clung to his legs until it had spent itself through the vents above. The night was dark and the sea was calm. The sombre silhouette of the land was relieved here and there by a pale patch of radiance from a distant village, and by the glow of Naples over the hills to the north. Dizzy with fresh air, Lunn and I stood on the bridge and breathed deeply in order to get used to the heady tang. Our canoe was brought on deck through the forward torpedo hatch and made ready, and after a final word with the CO we slipped away from the side of the submarine.

Taking as our leading mark a prominent peak on the skyline, we paddled steadily onward until scattered houses and a tower in the Roman town of Paestum could be identified. We were alert for sound or sight of movement on the beach and carefully scanned it with night glasses. When our soundings showed that the highest part of the sandbank was beneath us, we turned north and travelled slowly along the ridge parallel to the shore. Every dozen or so yards I would slide the leadline overboard, and 'Sally' would note the recorded depth on a pad strapped to his wrist.

There was a faint crackle of underbrush ashore as a bored sentry eased his muscles, and we in the canoe were suddenly very still. We waited for him to move again and prayed that he would not notice the grey smudge floating in the water so near to his post. To our consternation the throb of aircraft over Naples to the north, and the pale, steady, revealing radiance of parachute flares heralded an Allied air-raid. We crouched low in the bottom of the canoe and cursed.

The bombers departed and we headed gently out to sea, showing our slimmest silhouette towards the man on the shore and using the lightest of paddle strokes. The Allied invasion fleets were about to come north for the main assault. It was vital that security should be maintained and their destination concealed until the last moment. We were late for the rendezvous owing to a navigational error but paddled hard until the faint grey shape of 'Mother's' conning-tower could be seen against the skyline. Homing on 'Mother' after a special operation was always a ticklish business for both parties, as a submarine stopped on the surface in enemy waters is at its most vulnerable. In spite of the risks and anxiety, 'Mother' was always at the rendezvous when humanly possible to welcome Special Boatmen to safety and to that unforgettable stench of old food, diesel oil and unwashed sailormen.

Our reconnaissance completed the first phase of the operation. Our skipper, Mike Ainslie, and his First Lieutenant, 'Digger' Littlejohn, were anxious to get offshore into deep water and comparative safety as soon as possible, to await the arrival of the Allied fleets. No good poacher likes to go out the same way he comes in, and *Shakespeare* slipped carefully out of the bay at periscope depth round the northern flank of the minefield. Submariners were rarely happy with several people like us aboard on a major special operation. They must leave torpedoes behind in order to accommodate our canoes, divert effort from the main task of sinking enemy ships and suffer greater discomfort than usual in an already overcrowded steel tube. But the worst part was having to wait quietly near a hostile shore like a sitting duck, always with the fear of detection and attack before they could dive and get away out to sea. They have told me of the anxious hours spent waiting for the 'Pongos' (us) to reappear out of the darkness. 'Pongo' is the nickname given to the soldier by the Royal Navy. It comes, they tell me, from our resemblance to the orang-utan (*Pongo pygmaeus*).

We lived with the submariners in their Depot ships, protected from prowling brigadiers and sergeants-major, and were known as their pet submersible 'Pongos'. For our part we developed an immense admiration for them. They were quite crazy and used to do the most dangerous things, like being beastly to Italian destroyers and gunboats without provocation. We always felt that our own risks were quite enough without having to put up with theirs as well.

Safely away from Salerno, *Shakespeare* continued on patrol in the Tyrrhenian Sea off Corsica and Sardinia, on the surface by night and submerged by day. After about ten days she returned to the vicinity of Salerno to await the arrival of the assault fleet and the final phase of our operation.

Then occurred a sad and wasteful tragedy of war. A few

days before the Allied fleets were due to arrive, an Italian submarine came pounding south past us on the surface during the late afternoon. Our Captain did his duty and torpedoed her, probably killing all the crew. Four days later Italy surrendered and the Italian fleet fled to Malta to escape the clutches of the Germans. No one in our ship will ever know why that submarine was rushing south on the surface in such a hurry – to attack or to escape? – which is just as well for our peace of mind.

After dark on D-Day minus one, *Shakespeare* slipped inside the bay again between the minefield and the shore. We, the passengers, were dropped opposite the landing beaches in our canoes to act as guiding beacons for the waves of assault craft to come. Before dawn the next day, 9 September 1943, resting quietly on the swell, my Sergeant Thompson and I could hear the booming roar of engines and see the silhouettes of warships and troop transports against the horizon. We flashed our hooded torches to seaward and hoped that the onrushing landing-craft would not run us down. Our beach had been allotted to the American Fifth Army under General Mark Clark, and our job would be finished once the first wave of assault had passed us. We thought it wiser to avoid the fog of war among a lot of trigger-happy Yanks and paddled out quietly to a troop transport, away from the battle developing ashore. Not 'Sally' Lunn, however, who went ashore and joined in. And so back to base.

The United Kingdom

7

No. 2 SBS: Formation and Training

Roger Courtney returned to England in early December 1941. After some leave in London with Dorrise during the bombing blitz, he went north to Ardrossan-Saltcoats in Ayrshire to form No. 2 SBS. It became part of Brigadier R.A. ('Bob') Laycock's Special Service Brigade and officially came into existence on 1 March 1942. Roger wrote subsequently:

'I was protesting that everybody would accuse me of nepotism. It was then that Bob laid down a few rules about generalship. "If you think that your little brother is good enough to be your second-in-command . . . take him on; after all he is a regular and knows more about Army procedure than you do." Then he gave a few rules for "Special Service" which I have never forgotten:

'(1) Select the right man for the right job and let him get on with it.

'(2) Let him abuse you to your face if he thinks that things are going wrong, and that it is your fault and not his.

'(3) Tolerate no creepers.

'(4) Choose your other ranks more carefully than you would choose a wife, and trust them; also keep them in the picture as much as you dare.

'(5) Bring no petty charges; if a man is not up to scratch, return him to his original unit by the first available train.

'(6) Above all, you must be accessible at all times to

your officers and men; you must be Daddy; except on grave occasions let your second-in-command use the harsh words.

'Then Bob Laycock told me that majors at forty and over were to be considered fit only for office chairs or training centres – no more active operations for old ducks like me . . . I was later to have greater frights in training than I ever had in war.

'I started forming my new unit; my little brother, who had been a regular Adjutant, started to build up his administrative side, while I sat on selection boards. On these I had, as regular partners, two elderly captains and a full colonel; our selections were to be the pick of the commandos. I only wanted about thirty men to begin with and, in spite of some opposition, skimmed the cream.'

Luckily, the nucleus of No. 2 SBS was already available from 101 Troop to 6 Commando, which was absorbed and from which fifteen experienced Other Ranks were chosen together with Captain G.C.S. Montanaro (Royal Engineers). He left fairly soon afterwards on secondment to the Royal Navy on development work of a secret and amphibious nature, but not before paddling into Boulogne harbour in a canoe and sinking a German merchant ship with limpet mines, after scraping off the barnacles to make them stick to the hull.

No. 101 Troop had been formed at Glencoe in Scotland in April 1941 by Montanaro and Lieutenant Smith and moved to Dover in September 1941.

Ex-Guardsman Ron Sidlow recalls that punishments for minor misdemeanours in Scotland were a little bizarre. In winter they would have to go for a swim in the sea fully clothed. In summer they would be marooned for a few days on the burial island of the Clan Macdonald, presumably a bleak spot offering few home comforts. This turned out to be no deterrent to the lassies of Ballachulish, just over the water, who were pretty good in a dinghy and would come over on the quiet to join them.

At Dover 101 Troop were mostly engaged in helping the Royal Navy destroy floating mines by rifle fire, but two canoe pairs were used to make a reconnaissance on the night of 22/23 November 1941. This was in preparation for a raid the next night by a hundred men from No. 9 Commando on a coastal gun battery at Houlgate near the mouth of the River Seine. Lieutenant Smith and Corporal Woodhouse overturned in surf and were captured, while Corporal D.C. Ellis and Private Lewis missed the rendezvous and paddled back across the Channel to England. However, they had gathered sufficient information to confirm that LCA's (landing-craft assault) could land on the beach.

Roger Courtney continues: 'My first choice was any boy scout (especially ex Rover Scouts) – they need no explanation.

'Secondly, I went for ex-bandsmen in the Army who are known for their good shooting with any weapon, the reason being their training. The Kneller Hall boys have to slow march, quick march and counter march, tooting on the instrument meanwhile. They have also to watch their feet, avoid running into the leading trombone and read their music at the same time. This makes them excellent marksmen, because they have to do three things at once – aligning foresight, backsight and target at any range with any weapons.

'Thirdly I went in for studious and artistic types; to be super-sensitive was essential in our job when approaching an enemy coast because every nerve had to be a prickling antenna, and every pore an ear.

'The swaggering, tough type I rejected unreservedly . . . most of their toughness being displayed in pubs.'

Brother Roger's method of final selection was simple and highly unorthodox, being based upon the ancient truth '*In vino veritas*' – that very strong drink loosens the tongue and bares the soul. Roger would visit the nearest pub with the new recruit and fill him full of favourite liquors until all was revealed or he became speechless. 'Tug' Wilson was the only person known to have come off best and to have put Roger to bed. He became his second-in-command in the Mediterranean in 1941 and one of the best operatives ever to serve in SBS.

Omar Khayyám again has a fitting phrase, in Stanza 80:

> O Thou, who didst with pitfall and with gin (?)
> Beset the path I was to wander in. . .

'Soon I had my crews collected and we moved to fresh quarters; and I had an Adjutant, a Quarter Bloke and a clerk who could spell. The unit was complete, and in the ensuing three years it was to gain over ninety per cent in decorations and to lose only one man Returned to Unit (the dreaded RTU and the most effective disciplinary measure). We started furiously to train; there was the usual canoe stuff, which meant paddling and tumbling over in the icy waters of a Scottish loch. I had the idea that if a submarine's gun crew were knocked out, my merry men would be able to take over. The naval officer in command next door was a good chap and brightened considerably when I made the suggestion. In a few days my boys were banging away with four-inchers at targets which were being towed well out to sea.

'I also thought it necessary to train the lads to live on the land should they find themselves at any time stranded ashore in enemy territory. Bob Laycock had received a letter from an eccentric who was reputed to live on the grass off bowling-greens in South London. He offered to teach the commandos how also to lead the rich life: he was offered his railway fare up to Scotland and as much grass as he wanted, so that he might come and give us a demonstration.

'No reply was received to our letter, but about a week later a gnome-like old gentleman arrived at our headquarters on a patent bicycle. He must have been about seventy years old and had a brown leathery wiriness remarkable in a man of that age. He had come about five hundred miles in a week, but he apologized mildly for being late; he stated that he had stopped once or twice along the coast to sample the seaweed.

'We gathered around him. Most hedge weeds are safe provided they do not sport gaudy flowers; you must find them in the cool shade. Croquet lawns and bowling-greens are not to be recommended unless you like the taste of mowing-machine oil. To mix your salad you need a little oatmeal, a little sugar, a little vinegar or a little milk if you have no vinegar. The resulting mixture looks utterly revolting, but I must say it was filling. I stopped all our normal rations, and in three days the boys were screaming for steak. He offered to initiate us into the mysteries of seaweed, but we shook him by the hand and thanked him fervently, and he pedalled away back to London.

'It was essential to train the men to find a point on an enemy coast on a dark night by use of calculation and instruments alone, and it was just as important for them to find the dark shape of their submarine again; it might be lying two miles out to sea; this all called for a high degree of skill in tidal navigation, for the teaching of which we had various experts attached to us from time to time. This called for many trips up and down the coast, and one wet Sunday when we were setting up our tents we were sternly rebuked by a crofter lady for profaning the Sabbath. She turned up trumps, however, and organized the local fishing industry on our behalf so that we feasted on everything from lobster to lemon soles. Our mountain section returned this Scottish hospitality later by rescuing a party of hikers who had got themselves marooned on the face of a thousand foot cliff.'

On training during the summer we stumbled across the occasional fringe benefit in the heather. Alex McClair remembers a Scottish soldier clad only in his Glengarry and a pair of boots, with his lady-friend in nothing but a sweet smile. He parted from them with expressions of mutual esteem. A year later he had a similar experience on the Italian coast, except that the headgear was different. In this case he was obliged to tie them up with fuse wire and gag them – with suitable apologies.

'Meanwhile my trainees were being wafted away on mysterious errands. In those days a man carried the lives of his friends on the tip of his tongue, but it was better for all to know too little than too much. Therefore I asked no questions and invited no confidence. But it was good to see weary submarines returning to their Mother ships with the skull-and-crossbones flying proudly. On them were sewn the battle honours; there were bars for every ship torpedoed; there were crossed guns for every gun engagement, and to get an enemy submarine by either gun or torpedo meant an automatic DSO for the commander. One returning submarine even had a little engine sewn upon their Jolly Roger . . . they had pooped a train which was running along the Italian Riviera. But it made me proudest to see the many little commando daggers also sewn on, which meant that our chaps had been doing their stuff.'

Our team in training were called upon to exercise with

new submarines during the working-up period before their first patrol. On one occasion three teams were sent to the submarine depot ship HMS *Forth* to carry out a reconnaissance of beaches north of Troon in the south-west of Scotland.

Jimmy Foot recalls that he and his canoe partner, Company Sergeant Major J. Embelin (Royal Engineers), arrived off their beach after dark. They worked out compass courses to and from the target and embarked in the canoe in near-perfect conditions. Their landfall was accurate, and a start was made taking soundings to seaward from the water's edge from some two to three hundred yards. Somewhat to their surprise, they found a sandbank about fifty yards from the beach covered by more than two feet of water, with eight feet of water inside and a nice shelving run up on the seaward side. Next they checked beach gradients, sand consistency and beach exits, with a quick look at the ground beyond the sand dunes. During their time ashore a stiff onshore wind blew up and conditions continued to deteriorate. On the first run out they failed to make contact with their own submarine, but they were eventually picked up by one of the others on the exercise. They wrote their reports, mentioning the false beach offshore and saying that they did not consider the place suitable for tank landing. Their reports were sent to the planning staff, and later they were ordered to appear in person. They were told in no uncertain terms by a senior naval officer that, as the Admiralty chart did not show a sandbank, no sandbank existed.

A few days later they were taken by Roger Courtney to watch the landings on their beach, with threats of awful consequences should their report prove to be inaccurate.

At dawn the landing-crafts approached the shore; the ramps dropped and the first three tanks drove off into about three feet of water. They continued towards the beach but suddenly plunged bows downward until only the tops of their turrets were to be seen. The tanks were still there in mid-1944, as far as Foot can remember.

Actually, this exercise was a rehearsal for Operation Torch, the Anglo-American invasion of North Africa in November 1942. As a result of this fiasco, beach reconnaissance became popular with planners as a preliminary to assault landings. However, senior naval officers were often reluctant to accept the accuracy of reports by SBS operatives, probably an instinctive feeling that soldiers could hardly be expected to cope with such high matters.

This incident led to the hurried formation of the COPP (Combined Operations Pilotage Parties), composed at first of naval officer navigators with SBS paddlers, and commanded and inspired by Roger Courtney's companion off Rhodes in March 1941, Lieutenant-Commander Nigel Clogstoun-Willmott DSO.

Before he left the nest, the fledgling SBS operative was given 'Passing Out Instructions', which were to be kept and looked at occasionally:

1. You are now considered fit to operate on your own, and should be proficient in Navigation, Demolition, and Scoutcraft. You have been selected on your character qualifications as much as anything else and, as far as we can judge, you can be trusted to take responsibility and can be trusted on your own.

We are jealous of our good name, and our reputation is in your hands.

2. If you go abroad you will very largely have to administer yourselves. People are usually helpful, but remember if you have to deal with military establishment ashore, that the personal touch will get you more than a mass of paperwork.

3. If you find any way that our system can be improved, put it into practice and let us know the results, and we will do the same for you.

The SBS Depot is your servant, let us know what you want and we will let you have it by the quickest possible means.

4. Keep in touch. Good luck and good hunting.

8
No. 2 SBS in Europe,
1942–3

No. 2 SBS was officially formed on 1 March 1942 with
Major R.J.A. Courtney MC (King's Royal Rifle Corps) in
command, and with Captain G.C.S. Montanaro (Royal
Engineers) as his deputy, bringing him selected men from
101 Troop which had been operating from Dover. A
nominal roll is in Appendix F.

The Section scored its first success in April 1942 with a
raid on enemy shipping in Boulogne harbour, named
'Operation J.V.'. It had been decided to send two canoes
into the harbour, and these were to be manned by Captain
Montanaro with Trooper F. Preece, and Acting Lance-
Sergeant S. Weatherall with Guardsman R. Sidlow. In
Weatherall's own words:

'We studied aerial photographs of the harbour and
ships, two of which, one a four- to five-thousand-ton
vessel, were chosen by the Admiralty as being the most
valuable to attack. Two canoes were taken down to the
harbour (Dover) with sixteen limpet mines, activated by
acetone fuses, each canoe to carry eight limpets. The
canoes had already been "swung" at Hawkinge airfield.
This was done in order to counteract the magnetic
variation caused by any metal carried in the canoe, to be
rectified on the P8 RAF compass. Tropal suits were worn
as used by Spitfire pilots; these keep the wearer afloat up
to twenty-four hours should the canoeists capsize, and as
they were filled with kapok, they were warm to wear.

'The canoe and limpets plus weapons were put aboard

the motor launch (ML 102) while Captain Montanaro was at the Admiralty for the final briefing. The three of us waited on the quay for him to come, all with blackened faces. It was dusk when he arrived with some bad news – he called us together and said: "Well, I have come straight from the Admiralty, where there has been a conference, and they think it is too dangerous to send two canoes into the harbour." I remember doing a bit of cursing and swearing but the Captain, who never used bad language, took no notice of it but said simply, "I'm sorry, Weatherall, but it's not my fault." However, we did go on the ML and helped in the launching of their canoe, and also helped to get it aboard after the raid. As near as I can remember, the canoe was launched about a mile from harbour, and the ML hung about awaiting their return. I spoke to Preece about the raid at Ardrossan afterwards. He told me he thought one of the limpets fell off as they were attaching it. I surmise that the magnets had got de-magnetized one way or another. However, he certainly got the rest to stick on the steel plating of the ship after scraping off the barnacles. Each limpet was capable of making a hole up to six feet in diameter.

'They returned on a back-bearing, found the ML without having to make a search-square and went back to Dover. Aerial photographs taken the next day showed five tugs trying to tug the vessel onto the sandbank, but they failed to do so and it sank. I was told afterwards that it was laden with five thousand tons of copper or copper ore. Sometime later, when we were practising in the morse code room, the Captain came and sent the naval instructor out of the room. He then told us sadly that a hundred Frenchmen had been executed as a reprisal, the Germans believing that it was the work of the French Resistance Movement. Montanaro was admitted to the

Distinguished Order (DSO), and Preece was awarded the Distinguished Conduct Medal (DCM).'

Gerald Montanaro soon departed for some secret establishment, disguised as a Royal Navy Commander, and was seen no more in SBS.

This was the heyday of the inventors of strange vehicles. As a maritime nation, Britain naturally showed great interest in developing small craft capable of penetrating enemy defences above and below the surface of the sea. While most of this effort was naval, the SBS was called upon to provide volunteer guinea-pigs during the developmental stage, and later for training as operatives.

Stung by a successful attack in 1941 on British battleships *Queen Elizabeth* and *Valiant* in Alexandria harbour, the Admiralty had given priority to the development of a British counterpart. This was called a 'chariot'.

In April/May 1942 Second Lieutenant J. Kerr (Highland Light Infantry) and Sergeant D. Craig (Royal Engineers) joined the 'Charioteers' from SBS to be trained to attack enemy ships-of-war sitting astride submersible torpedoes with detachable warheads. These 'chariots' were carried on the decks of submarines or slung under small surface vessels, either naval or civilian. When within striking distance of the target, they were released and attacked under their own power. They were joined in training by Corporal J. Allender MM (Duke of Wellington's Regiment) from SBS.

At the end of 1942 Craig and three naval 'Charioteers', with extra as reserves and dressers, sailed with the famous Norwegian blockade runner 'Shetland' Larsen to attack the German battleship *Tirpitz* in Asenfjord near Trondheim in Norway. The two chariots were secured underneath Larsen's fishing-smack but broke loose and sank in a first-class storm which arose when they were only ten miles from their objective. The fishing-smack was then scuttled and the party made its way on foot across Norway and into Sweden. Craig got back to England in January 1943.

At the end of December 1942 Jock Kerr sailed from Malta in HMS/M *P.311* as a member of three chariot teams planning to attack Italian cruisers anchored north of Galeria in Corsica. *P.311* was lost through enemy action before reaching the target area, and the crew and passengers were all killed.

The fascinating story of the 'Charioteers' is told in *Above Us the Waves* by C.E.T. Warren and James Benson.

By the end of 1942 the SBS contingent had all left the western Mediterranean to regroup at Hillhead. Their place with the 8th Submarine Flotilla was taken in early 1943 by 'Z' SBS, whose operations are described in Chapter 5. No. 2 SBS was then reinforced with officers and men recruited from other Commandos and began a programme of intensive training. Captain Basil Eckhard was permanently seconded to COPP nearby at Hayling Island as training officer responsible for the advanced instruction of Royal Engineer officers and men destined for beach reconnaissance, their basic canoe training having been given by SBS headquarters at Hillhead.

It had been decided that submarines were unsuitable for small-scale raiding in the English Channel and, in consequence, only fast surface craft were used.

On 2 March 1943 Lieutenant David Smee (Royal Artillery) and Second Lieutenant A.R. McClair (Essex Regiment) sailed in a motor torpedo boat (MTB) to reconnoitre the Anse de St Martin in the Channel Islands. However, searchlights and gunfire showed the Germans to be wide awake, and the operation was abandoned.

At the end of July 1943 Captain R.P. Livingstone, CSM Stan Weatherall, Lieutenant D. Sidders (Royal Welsh Fusiliers) and Sergeant A. Salisbury were sent to Dover. This was the launching point for Operation Forfar Love, to kidnap a German soldier from the long pier at Dunkirk and bring him back for interrogation. Stan Weatherall describes the experience:

'We practised with a three-man plywood canoe and one of our usual ones (Cockle Mark 1**) on the Prince of Wales' Pier in Dover harbour, using a steel sectional ladder hooked at one end, the rungs just wide enough to accommodate an army boot, also an American .45 calibre rifle that had luminous night sights. It was thought that the Germans might have Frenchmen working for them, pressed or voluntary, and we were given instructions not to molest them in any way. Asked if we could use knockout drops, the answer was definitely "No", because it might give the enemy an excuse to start chemical warfare if they found out.

'On the night of 3 August we loaded the boats and gear onto a motor gun-boat (MGB) and left the harbour at 9.30 P.M. and set off across the Channel. At 11.45 P.M. we launched the canoes and paddled towards the pier about a mile distant, steering by P8 compass, and found there was a small searchlight shining from the end of it. We had no option but to enter the beam, but as we paddled, it followed us. Most probably the canoes were not seen, but the flash of the paddle blades might have been, and the Germans knew there was something there that should not be. The beam continued to follow us, and as the Captain had given instructions not to make this a do-or-die job, he gave the order to withdraw. As we came back on a reciprocal course, the light ceased to follow us, and we came to the conclusion that the lamp must have been on a fixed arc, which allowed us to get back into the safety of the darkness. We kept in touch with each other by walkie-talkie, and Dickie Livingstone's last message was, "Steer North until daybreak and then head West." This was because we could not find our parent craft, the MGB, and because Doug Sidders' radio got waterlogged. We learned later that our MGB had got into a scrap with three E-boats and left the area and returned to base.

'The "Rhud", a turbulent stretch, caused us to ship some water and we had to bail out a lot. Just after we cleared the "Rhud", "Dickie" began to be sick, caused by taking (I understood) a bromide tablet instead of benzedrene. At about 2 A.M. I took over the compass and paddled as "Dickie" was in a very sorry state. After clearing the "Rhud", we observed three vessels heading east, a tanker, an escort ship and a supply vessel. At daybreak we began to head the canoe west.

'At 8.30 A.M. we saw a Spitfire, so lit a smoke float and waved it up and down on the end of a paddle, but it failed to attract the pilot's attention, or so we thought. At 11.30 A.M. two Spits arrived, so I lit a second smoke float. We were seen and had the two planes circling over us; then one left to circle the other canoe, which had fired a Very light, about a mile behind. Within a very short time four more Spits arrived on the scene, bringing with them a Walrus seaplane which landed. Four of the Spits peeled off; we saw them dive and heard their cannon fire and were told afterwards that they shot up two or three E-boats that were on their way in the direction of our smoke. We boarded the Walrus and sank the two canoes, as we could not take them on the plane. We landed at Hawkinge airfield.'

By the end of 1943, planning and preparations were well advanced for Operation Overlord, the massive invasion of Europe planned for mid-1944 as the 'second front' to relieve the pressure on the Russians. A series of beach reconnaissances was carried out by COPP on the vital Normandy beaches in X-craft midget submarines. A series of deception raids was also carried out under the covername Hardtack to distract attention from the COPP reconnaissances. On one of these, Hardtack 28, Captain Philip Ayton of No. 2 SBS was severely wounded by a landmine during a raid on Petit Port in the Channel Islands, and he died on return to England. He was post-humously awarded the Croix de Guerre with Palms. The party travelled by powered dory, and Ayton was accompanied by Sergeants D. Roberts and Carver, also of No. 2 SBS, Sergeant Unwin of SS Group Signals, and four Frenchmen from No. 10 Commando.

Corporal J. Parkes was killed the same night during another deception raid, Hardtack 2, on Gravelines near Dunkirk, to the best of my knowledge.

9

The Sardine Men

By Major R.J.A. Courtney, MC, OC No. 2 SBS

The Welman midget craft was designed by the British Army for attaching limpet mines from its nose to the bottom of enemy ships. The one-man crew had forward-vision armoured glass in the conning-tower and four portholes, steered by joystick, and its tanks were trimmed and its bilge pumped out by foot- and hand-pumps. It was launched by derrick from a transport and floated off a Welman submarine freighter. After diving below the enemy, the operator adjusted the trim and allowed high-pressure air into the buoyancy tanks, forcing the charge (weighing 560 pounds) up and against the enemy hull, where it was held by magnets. The heavy drop keel was detached in an emergency, allowing the Welman to surface even if partially filled with water.

While the light canvas and rubber canoe was still the final answer for most problems connected with clandestine landings, Brother Roger and his SBS were continually on the look-out for better craft and new weapons. He was therefore very popular with inventors of dangerous toys, the more so because he was prepared to try them out himself under practical test conditions. They sold him completely on the Welman and, after some high-level wrangling, three were ordered for the Navy for trials and three for the SBS. In Roger Courtney's own words:

'She was not much longer than one of my canoes, and when I climbed through the hatch there was just room for my shoulders; and when the hatch cover was closed with a clang about two inches clearance above the top of my head. It was rather like the cockpit of an aircraft in its way. Between my knees was a joystick, and beneath my feet the rudder bar. In front of me was an instrument panel with dials which indicated direction, engine speeds and air pressure etc. And a nice little depth gauge which was going to cause me a lot of anxiety in the future. Behind me was the power unit and rows of batteries.

'She was naturally too small to carry torpedoes but had a 560-pound limpet armed with powerful magnets with which you firmly attached yourself to the bottom of your victim, after which you started to unscrew it and yourself by an internal arrangement. This action also set the fuse going, and then you supposedly scrammed, leaving the fizzing charge stuck to the bottom of the ship. I often used to wonder what would happen if, when you had your conning-tower hatch pressed firmly against the ship's bottom, you got the charge half unscrewed, thus starting the fuse, and then got stuck . . . a little imagination is an uncomfortable thing.'

After preliminary trials by Captain Noel Kennard and Captain Eric Lunn of SBS in Staines Reservoir near London, the six midget submarines travelled north by road, heavily disguised and guarded, and all finished up in the far distant Loch Corrie. Lunn recalls that there was a lot of trouble with the compasses and that as a result he spent a very unhappy hour stuck in the mud at the bottom of the reservoir. The line attached to the indicator buoy had wrapped itself round the propeller shaft while he was disoriented and going round in small circles. Though helpless on the bottom, he was able to cut the line by pressing the self-starter continuously and popped up to the surface, to the relief of all concerned.

Again Brother Roger's description: 'Real sea practice in a deep Scottish loch was a very different matter from playing about in the gentle waters of the South.

'For one thing you knew that if your HP air failed or something else went wrong, one could go down and down and down, and still go on going down until outside water pressure scrunched one like an old biscuit tin . . . I had heard old submariners talk of hearing ships that they had torpedoed in deep waters, crackling and crumpling as they sank to that unbearable level of pressure.

'Our submarine kindergarten, however, was the sunlit shallows of the upper loch, and this was great fun. For the amateur one-man submariner it was a delightful playground. To steal through the marine undergrowth and chase fishes; to see ridiculous web feet and absurd bottoms cruising above one; to cruise silently a foot or two above the dappled light of the loch bed and startle crabs and lobsters and other marine monstrosities crawling their weary way from A to B. But these were only the shallows; deep-water experiences yet to come.

'After we had graduated in our playground, there came other and grimmer tests.

'For claustrophobia we were ordered to sink to the bottom of the other end of the loch . . . one hundred feet, and there to keep ourselves amused for an hour. There was a fairly powerful little light behind each of us so that we could see to read our instruments; one could also read a book by it.

'One by one we sank gently down into the darkness until with a slight grinding bump we all hit the bottom together; I could see the light of my immediate neighbour flickering weirdly through this dark underwater world. I had a photo of (wife) Dorrise pinned to my instrument panel for luck, and settled down to read *Wind in the Willows* which is a favourite of mine.

'Down there, with my motors shut off, everything was very silent; it was not really necessary for just one hour, but every so often I would give a twist at the oxygen to freshen things up a little. I had just got to the point where Mole gives his Christmas party when there came a gentle tapping at my windows. The hair was just about to rise on my head when I saw a number of gaping faces pressed against the glass; attracted by the light, most of the local fish had come to investigate the strange monster which had entered their domain.

'When the hour was up, we blew tanks and surfaced gratefully; in my anxiety to reach the surface, I blew too heartily and fairly bounced out of the water among a flock of gulls which fled screaming with terror up the loch. It was good to open the hatch and suck in the sweet Scottish air once more; the sky was overcast and it was raining, but it couldn't have mattered less. About a mile away was the Depot Ship with smoke creaming lazily from her funnels. I had a vision of a cosy wardroom and good cheer, and with my companions making a bad second and third, I popped up the revs and headed for home.

'The next experiences of the Sardine Men, as we were known by the Human Torpedo Men, whom we called the Jeep Men, were to be even grimmer.

'The next test was to get through the anti-submarine and anti-torpedo nets specially devised for our discomfort by our dear friends in the Navy. I must say that they usually had a diving tender and a couple of divers standing by to succour any poor Sardine Man who might get tangled up.

'Our first try was a most harrowing affair; there were two very cheerful divers and three very miserable

Sardines. The obstacle was pretty awkward. First there came a net which was buoyed from the surface to fifty foot depth, and then another which was buoyed from the fifty mark to a hundred foot; and the third net was like the first, all about sixty foot apart. Usually these nets have explosive charges attached to them, but even the devil who devised this torture for us stopped short at that.

'We went through this ordeal one at a time, and in order to count noses, no Sardine was allowed to start before the other Sardine had clocked in on the other side of the obstacle.

'My turn came, and I nosed up to the first line of buoys. I was feeling thoroughly miserable as I flooded my tanks and sank. To keep trim and distance I had to keep my motors going slowly at about quarter speed . . . now a little ahead and now a little astern. The net was a filthy-looking affair of thick steel mesh covered with green slime and barnacles, and as I went lower and lower, and as it got darker until I could hardly see those deadly meshes, I wondered if I would get stuck; I heard my bow scrape once or twice and my heart was in my mouth. At last the end of the fifty-foot bit came in sight . . . it had green streamers hanging from it. I shot forward and under it, and blew tanks to get over the next one which was buoyed from fifty feet to one hundred. Now in this kind of business, a miscalculation may send you down and down to the ocean bed to be lost for ever; on the other hand a miscalculation in the opposite direction may cover you with ignominy.

'In a frenzy of relief I turned too much high-pressure air and rose towards the surface like a cork. I saw the top of the one-hundred-foot net shooting down past me and had just time to save my honour in the next fifty feet by flooding all tanks, going full speed ahead and wiggling my hydroplanes. I hit the next net with a terrible bump . . . my engine stalled, and my tanks having flooded, I found myself in an upside-down position with my legs in the air and gazing earnestly up at my instrument board. My depth gauge was going round like the minute-hand of a clock, and I was sinking like a stone – stern first.

'I was now pulling every plug there was, but it was too late; I saw the bottom of the fifty-foot net go up past me, and I hit the floor with a thump that made my teeth rattle. Fortunately I landed on my keel or I would have been still there now. It took me some little while to recover my nerve, and then I gave her just a soupçon of HP air; just enough to get her off the floor, and then half speed ahead . . . I was beginning to learn at last. I arose like Venus from the waves to receive the congratulations of my fellows.

'Our next trial was an attack on one of our super battleships; all six of us participated this time, half Navy and half Army. The idea was to see whether she could pick us up with her radar or listening devices; it encouraged us to find out afterwards that she could do neither with either.

'The bottom of a super battleship looks rather like an inverted football ground and looks also rather rude. For a change it was a brilliant sunlit morning, and as we sailed under her at fifty feet, visibility was practically perfect at that depth. On the way back I passed too close to the anchor cable and got hooked up by my tail fin. I had several moments of blind panic, and sweat poured off me in a clammy stream. Some advice which I had received, then came back to me: "When in doubt, take your hands and feet off the controls and reason it out."

'I took my feet off the rudder bars, put my hands firmly on my knees and had a good pray. Naturally I could not see behind me to find out how badly I was hooked, so I would have to go by guesswork only. When I had slightly recovered my nerve, I tried her gently backwards and forwards on the motors, meanwhile blowing tanks a little or flooding them. While I was doing this, one of my companions slid darkly past me on the way home; I hoped he would report my presence and my predicament.

'I tried everything I knew, but still could not become unstuck . . . then the worst happened; something behind me fused and there was a smell of burning rubber; in a moment I was choking with smoke and turned on all the oxygen. In an agony of desperation I blew all tanks and went full speed astern.

'Something snapped and I bounced to the surface in a most curious position to the great astonishment of an Able Seaman who had been slung over the bows with a pot of paint. I went limping back standing half way out of the hatch and steering with my feet, and breathing God's fresh air.

'My troubles, however, had been petty compared with those of the gentleman who had slid past me when I was entangled with the cable. As he was coming alongside the Depot Ship HMS *Titania*, he thought he would do a few little "Porpoises", which were our equivalent to the RAF Victory Rolls; something went wrong with his HP air and he sank like a brick to ninety feet – up to his conning-tower in soft mud. With great presence of mind, well knowing that it was his last chance in life, he turned on the little valve at the conning-tower hatch and let the water in; he undid the clamps and let the water rise to nose level before he pushed; pressure being equal, it was a success and he wriggled to the surface like a frog.'

Shortly afterwards the series of tests on Welman craft was discontinued, and Brother Roger and his party, consisting of Livingstone, Foot, McClair, WO II Weatherall, WO II J. Galloway and Sergeants Salisbury, Penn and Smith, returned to base, having fulfilled their function as guinea-pigs. There is some record of the Welman having been used on one occasion by the Norwegians but, as far as we know, without success.

10
No. 2 SBS: The Final Stage

In September 1942 No. 2 SBS moved from Scotland to Hillhead in Hampshire, a small village on the coast of the Solent opposite Cowes. The headquarters were established in an isolated private house with access to its own beach and with sufficient grounds to accommodate stores and sheds for motor transport and canoes. 'Dicky' Livingstone arrived from Scotland with sixty men. He succeeded in wheedling a large flagstaff out of a firm of boatbuilders in Portsmouth who were working on new prototypes of operational craft. With due ceremony the Union Jack was hoisted for the first time at our new location. The effect was marred a little when the local Home Guard, composed of old gentlemen festooned with First World War medal ribbons, pointed out that it was upsidedown. They offered their help if the Army commandos were really in distress and had not just made a mistake.

In order to cut down administration and to foster independence, all officers and men were given a consolidated cash allowance sufficient to maintain them in reasonable comfort. They were all billeted in private houses and well looked after by landladies in surrounding villages. Brother Roger chose the local pub, the Osborne View Hotel, and this became a nightly rendezvous for many of us. It was competently managed by a lady named Marjorie Copp, whose husband Denis was mostly away in the War with an anti-aircraft battery. She was aided by her elderly maiden aunt, Em. Marjorie had seen it all but retained a lively and caustic sense of humour which coped with any emergency. She rapidly became our guide, philosopher and friend. Aunt Em was a gem of pristine innocence, and Brother Roger used to pull her leg. On his way to the bathroom one day, he met Aunt Em and suggested that she might like to come and scrub his back – then she would be allowed to play with his little rubber duck. 'Fancy a grown man like that having a little rubber duck,' said Aunt Em.

Life at Hillhead was pleasant for officers and men – a welcome haven in which to rest and retrain after operations and before we were all sent to the Far East for the war against the Japanese. We were tucked away in an inaccessible corner of Hampshire and rarely bothered by visits from senior officers. Titchfield, Fareham and Lee-on-Solent offered the quiet enjoyments of a small country town, while Portsmouth, Southampton and London were not too far away for week-end leave. There were a few diversions of a sporting nature in our local river – notably a successful attempt by Lieutenant Philip Ayton to fish for salmon with plastic explosive, and by Sergeant Jack Hutchinson to teach a chum how to tickle trout. In both cases they were surprised by the local bobby. Ayton was caught clutching a stunned salmon and could only mutter that he was giving it artificial respiration. Hutchinson was thanked for the lesson, which the Law had observed from behind a bush, and told to put it back.

During this period we invented a special pay book for members of SBS overseas. Our officers and NCOs were often sent abroad in penny packets at short notice and, not being attached to any orthodox Army formation abroad for pay and administration, they sometimes experienced difficulty in obtaining money. Our SBS pay book, approved by the Paymaster at the War Office, enabled them to draw money up to a fixed sum per month from any British service establishment and even from British Embassies. In the pay book paymasters were instructed to hand over the money required, up to the balance outstanding. Mostly this worked well enough. However, one paymaster in Cairo refused point-blank to provide any cash for Alex McClair against the SBS pay book, when he was on his way through from Ceylon to Malta armed with the highest travel authority. Instead, to Alex's astonishment and joy, he was given the equivalent of a modern credit card at Shepheard's Hotel (the best in Cairo in those days) for the few days he was staying. Happy Alex lived it up in considerable comfort, drawing such cash as he required. The final account seems to have been lost in the fog of war as it never came home to roost.

As planning for the invasion of Normandy was reaching its final stages, the training of SBS operatives concentrated on deeper inland penetration of enemy territory than had previously been thought necessary. In one exercise to increase self-reliance they were told to report to Edinburgh in one week's time properly dressed. Before leaving Hillhead, their AB 64s (Army pay books) were removed and they were put on their honour not to carry any money with them. Most of them made their way with friendly long-distance lorry-drivers but one lucky fellow hitched a ride with a fast blonde in a fast car. Her pillow talk included full details of all the aerodromes *en route*, including the numbers and types of planes, and the bedroom idiosyncrasies of many of the pilots. Sighing deeply with regret, he dutifully made out a report for Security when he had returned to Hillhead.

On another occasion Roger staged an attack on objectives in the Isle of Wight. At that time the Chief Constable of the island had also, before the War, been Chief Commissioner of the Palestine Police in Jerusalem.

Roger had been his personal bodyguard. Like Tweedledum and Tweedledee, they proposed to have a battle. Roger described the contest as follows:

'We had arranged for any favourable night in a ten-day period. The attack was to be made across the Solent by canoe, and landing places would be of our own choice. Certain vulnerable points all over the island were selected for attack. To make things easier for the enemy, and to protect innocent soldiery from summary arrest, we had agreed to have small white diamonds sewn into the backs of our battledress.

'In our particular mode of operation there was attack by stealth and attack by bluff. We divided fifty-fifty, and I drew a card for the latter. The Chief Constable, meanwhile, had not been idle. We guessed that he would warn all police and Home Guards to be on the alert for soldiers with small white diamonds on their backs but did not think he would put a news flash on the screens of the island cinemas informing the general public.

'Came a suitable night with a calm sea and a quiet drizzle. In line with my bluffer role, I had stripped off my commando flashes and donned a forage cap instead of the green beret; I carried a groundsheet and a kitbag stuffed with straw to help with the pretence.

'We landed undetected at about two o'clock in the morning; the stealthy party left immediately on a compass bearing to their objectives: I curled up and went to sleep in an abandoned bathing-hut. At dawn I nibbled a bar of chocolate and sucked a couple of milk tablets, and then set off eastward. It was still drizzling and I was thankful to wear the groundsheet which covered the fatal diamond; my kitbag I carried jauntily on my shoulder; it weighed nothing at all.

'By and by I passed a garden cottage in which an elderly

countryman was digging up a row of potatoes. "Morning," says he. "Morning," says I. "Coming off leave?" "Aye." "Boat's a bit early ain't it? Don't usually come before eleven." I hurried on. After about three quarters of an hour he overtook me, driving a battered old Ford van loaded with potatoes and green vegetables. "Going my way?" says he. "Going Totland to rejoin my unit." "That would be the Buffs?" "No, the Fusiliers." "Give me your kitbag and jump in."

'We drove a little way in silence. Suddenly he looked down and said, "Nice pair of boots you've got," and to my horror I realized that I was wearing the special issue to commandos. With a sudden twist of the wheel, he ran straight into a police station yard where there was a police sergeant picking his teeth in the doorway. "Who was that?" I said to the police sergeant after I had been locked in a cell minus my trousers. "That was Sergeant Jenkins of our Home Guard, sir." Half the stealthies got through and half the bluffers, with the majority of the captures being made by the Home Guard.'

In the autumn of 1943 SBS was lucky enough to receive an intake of recruits from other commandos. These were already experienced raiders and highly trained in all arms, demolitions, sabotage, signalling, mountaineering, cliff assault and unarmed combat. In addition they had trained and operated in a variety of small surface craft. Some had recently taken part in Operation Forfar Beer, a cutting-out raid for intelligence purposes on the French coast near Etretat, under Captain N.G. ('Trapper') Kennard of the SBS, who arranged for their transfer to us afterwards.

They were promptly given revision courses in canoeing, demolition, navigation, signalling, compass swinging and booby-traps. Only detonators were used as 'charges' for the latter, and training was carried out in a row of beach huts near the headquarters at Hillhead. Sometimes the booby-traps were overlooked and not dismantled – a detonator under the lavatory seat activated by a pressure switch is said to be a better cure for constipation than syrup of figs.

After they had been vetted and approved by Roger Courtney, they were sent to Padstow in Cornwall in December for advanced navigation, surf training and night operations under Captain W. Armstrong and Lieutenant J.P. Foot of the SBS. Bill Armstrong was an ex-Merchant Navy officer who taught navigation and boat-handling. He was in his late thirties and was a hard taskmaster – advisable when instructing a bunch of high-spirited young men in the art of canoe-handling in the bitter winter surf and Atlantic rollers. He was a cheerful character and seems to have been well liked by his pupils.

The day of Operation Overlord, the Allied landing on the French coast, was not far off, and SBS personnel were engaged in a series of beach reconnaissances and raids across the Channel in support of COPP reconnaissances of Normandy beaches. We did not know at the time that the operations in which the SBS took part were a small piece of a vast deception plan designed to delude the Germans and to deflect their attention from the COPP recces, which were the vital ones.

COPP, still under Commander Nigel Clogstoun-Willmott DSO, DSC, had progressed far from its small beginnings off Rhodes with Brother Roger in March 1941. After Torch, beach reconnaissance and pilotage became popular, and the Planners suddenly demanded fifty teams to be equipped and trained by Christmas or by Easter 1943 at the latest. Willmott insisted that four or five months were necessary for the adequate training of new entries and, with youngish specialist RN navigators and Royal Engineer Army officers in short supply, they had to

Major Roger Courtney MC, OC No.2 SBS, in 1943

With Dorrise, just married, London, 1938

Roger Courtney's grave, Hargeisa, Somaliland

Major R ('Tug') Wilson DSO, 1955

At Hillhead, 1943: *From left to right:* Flight-Lieutenant Roy Thompson, RAF, Medical Officer; Major Mike Kealey; Lieutenant Philip Ayton; Major Roger Courtney, CO; Lieutenant David Smee; Captain Doug Sidders; Lieutenant Commander I J Wymer

A 'folboat' being lowered down the forehatch of an S Class submarine

Craftsman Geoff Wood with Mark V engine and Corporal Bill Merryweather at M aungye, Burma, 19

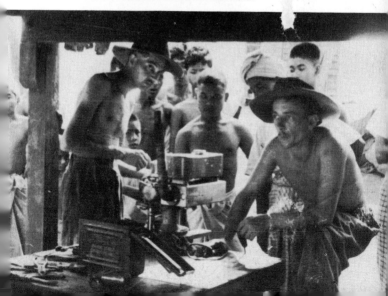

Sergeant Sandy Tough firing Vickers 'K' gun with Corporal Sid Longhurst as his No.2, Burma, 1945

Major E J A ('Sally') Lunn MC (front) and Lieutenant the Hon. John Rodney in Mark VI canoe, 'A' Group SBS, Burma, 1945

No.2 SBS at Hillhead, late 1943

Osborne View Hotel, Hillhead, 1943-44

Craftsman Geoff Wood in Mark 1 Folboat (2-star) canoe, Ceylon, 1945

Skeleton frame and complete hull of Mark 1** canoe: length 17 feet; maximum beam over woodwork 2 feet 5 in; total weight fully rigged including paddles maximum 122 lb

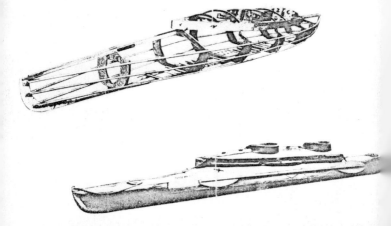

Bamboo airstrip, Bawang Valley, Central Borneo: *(above)* HQ Semut 1 SRD, 1945 and *(below)* Blowpipe platoon

Semut 1: Major Tom Harrisson and HQ staff on bamboo airstrip, Bawang Valley, 1945

Corporal Ron Westow with Mark VI canoes and Vickers 'K' machine-gun, Burma, 1945

be content with ten teams. The Sappers were held on SBS establishment for administrative reasons and wore commando SBS shoulder flashes and the green beret. Captain Basil Eckhard of SBS was lent to the COPP Depot at Hayling Island as senior soldier in charge of security, PT and combat and canoe training until he was forcibly put on the sick list by the medical officer in July 1943 suffering from overwork. His place was taken by Major Logan Scott-Bowden (RE) who, with Sergeant Bruce Ogden-Smith (East Surreys), was later to swim in to vital Normandy beaches in January 1944 under the noses of the Germans to obtain samples of sand and rock. This was in preparation for Overlord, which took place in June that year. Scott-Bowden won the DSO and MC, and Ogden-Smith the DCM and MM.

Willmott also insisted on having qualified navigators and Sappers at the sharp end of each COPP reconnaissance team. The main reason was that, if an ordinary young naval or infantry officer came back with technical information of great importance and possibly at variance with what was hitherto believed (e.g. from Intelligence, scientific/geological research etc), he was going to be disbelieved at higher levels and at least 'bullied' or pressurized. From experience it was found that admirals and generals were more willing to take the word of a professional navigator or engineer than they were of the 'amateurs' of the Special Boat Section, however enthusiastic. In addition, COPP teams would always find a higher court of appeal in the shape of a Fleet Navigation Officer or CRE (Commander Royal Engineers) in case of argument, whereas the SBS tended to be nobody's baby. By June 1944 COPP was a well-organized show of 174 officers and men with an impressive record of successful beach reconnaissances.

Friendly liaison between SBS and COPP continued until the end, with SBS helping out with stores and paddlers in emergency and with basic training in canoe work. This liaison was cemented by the really firm friendship which had developed between Roger Courtney and Nigel Clogstoun-Willmott, despite their very different temperaments and outlooks. These were clearly brought out in the mottoes of their respective units: '*Nobis Tutus Ibis*' ('With us you go in safety') for COPP and '*Excreta Tauri Astutos Frustrantur*' ('Bullshit Baffles Brains') for the SBS.

The other 'private army' with which we had long been associated was the Royal Marine Boom Patrol Detachment (RMBPD), founded and nurtured by Lieutenant-Colonel H.G. Hasler DSO, OBE, RM, known then and later in transatlantic yachting circles as 'Blondie'. He himself had led a particularly hazardous raid by canoe on Axis shipping in Bordeaux harbour in October 1942 (Operation Frankton). However, by 1944 the unit was mainly engaged, as far as I know, with developmental work connected with assault landings. Roger and 'Blondie' did not see eye to eye over equipment to be carried in canoes. Roger felt that 'Blondie' was far too gadget-minded and that a frail canoe bobbing up and down in a choppy sea off an enemy coast was no place for non-magnetic anchors and masses of signalling gear and wiring within which the operative could strangle himself. A survey of casualty ratios between the various Navy, Army and Marine small boat sections would be interesting. Nigel Clogstoun-Willmott was another gadget man, but the specialized and technical nature of beach reconnaissance did require more complicated aids than our simpler operations. Roger, whose sense of humour was irreverent and who lacked respect for 'Sacred Cows', used to describe the Royal Marines as having been 'egg-bound with tradition since the Battle of Trafalgar, when they wore funny hats, did good work with muskets, and with fingers in ears let off pieces of ordnance'. However, he who laughs last. . .

11
Canoes and Canoeing

It all started in June 1938 with a collapsible German canoe called *Buttercup* in which Brother Roger and his wife Dorrise travelled down the River Danube to the Black Sea on their honeymoon. *Buttercup* was the subject of the discussion with Admiral Sir Roger Keyes which led to the demonstrations described in Chapter 1. She was the fore-runner of all war canoes later improved and developed for clandestine operations mounted against enemy-held coasts. As the war went on, these were increasingly mechanized, hung around with gadgetry and subject to break-down. They culminated in 1944 in a submersible motorized canoe (MSC) operated by one man in diving-gear. Ironically named *Sleeping Beauty,* it was described by trainees as tricky, difficult to handle and notoriously unreliable. In fairness to the inventor it must be said that this opinion came mainly from trainees who had failed to pass ruthless selection tests in Australia for an operation planned against Japanese shipping in Singapore harbour for October 1944. It is believed that the MSCs were never actually used on this raid, but as the 23 men who were finally chosen for it never returned, their opinion of performance under operational conditions is not known.

We of Nos 1 and 2 Special Boat Section preferred to rely on simplicity, physical strength, seamanship and agility for survival and good results. You will note that physical fitness is not included in the list. To a person who is accustomed to fresh air, sunlight and hard exercise, the conditions in a submarine on patrol will produce a swift and violent reaction in the shape of constipation, physical lassitude and mental lethargy. Therefore it was inadvisable to take violent exercise for at least two weeks before embarkation. Gentle exercises to keep our paddling and leg muscles in trim would help us during the operation, but otherwise we did not hesitate to eat, drink and be merry. We found that a tin of glucose powder was a useful adjunct to our stores. The Commander of COPP, a typically clean-living and athletic naval officer, did not agree and made us run up and down the Rock of Gibraltar before breakfast every day. We of the SBS, the 'brutal and licentious soldiery', managed to slink away after a period of passive resistance to canoe and swim instead.

Buttercup was modified to Roger's design, and the type became known as a 'Cockle Mark 1'. It was made of rubberized canvas on a wooden frame, weighed about fifty pounds, could carry two men and was sixteen feet long. It was said to be very fragile, very fast and silent, but prone to turn turtle. The greatest disadvantage was in the beam of thirty inches, which was too large to allow passage fully erected through a submarine's forward torpedo hatch.

The final and, to us, most satifactory development of the folboat type was the Cockle Mark 1** (Two star). This incorporated a rigid frame with an adjustable cross member, allowing the beam to be reduced by two inches when passing through the hatch before refixing for launching. It was fitted with bow, stern and longitudinal buoyancy bags and weighed stripped about a hundred pounds. We sometimes used to strengthen all open-topped frames with wood and cut off the longitudinal bags to reduce weight and increase speed. This also eased exit through the forehatch. It satisfied the prime requirement of the submarine captain that as little time as possible should be spent stopped on the surface close to an enemy coast while launching or recovering folboat parties. The ingenious Australians removed the inflatable buoyancy bags from the bow and stern compartments and replaced them with coconuts. These acted as a combination of reserve food supply for the men, and flotation aid for the canoe if holed by a bullet.

A folboat-type canoe is canvas decked with a fairly narrow beam and with a long bow. The gunwale is low amidships and aft, and the foredeck slopes up sharply to a central ridge line. The cockpit has a watertight cover, with manholes for the crew. The crew sit facing forward, enabling them to keep a good look-out ahead as well as on the beam. Unfortunately, a forward-facing sitting posture is tiring and the least effective when propelling a small boat by muscular effort. The best speeds can be obtained only by using double paddles. But this method has the disadvantages of being comparatively noisy and more visually noticeable at close quarters. An effective compromise was found by using double paddles for the long passage and by breaking these apart and using them singly when stealth was necessary. British canoeists also favoured feathered double paddles to lessen noise from water slap and to reduce windage. The Australians, on the other hand, preferred to use only single paddles of the Canadian canoe type shaped to a point. The blade was pared to a knife edge so as to eliminate slap and drip. It was found that double paddles with a copper or brass joint must be used in preference to those fitted with stainless steel. This avoided unpredictable compass deviations – a matter of some importance when homing to a submarine on a dark night.

Getting into and out of a folboat from the forecasing of a trimmed-down submarine a few miles off an enemy coast with a sea running required no mean agility and a cool head. The painter and stern line would be in the hands of two naval ratings. It was important that they allow the canoe to float free with the swell. If the lines were drawn tight, it would capsize. Care was also taken not to let it ride too near the foreplanes in case it was swept under them and smashed. It took nice judgement to step into the centre of a canoe as it surged against the casing and to collapse oneself onto the bottom before one fell overboard. Then grasp the paddles and away clear before settling down for the long haul to the beach. Equally tricky was the disembarkation on return. Throw the bow and stern lines up to the casing party and hand up heavy gear. Then legs under, and hands on the gunwale at the point of balance. Wait for the surge of the swell against the forecasing to propel him upwards and inwards, never pausing with one foot still in the canoe if he did not want a ducking.

Capsizing also had its problems. The two-man crew must allow the folboat to roll right over quickly until the keel was uppermost, trapping the air inside. If checked halfway, when it was on its beam ends, it would take in much more water. The next and most urgent step was to retrieve the paddles. Thereafter the canoe would be flipped over and bailed out until it was possible for the crew to climb back in. No. 2 first over the stern, and No. 1 afterwards over the bow, and resume passage.

Negotiation of surf was also of vital importance. We found this during the secret landing of the American General Mark Clark and his party near Algiers in 1942, described in Chapter 4. In the Mediterranean we experienced two main sorts of surf. They both varied in intensity, of course, with the slope of the beach, and with the length, height, steepness, speed and direction of the waves. Over a shallow, gently shelving beach the waves are fairly far apart with a long breaker zone and crests of decreasing height. A skilled crew could ride in on the waves with the front man working hard to keep up and the rear man steering with his paddle, keeping the stern always square to them. If there was a danger of taking water, they leapt overside when they were in their depth and lifted the canoe over the breaking crests as they eased it into shore. There was little backwash on a shallow beach to hamper them.

The same process was reversed for coming out, except that they waited in the canoe just inside the line of large breakers until a calmer patch arrived. They then paddled quickly out square to the waves until beyond the breaker zone. They held their paddles above their heads when meeting each breaker to prevent them being torn out of their hands.

Over a steeply shelving beach the waves are closer together and higher. The breaker zone is shorter and more violent, with strong undertow and backwash. In this case, going in, it was best to wait just outside the breaker zone with the bow pointed to seaward. When several of the biggest waves had passed, then backwater the canoe fast towards the shore. To do this without being swamped, it was necessary to back paddle hard between the crests, then to stop and paddle forward into and over each one as it came in to loom over us, always keeping the bow square to it. When the water became sufficiently shallow, we would leap out and lift the canoe over the crests and on into the shore. Coming out from a beach through 'dumpers' is more difficult, as we found out in North Africa with General Mark Clark. To try to paddle out through them unaided is to invite disaster. However, when serving earlier in the (then) Gold Coast, I had noticed how surf boats were launched by Africans through the Atlantic swell. We copied them. Four men of our shore party carried the canoe on their shoulders, clinging together, as far as they could through the worst of the breakers. Beyond these the two crew members, clutching their paddles for dear life, were heaved into the canoe. Given a shove, they were last seen paddling madly up the slope of a large comber and over the top into the night. It worked.

To minimize the chance of detection on landing, it was important to choose the disembarkation point with care. Detailed pre-operational intelligence on the location of enemy sentries was generally not available. We would try to plan on the principle that a quarter or no moon period with a slight lop on the water would hamper the sight and hearing of patrols and look-outs. In addition we would try to choose a landing point near a rocky outcrop or a patch of mangrove, the principle being that a tired and sleepy sentry would prefer to walk on nice soft sand. 'Roll on f . . . ing death' was the attitude of the bored British soldier on such duty, and we hoped that the Jap, German or Italian would feel the same. During daylight we would examine the shoreline closely through the periscope of the submarine, as near in as possible with safety. We made a panorama sketch in silhouette of the terrain as it would look at night from canoe level. This we would memorize.

Once ashore the canoe would be carried immediately into cover and turned round to face the sea, with the paddles ready, for a last-minute getaway. Footwear was important – in winter we wore knee-high rubber and leather commando boots over the legs of our many-pocketed overalls, and in summer rope-soled shoes or felt-soled boots. Rubber sandshoes squelch loudly when full of water, and many Australians preferred thick woollen socks instead. These were silent and left less noticeable footprints which could more easily be erased by sweeping with a leafy branch. There was even one experienced operative in Australia who carried his own special home-made sand-rake.

We know that a heavy smoker is not conscious of the smell of stale tobacco smoke clinging to his clothing and hair. But even non-smokers do not realize the extent to which their own body smell can give them away, not only to dogs and other animals but to human beings. Asiatics often regard the smell of a white man as different and distasteful. This was an ever-present danger when operating in South-East Asia and South-West Pacific. Even in European waters the bouquet surrounding one's person after two or three weeks in a submarine was almost tangible and likely to alert the dumbest dawn patrol. It was therefore our practice to lie up in concealment on the leeward side of the footpath which usually ran close above the high-water mark on most beaches. We tried to avoid getting to windward of villages and farm dogs.

Retiring to seaward after a clandestine landing was always a time of nervous tension and anxiety, not only from the risk of being shot at from the shore but also because an enemy patrol boat might arrive and prevent our submarine from keeping the rendezvous.

Our good friends the submariners would take the most appalling risks on our behalf to pick us up after an operation. But it was accepted by all concerned that we were expendable and that they were not, the safety of the submarine and crew being far more important. In the early days we would paddle out hopefully from the shore on a reciprocal compass bearing, flashing a shaded red or blue torch to sea every few hundred yards, hoping that 'Mother' would pick it up and move across to meet us on our line of approach. Later we were equipped with a battery-powered RG lamp fitted with an infra-red filter, with which we signalled hopefully into the gloom. In both cases we must hold the light up as far as possible, particularly when there was any sizeable sea running, otherwise we would almost certainly not be seen by the look-outs on the conning-tower. We would normally hope to pick out the silhouette of the submarine against the sky ourselves, provided that the night was clear. In mist or rain neither the infra-red lamp or the shaded torch was effective. All would then depend upon the skill of the submarine's navigator in calculating the effect of the changes in wind, current and tide since we had left him, and upon the accuracy of our compass course, to bring us together before dawn. As a last resort we would drop grenades over the side at pre-arranged intervals in the hope that the bangs would be located by his hydrophones.

It could, and sometimes did, happen that a rendezvous was missed and through the fault of neither party. Captured commandos were usually interned by the Italians, shot by the Germans and tortured and beheaded by the Japanese, but occasionally SBS was lucky.

However, by the beginning of 1943 a better answer was found by SBS by which the submarine homed on the canoe instead of vice versa. This was a simple device which we christened 'The Bongle' and which consisted of a metal rod of fixed length for underwater sounds. This could be picked up by the submarine's Asdic at about seven miles and by her hydrophones at about two miles. The rod was struck by a simple mechanical hammer turned by a handle whilst the contraption was held over the side of the canoe. I spent many an hour on trials sitting in the middle of the Solent bongling away until

'Mother' appeared out of the mist. It eventually became standard equipment for COPP and other special boat parties.

If only we had known, we could have got the idea for 'The Bongle' much earlier in the War from the Solomon Islanders. When short of cash they sit in a canoe in a convenient and blockable bay, thread two pieces of lace coral on to a knotted stick, and pump it up and down in the water. The resultant clicking of coral is apparently an invitation in porpoise language to a love-in. During the mating season it attracts hundreds of porpoises, which come dashing into the bay for a cuddle. The islanders, who value porpoise teeth as a minor form of currency, capture them and extract one or two teeth before releasing them to live and love again. There was a time in the Solomon Islands when the gift of a porpoise tooth by a young man to a maiden during sexual initiation ceremonies was a sign of mutual appreciation and the length of a girl's necklace of teeth a measure of her performance.

As you may imagine, we were much sought after by inventors of strange gadgets. Special boat men as a species were considered by orthodox staff officers to be eccentric, a bit of a nuisance and not quite respectable. We were therefore regarded as a convenient captive audience for enthusiasts of all kinds, some of whom endeared themselves to us as fellow eccentrics and helped to lighten the tedium of training. We had our favourites. One was the old gentleman who cycled up to Scotland to teach us how to live on grass. Another was the late Sir Malcolm Campbell, the veteran speed ace, whose visit to COPP is happily described in *The Secret Invaders* by Bill Strutton and Michael Pearson (1958).

'Sir Malcolm brought along his own "beach tester". It was an enormous bar with a handle and a foot pedal. You pushed it into the ground, then stepped on a trigger which tripped a clapper. Then you counted. The time its spike took to penetrate the sand determined its bearing capacity. Sir Malcolm had used it on Daytona Beach to test the sand for *Bluebird*. The COPPists called it "Campbell's Pogo Stick". They could hardly manipulate it standing upright on an enemy beach, so they tried it lying down. Usually it used to leap with a loud twang and smack them under the chin. Its clapper made a noise like thunder. Under the eyes and ears of the Germans it would work like a burglar alarm – but they did not like to tell Sir Malcolm that. He was so eager to help. So they suggested that it was rather a hefty piece of gear for any swimmer to drag with him inshore, laden as he already was. In a few days Sir Malcolm was back with an enormous mandolin-shaped affair made of cork. He loaded one of his pogo sticks on this and said, "There, you can pull it behind you."'

In 1944 Sir Malcolm visited Ceylon and came to SBS with a new invention. This was two canoes joined together by a platform in the middle. The motor worked an oil pump as well as the propeller and had pipes running into it. The whole could be lifted up high and dry when coming into the beach so as to keep one's feet from getting wet. The only drawback was that the motor had an audible high-pitched sound, which could be heard a good way off and it was therefore no good for landing on an enemy beach.

I believe it was also Sir Malcolm who invented the miniature torpedo, used by SBS on Operation Reservist in Oran harbour in November 1942 and by 'Tug' Wilson in Crotone harbour two months previously. Although ingenious in theory, it did not work in practice. Lieutenant Eric Lunn recalls that it just did not function in the slightest rough water and tended to go round in circles. When the engines cut out, it was supposed to sink of its own accord. During the assault in Oran he was horrified to see one afloat near the quay when he was being marched off to prison by Vichy French marines. It is a pity that the SBS were not consulted during the period of its development but were used as operational guinea-pigs and some captured to no purpose.

Despite his well-founded suspicion of gadgets, Brother Roger was prepared to try anything once. He and other operatives of SBS were engaged at various times on the trials of such perilous means of under-sea transport as the Welman one-man submarine and the 'chariot' human torpedo. Fortunately for them the motorized submersible cnoe (MSC) named *Sleeping Beauty* had not yet been developed.

Australia and the Far East

12

'Z' SBS with SOE (Indian Ocean), 1944

In the autumn of 1943 it was announced that a new Supreme Command of South East Asia had been created. Lord Louis Mountbatten was to be Supreme Commander. He foresaw that there would be considerable scope for the small, highly specialized units which had grown up under his umbrella at home. As a naval officer he had long held the opinion that amphibious operations were the traditional role of the Royal Marines. He had been instrumental in planning for Royal Marine Commandos gradually to replace the commando units created and run by the Army since 1940. In fact, as early as 20 May 1943, a Combined Operations Headquarters' Minute advocated the amalgamation of small boat parties into one special boat unit. It went on to suggest that the (Army) Special Boat Section should be seconded to the proposed unit to continue their work. But no further reinforcements should be demanded from the Special Service Brigade (also Army). It recommended that, to keep the unit going, Royal Marine personnel should be drafted to reinforce it if required. 'In this way the military interest would gradually die out; and the Commanding Officer (of the new special boat unit) may find it possible to amalgamate this Section to the Royal Marine Boom Patrol Detachment and possibly the Royal Navy Boom Commandos.' This was incorporated in a final Minute to Force Commanders dated 1 November 1943.

Of this, of course, we in SBS were blithely unaware. We

carried on with business as usual in the Mediterranean and with training at home. In January 1944 'Z' Special Boat Section was posted to Ceylon to work under Force 136 of the Special Operations Executive (SOE), responsible for provision of operational intelligence and fostering guerrilla activity in the SEAC (South East Asia Command) area. We were attached to the 4th Submarine Flotilla at Trincomalee.

At that time 'Z' SBS consisted of Captains E.J.A. Lunn MC, N.G. Kennard, A.R. McClair and W.G. Davis, Sergeants N. Thompson MM, J. Gilmour, J. Galloway and F. Preece DCM, and myself. In mid year we were joined by Lieutenant J.P. Foot MBE, Sergeants Blewett, and G.C. Ellis MM, and Trooper B. Moores. Meanwhile, plans were being implemented to co-ordinate small-scale raiding parties under SEAC. These were to be based in the north of Ceylon under Royal Marines control. Instead of being called the Special Boat Unit (SBU) as previously suggested, the name was changed to the Small Operations Group (SOG).

So in the spring of 1944 the officers and men of No. 2 SBS, training for the Far East at Hillhead on the Solent, were invited to transfer to the Royal Marines. Brother Roger was given the job of putting the proposal to them. The British soldier has his regimental pride. Ours were drawn from some of the most famous English, Scottish, Irish and Welsh regiments. The tone of their response was set by one of our best canoeists. Resplendent in kilt and sporran, he said, 'Sorr, I have always been in the Argylls and would like to stay in the Argylls if ye don't mind, sorr.'

While this was happening at home, I was confronted in Ceylon by a Royal Marine colonel with what amounted to an ultimatum. With courtesy I also declined the honour of becoming one of 'His Majesty's Jollies', as did my officers and men.

While this plot was thickening, I composed an impassioned memorandum to SACSEA (Supreme Allied Commander South East Asia). I pleaded that it would be a misuse of the unique experience of SBS personnel in small-scale clandestine operations if we were to be put under the control, for operations as well as administration, of Royal Marines less experienced than ourselves. Morale would inevitably suffer. Brother Roger was also fighting the rearguard action at home, neither of us realizing that the battle had been lost twelve months previously.

I made a personal and unsuccessful appeal to Lord Louis Mountbatten (by then known as 'The Supremo' to the outer circle of his admirers, and as 'Dickie' to the inner). I was passed on to a staff officer and got nowhere. Again, Omar Khayyám has the apt aside to offer, in Stanza 71:

> The Moving Finger writes; and having writ,
> Moves on: nor all your Piety and Wit
> Shall lure it back to cancel half a Line,
> Nor all your Tears wash out a Word of it.

Thirty-seven years later, in the Public Record Office in Kew, I discovered a copy of my memorandum. It bore 'The Supremo's' initials thereon and the letters 'N.A.' (No Action).

I was equally intrigued to see in the PRO a letter dated 19 June 1944 from the SACSEA Chief of Staff, Major General G.E. Wildman-Lushington CB, CBE, Royal Marines, to the then Chief of Combined Operations in London, Brigadier G.J. Robinson OBE, MC, which stated, *inter alia*, 'As you say, the Courtney brothers are not very easy to assimilate.' However, a less indigestible officer was available in the person of Major (later Lieutenant-Colonel) M.R.B. Kealy (Devonshire Regiment). He had been left in command of No. 1 SBS in the Mediterranean after Roger Courtney's departure and up to the end of 1942. Then they had been finally absorbed into the Special Air Service and reborn thereafter as the nucleus of the Special Boat Squadron under Lord Jellicoe.

SOG came into being officially on 12 June 1944 under the command of Colonel H.T. Tollemache, Royal Marines (now retired as Major General Sir Humphrey Tollemache Bt, CBE, DL), with Lieutenant-Colonel H.G. Hasler DSO, OBE, Royal Marines (Roger's old 'Blondie'), as second-in-command. At its maximum SOG consisted of four COPP parties, three Army SBS groups, a formation of Royal Marine Commando assault troops known as Detachment 385, and four Sea Reconnaissance Units. Until disbandment in October 1945, SOG carried out nineteen independent operations mounted by its own headquarters. No less than 154 minor tactical raids under command of Local Force Commanders of the 11th Army Group on the Arakan Coast and on Burmese rivers were also carried out. Of these at least eighty were the share of SBS and are described in the next chapter.

Meanwhile, 'A' and 'B' Groups of the SBS sailed in April 1944 for Ceylon under Major Kealy. They were followed by 'C' Group, leaving No. 2 SBS HQ on the Solent to be wound up on 19 May 1944.

'Z' SBS, already in Ceylon with Force 136, was then split up. Lunn eventually joined SOG in January 1945; McClair, Foot, Sidlow, Gilmour, Blewett, Ellis and Moores remained with Force 136; Kennard, Davis, Thompson, Galloway, Preece and I sailed for Australia in HMS/M *Clyde* at the end of July 1944. *Clyde* had seen

better days and is rumoured to have settled down happily
in retirement in Fremantle harbour upon a steadily rising
bed of empty gin bottles.

Brother Roger was not encouraged to stand in the path
of progress and was shipped off to the British Military
Administration in ex-Italian Somaliland. His indomitable
wife, Dorrise, had contrived to join the FANY (First Aid
Nursing Yeomanry) to be with him in Ceylon and had
wangled a passage to Colombo. She was obliged to wangle
a passage back again and was next heard of in a place
called Jigjiga (believe it or not) on the Abyssinian border.
Life with Roger was never dull. 'Tug' Wilson, who knew
him better than most, has written: 'It was with him that
just anything could be tackled. The impossible became
downgraded to improbable, then probable, and finally
almost a piece of cake.' Like many a pioneer, he sowed
for other men to reap. He used to quote Stanza 28 of the
Rubáiyát:

> With them the seed of Wisdom did I sow,
> And with mine own hand wrought to make it grow;
> And this was all the Harvest that I reap'd –
> I came like Water, and like Wind I go.

McClair and Foot remained at Trincomalee with Force
136 (Special Operations Executive) and were joined for a
short period by Lunn. They were kept busy ferrying
agents and stores and preparing for Operation Zipper –
the main assault being planned by South East Asia Command (SEAC) for the re-occupation of Malaya. This
never came off because of the Japanese surrender.

McClair relates that on one such operation the pre-
arranged password for the pick-up was, 'Did you hear the
nine o'clock news?' The gun-crew of the submarine were
alert to blow the approaching boat out of the water if the

incorrect answer was given. Came the reply, 'What the f . . . ing hell are you talking about?' McClair dropped flat on the forecasing, yelling, 'Don't fire,' but the sailors had recognized something familiar and un-Japanese in the words and all was well.

Standard escape gear, concealed on the person, for such operations was 2,000 Japanese Straits dollars, twenty gold sovereigns, six compasses bedded in rubber, six linen maps, five Union Jacks on silk, four messages in Chinese, and five 'L' cyanide tablets. These latter aids to self-destruction were more important in the war against the Japanese than they had been in the Mediterranean.

Jimmy Foot was occupied in Ceylon mainly as boating instructor. After VJ Day he was sent to Siam via Calcutta to work partly for Force 136 and partly for the Civil Affairs Section (Malaya). The job was to collect, feed and eventually repatriate civilian native labour which the Japanese had brought from Malaya and the Dutch East Indies for work on the railway. He found himself acting as liaison officer with the Japanese Railway Division at Chumporn. He writes that he had a most enjoyable six months supervising the repair of railway bridges. By January 1946 most of the displaced persons had been moved to the area of Bangkok, where he happily spent the next four months – with some leave in Penang, Singapore and Kuala Lumpur.

Alex McClair and his longtime canoe partner, Sergeant Ron Sidlow, continued to live in HMS *Maidstone*, our old home in Algiers days, and its accommodation ship, *Wu Chang*.

At the beginning of March 1944 they flew to the eastern Mediterranean with Eric Lunn and Sergeant Jock Gilmour to carry out the simulated beach reconnaissances described in Chapter 5. As a result of these, McClair was Mentioned in Dispatches.

On 10 June they returned to Trincomalee and were accommodated by Force 136 in Camp W, where they remained until December 1945. Meanwhile Eric Lunn had sought fresh fields and eventually took command of 'A' Group SBS in January 1945. Sergeants Gilmour and Newsome remained in Camp W.

McClair spent most of his time in Camp W training with inflatable rubber dinghies to find the maximum load with which they could be operated. The operational role of 'Z' SBS with Force 136 was that of ferrying agents and stores into Malaya from submarines. The number and quantity of each that could be carried, in the minimum number of trips, were of great importance.

Someone had invented a wooden cradle to which an outboard motor could be attached on the dinghy at the back. On their first ferry operation to Malaya the three SBS pairs failed to take a party of agents ashore as their outboard motors refused to start after travelling in the high humidity in the submarine for a couple of weeks. Eventually one did start with a mighty roar and jumped off the cradle. They were brought back to Ceylon for another try and housed in a section of Camp W next to another party which was about to be inserted before it. This was a serious breach of security and Alex McClair complained to Colombo headquarters of Force 136 but got into hot water for it. He was subsequently proved right, as the other party was captured by the Japs as soon as it landed.

Unaware of this disaster, McClair and his team sailed with his own party in HMS/M *Severn* to have another go, and the Captain of the submarine took them to within two hundred yards of the jetty at which they were to land. They loaded the rubber dinghies with men and stores and started the outboards when suddenly the Captain yelled to

him to re-embark, slash and sink the dinghies and abandon the operation. Back on board, a frustrated and
furious McClair was told that they had received a signal
from base ordering immediate cancellation.

He did not learn the reason until after the war. The first
party had been captured on landing and had given away
under pressure every detail of McClair's party and its
proposed place and date of landing. The Japs were there
behind the jetty waiting in ambush, but the submarine got
away so quickly that not a shot was fired. There was a very
brave Malay called Lieutenant Ibrahim ben Ismael, who
had been transferred from McClair's party to the other.
He pretended to collaborate with his captors and offered
to operate the radio for them to send back false information to Colombo. In the course of transmissions he
managed to warn Colombo that his own party had been
captured and that the next one was compromised. So well
did he deceive the Japanese that they actually gave him
money and clothes after the surrender to help him escape
from the British, as they were sure that he would be
executed as a collaborator.

Having survived the war he rose to the rank of General,
and became Chief of the Malaysian Armed Forces. In
October 1982 he attended the Annual Dinner of the
Special Forces Club in London as a special guest,
welcomed for his 'most outstanding war record, with
Force 136'.

The perils of the sea in submarines were not confined to
mines, bombs and depth-charges. On one trip to Malaya,
McClair remembers hearing the coxswain complaining
that a sailor was persistently malingering and refused to
get out of his bunk. The next day the man was dead and
another one down with similar symptoms. Naval officers
are not doctors, and medical attention aboard is normally

limited to castor oil for constipation, so the officers pored through their medical books and sent a signal to base describing the symptoms and asking whether it could be cholera. You can imagine the devastation that could be caused by an outbreak of cholera inside a submarine far from home, and they were ordered to return forthwith. They were met by a destroyer with a doctor and a complete spare crew, and all hands were evacuated from the submarine. Apparently nobody else contracted the disease, which turned out to be heatstroke.

As a change from visiting Malaya, McClair and Sidlow were flown by Catalina flying-boat across the Indian Ocean to a small island in the China Sea. From there a small party of Thais accompanying them went to the mainland to collect some fifteen to twenty Thai Army officers to bring back to Ceylon for training in counter-espionage. They were all due to be picked up by the Catalina that night before the monsoon broke and marooned them there for some time.

The Catalina did not arrive on schedule but the monsoon did not break the next day, and the aircraft arrived that night. The Thais brought masses of luggage with them, which they refused to abandon, and McClair had to throw it overboard from the dinghies on the way to the flying-boat. Even so, the aircraft was so packed with the men that several of them had to stand all the way back to Ceylon.

13

'Z' SBS in Australia and Borneo

The men of 'Z' Special Boat Section who accompanied me
to Fremantle in HMS/M *Clyde* in mid 1944 were: Captains
N.G. Kennard and W.G. Davis, Sergeant (later WO II)
N. Thompson MM, Sergeant (later WO II) J. Galloway
and Sergeant F. Preece DCM.

I was whisked over to Melbourne to the Services Re-
connaissance Department (SRD) which was the SOE
(Special Operations Executive) equivalent in Australia of
Force 136 in Ceylon. I became Staff Officer Grade II
(Plans) under Lieutenant-Colonel J.E.B. Finlay (Royal
Welch Fusiliers) who was my GSOI. After the War he
returned to his old job in HM Customs and Excise in
London, where he rose to be Director of Personnel. He
taught me a lot – chiefly how to think straight and not to
take anybody too seriously.

During the Australian summer of 1944–5 we shared a
dilapidated weatherboard bungalow near the sea, renamed Fincourt (get it?) in a suburb of Melbourne called
Beaumaris. In those days Beaumaris was comparatively
undeveloped and consisted mostly of T-trees and scrub.
However, the family mansion in whose ground we lived
possessed a small chicken-farm, guarded by a fierce
Irishman and his fierce dog. As all we knew how to cook
was eggs, it was my duty as junior officer to run the
gauntlet of the dog, who seemed to dislike British majors.
Leaves were spent on a property in the western district of
Victoria, run by a kindly but formidable lady and her

three daughters, father being away at the War. The girls were all adept at managing sheep and were expert horsewomen. Being unacquainted at that time with the Australian sense of humour, I was unwise enough to make modest mention of my horsemanship, based on a few days at Gunner Riding School in the Territorial Army in the early thirties. I was led out into a paddock and placed upon an allegedly docile beast which promptly threw me headfirst onto a rock.

The remainder of 'Z' SBS, who were joined by CSM Jimmy Jones from Ceylon, stayed in Fremantle and were absorbed into the training and operational pool of SRD, on attachment to the Australian Army. 'Trapper' Kennard, a large, quiet Scot from the Argentine, was employed from January 1945 as officer-in-charge of Optician. This was the cover name for the attachment of six special task canoe operatives from SRD to the British Submarine Flotilla in Fremantle. They would accompany submarine patrols, normally in pairs, to carry out such tasks as limpet-mine attacks on shipping inaccessible to submarines, railway sabotage, beach reconnaissance and similar activities. Optician was duplicated by Politician, with attachment of SRD personnel under Major W.T.L. Jinkins (Australian Army) to the American Submarine Command South West Pacific Area (SWPA). 'Trapper' Kennard sailed from Fremantle early in 1945 in HMS/M *Telemachus* as dispatcher, to launch a Eurasian agent into northern Java. Owing to bad weather and engine trouble, the insertion was postponed until May 1945 in a different submarine and without a dispatching officer.

Also in early 1945 the US Navy Submarine Command (CTF71), by which Optician/Politician was controlled, moved from Fremantle to Subic Bay in the Philippines. A request was made to the US Admiral for permission to establish an SRD base in Subic Bay to continue the operations. Permission was granted.

Sadly, during a submarine patrol by USS *Bream* from 11 March to 17 April 1945, an Australian canoe pair from the Politician team failed to return from a limpet-mine attack on a Japanese convoy. The Japanese tried to lure the submarine close to shore by means of a fake radio message in English, but this was detected and *Bream* retired undamaged but after a severe depth-charging. Following this news, CTF71 decided that Politician/Optician types of operation were too risky for US submarines and would be discontinued. An SRD move to Subic Bay would therefore not be necessary.

Such risks were par for the course and accepted as part of the game by British submariners. American submariners were no less adventurous, and I suspect that the decision was influenced by political pressure from American GHQ. General Douglas MacArthur and his senior Intelligence staff tended to be anti-British and looked upon SRD as a British Trojan Horse. While SRD could be tolerated in the South West Pacific, by then a sideshow, its presence on the approaches to Japan was another matter.

Nevertheless, this ban on Politician/Optician and the consequent cancellation of SRD's move to Subic Bay, did not apply when co-operation was requested by Mountbatten's South East Asia Command. In early August 1945, Kennard sailed with Major Jinkins and thirteen other Australian operatives on USS *Hawksbill* on Operation Crocodile. This was carried out at the request of Force 136 in Ceylon and was for the purpose of establishing a series of bases in the China Sea between Borneo and Malaya. Support could then be given to clandestine parties operating in Malaya, and intelligence of enemy movements could be obtained. The submarine visited Tamelan Island, and Djemadja Island in the Anambas group and intercepted and interrogated several natives on shore and from prahus and junks. As a result of these interrogations, a landing party was put ashore at Terempah, the Japanese garrison having fled to the hills. Enemy stores and four hundred drums of petrol were burned, and the submarine destroyed a Japanese radar station by gunfire. On 14 August 1945 the Japanese Government capitulated and Crocodile was abandoned.

WO II Norman Thompson MM (Royal Engineers) had been my canoe partner since the early days of 'Z' SBS in the Western Mediterranean. In May 1945 he became one of the party allotted to SRD for short-term intelligence operations in the area of Brunei Bay on the north-west coast of Borneo. These were in support of the landings to be carried out by 9th Australian Division the following month. Phase IIB of these operations, of which the collective cover name was Operation Stallion, was the extraction of natives from villages in the Kimanis Bay area and from sea-going prahus *en route* between Labuan and Brunei.

The party landed in a Catalina flying-boat in Kimanis Bay, just north of Brunei Bay, at dawn on 8 May 1945. They went ashore in the vicinity of Kimanis village and made a fruitless search of a Japanese-occupied house inland from the beach. As the time limit given by the captain of the aircraft was 1½ hours, the party leader decided it was not possible to cover the distance of one mile over difficult country to Kimanis village. They therefore returned to the aircraft, bringing with them for interrogation one native from the Kimanis area.

I am indebted for much of the above information to the SRD official history Part II (Operations) released by Australian Archives in Canberra.

Incidentally, the prefix VB (Victoria British) was used before the personal army numbers of British Service Personnel seconded to the Australian Forces and serving with SRD. Out of Australia in operational areas we wore Australian Army jungle-green uniforms, with berets or slouch hats, on which we were allowed to wear our own regimental badges. All British Army personnel were granted local rank in the Australian Military Forces. However, this close integration with the AMF during the War did not entitle those of us who settled in Australia afterwards to the post-war benefits enjoyed by our Australian comrades.

The operations carried out by the SRD in the Borneo area were, with the sole exception of the Jaywick raid on Singapore, the most successful of all the missions undertaken by the organization. Most of the Borneo operations were conducted in British territory and were led by officers who, before the War, were employed there. SRD was the only organization of its kind operating in this area, and when the reconquest came about, it was performed by Australian Forces, SRD working directly under the Australian command.

The most important of these operations were Agas (Sandfly), covering British North Borneo, and Semut (Ant), covering Sarawak. Both were inserted in March 1945 for the purpose of providing pre-invasion intelligence and of fostering resistance against the Japanese occupying troops. The only ex-SBS member involved was WO II Norman Thompson MM, who was landed by Catalina flying-boat at Jambongan Island in north Borneo to join Agas. He travelled to the forward headquarters south of Bongaya where he was employed in training guerrillas. Thereafter, until 24 August 1945, he and his guerrillas took part in skirmishes with wandering Japanese parties, who were unaware that hostilities had officially ceased on 15 August. With the remainder of Agas I party he arrived at Keniogan Island on the north-east coast on 24 August, from where they were evacuated by Catalina on 18 September 1945.

The Carpenter project for operations in the area of South East Asia Command (SEAC) was planned by Force 136 (India), which provided some of the equipment and most of the personnel. It was supported logistically by SRD which also supplied the ferry party. This was composed of the other members of my own 'Z' SBS who had come over with me from Ceylon and who had been training in Western Australia ever since. They were Captain W.G. ('Bill') Davis, WO II John Galloway and Sergeant Freddie Preece, DCM.

Carpenter's area of operations was the south of the state of Johore in Malaya. In this region Chinese Communist guerrillas had organized themselves in a strong and widespread resistance organization known as the All Malayan People's Anti-Japanese Forces (AJF), and a number of British officers and men were known to be living with the AJF units.

The task of the Carpenter party was to set up a base in the south-east of Johore from which radio contact could be established with Colombo. Thereafter, they were to contact the AJF and to train and organize the guerrillas for attacks on enemy communications and installations.

On 21 September 1944 HMS/M *Telemachus* sailed from Western Australia with Carpenter I, commanded by Major W.B. Martin (British Army). The final insertion plan provided for the disembarkation of the whole party and half the stores on the first night. On the second night the boat party was to rendezvous with the submarine and

discharge the remainder of the stores, after which the
ferry party would return to the submarine. If *Telemachus*
failed to close the coast on the second night, it would
return again on the fourth. The party leader, however,
arranged to take ashore on the first night all essential
equipment, against the possibility of subsequent rendezvous not being kept. Similarly, 'Bill' Davis, commanding
the ferry party, was prepared to be stranded ashore with
his men – a wise precaution. At 2000 hours on 5 October
1944, *Telemachus* surfaced three miles off Tanjong Balau
on the east coast of Johore about thirty-five miles north-
east of Singapore. The disembarkation procedure was
carried out without mishap, and the submarine put out to
sea at 2128 hours.

The official history of the SRD relates that, 'At 2000
hours on the following day (October 6th), *Telemachus*
surfaced about one and a half miles north-north-east of
the rendezvous and cruised slowly towards it. At 2023
hours, hydrophone effect which resembled the motors of
the rubber boats (in which Carpenter had disembarked)
was heard on two different bearings. For an hour the
submarine stalked these indications without success.
Again at 2150 hours, indications of a fast approaching
vessel of anti-submarine character were recorded and the
Telemachus put out to sea. At 0032 hours on 7 October,
while stowing the submarine's special ladder, six float
planes passed close to the vessel. The Commander then
decided that there was a strong possibility of the operation
being compromised. A further attempt to rendezvous with
the party would be an unjustifiable risk to the submarine
and a grave embarrassment to the party if in hiding. The
vessel therefore proceeded on its next assignment.'

During the secret war against the Japanese in the Far
East it was not often that a ferry party stranded ashore

was able to survive and give its side of the story. I am indebted to 'Bill' Davis for a copy of his Ferry Party Report compiled after his evacuation to Ceylon in February 1945; this is reproduced in full in Appendix B.

It is evident from his report that the breakdown of the outboard motors, which were always tricky to operate after the humid conditions met inside a submarine on patrol, caused his party to reach the rendezvous area at sea some two hours late. *Telemachus* had already encountered the three barges or patrol vessels later seen by Davis, at about 2200 hours, and had retreated seawards after hearing indications of another vessel of anti-submarine character approaching the rendezvous. Half an hour late Davis's party arrived in the same area and was chased by the three vessels. It was significant that six float planes passed close to the *Telemachus* only two hours later and, unusually, in the middle of the night, surely more than a coincidence. Davis has told me that the Japanese knew the names of the whole of the Carpenter party within two weeks of their arrival and had put a price on the head of each of them. With such a good local information service, one wonders whether the Japanese had not been warned by the vessels encountered by Carpenter on the way in the first night and set a trap on the second. It was known that a network of patrols and coast-watchers had been organized among local natives in occupied territories by the Japanese. Great were the hazards to agents and submarines from collaborators and from the well-laid Japanese ambushes which inevitably followed their betrayal.

Captain Davis and the ferry party were finally evacuated to Ceylon in February 1945 in HMS/M *Thule*. After four months of smoking tobacco made from pawpaw leaves, and a diet of rice and monkey, rice and pawpaw, rice and fish, rice and green vegetables, and rice and pineapple, they were glad of a change. Galloway and Preece did not return to Australia but Davis was posted to advanced SRD Headquarters in Morotai in the Halmaheras as GII (Operations). Major Martin had been killed by the Japanese when they penetrated the camp area on 25 January 1945 after a supply drop by Liberator aircraft. The guerrilla forces in south Johore were officially disbanded early in December 1945 but re-emerged in 1948 as part of the Malayan Peoples' Anti-British Army (later called the Malayan Races Liberation Army).

Meanwhile I was employed as GSO 2 (Plans) at SRD Rear HQ in Melbourne and, in the Australian spring, lived just round the corner at the Botanical Hotel in suburban South Yarra – known to all as the Bot/Hot – which was our favourite watering hole. In 1944 British officers in uniform were rare, and therefore interesting, and were encouraged by the local ladies to wage the 'Battle of Toorak', as it became known, Toorak being the Melbourne equivalent of Mayfair in London, where our sleazy Pommie charm had some attractions – in the absence of the more rugged Australian variety, which anyway was away at the War.

In November 1944 Allied operations had moved away from Australia, and it became necessary for SRD to operate from advanced bases overseas. So in February 1945 SRD Advanced HQ moved to Hollandia in Dutch New Guinea, and in March to Morotai in the Halmaheras as part of the Allied Intelligence Bureau under General Douglas MacArthur's General Headquarters South West Pacific Area (GHQ SWPA). By that time the operational sections of the SRD had been reorganized and I was appointed to command Group 'A' – responsible for the Northern Celebes, Macassar Strait, Borneo, China Sea (excluding Malaya which was under Mountbatten's South East Asia Command (SEAC)), French Indo-China and the China Coast. However, in early 1945 the role of SRD became entirely para-military, and almost the whole existing effort was directed in support of 1 Australian Corps' operations in Borneo. Group 'A' activities were therefore concentrated in the China Seas, British North Borneo (renamed Sabah post-War) and Sarawak. We had two Country Sections – BNB, under Flight Lieutenant Paul Bartram, and Sarawak, under Captain A.G. Crowther, and all signals to and from parties in the field were to be routed through Group 'A' Headquarters.

On 10 June 1945 the 9th Australian Division, of Western Desert fame, landed on Labuan Island in Brunei Bay on the west coast of Borneo. Two weeks later we moved there from Morotai and established our tented camp on a bluff overlooking a nice sandy beach at the north end of the island away from conventional military formations.

The history of the SRD and its operations has no place in a story about the Special Boat Section of the British Army Commandos, except in so far as individual members of the SBS were involved in Australia and Borneo. However, for those who are interested in the sideshow that was Borneo in the later stages of the War, I would highly recommend *The World Within* (1959) by Tom Harrisson, individualist, author and anthropologist, whose graphic description of life among the head-hunters gives a good idea of conditions prevailing behind the Japanese lines at the time.

He and other party leaders of Semut and Agas operations were men of highly independent character and, although I was officially their Commanding Officer, my command was very nominal. My role was that of meat in the sandwich between Semut and the somewhat legalistic and conventional senior staff officers in the 9th Australian Division Headquarters. According to the official history of the SRD:

'Prior to the invasion of Borneo Headquarters 9th Australian Division seemed to possess little appreciation of the potentialities of Semut, with the result that there was little forward planning, and full use was not made of Semut for close support of the assault. However, after "A" Group SRD moved to Labuan on 28 June 1945 and came under command of 9 Australian Division, co-operation was close and satisfactory at all times . . . relations with the 9 Australian Division staff were excellent and other branches of the Staff assisted with arms, stores, and advice where possible.

'It was found advisable to keep all operatives in the field well away from close contact with Australian Army localities, as the slightly unorthodox outlook of individualistic Semut junior leaders was prone to irritate the more orthodox type of battalion commander.' This was an understatement.

One of our junior Australian party leaders in the fighting zone had been held responsible for the killing of a Jap collaborator by his guerrillas. Our infuriated General, a lawyer in private life, ordered his immediate arrest and trial for murder. We advised our man to leave speedily for the jungle and get lost, whereupon our General, balked of his prey, intended to arrest me as the next best thing. This ridiculous affair was settled by direct order of the Commander-in-Chief and no action taken.

The Air Officer commanding I Tactical Air Force Royal Australian Air Force (AOC 1 TAF RAAF) was a famous and fiery officer, now retired as Air Chief Marshal Sir Frederick Scherger KBE, CB, BSO, AFC. He was at all times kept acquainted with the movements and intentions of Semut parties and showed the greatest co-operation and interest. The RAAF was hard put to find sufficient profitable targets and welcomed close co-operation with SRD. Personal relations with the AOC were cemented with Sunday curry lunches at our camp prepared by our native cooks, and with banana wine brewed on the mainland. It is no exaggeration to state that, without the generous assistance given by 1 TAF RAAF in close support, transport aircraft and Catalina flying-boats, Semut operations would have been impossible to maintain during the difficult period following the confinement of 9th Australian Division to a very limited coastal area.

During close support full use was made of the Japanese habit of retiring into the jungle when attacked by aircraft. During the night prior to an assault, the native troops and Dyaks would surround the Japanese perimeter and conceal themselves in the jungle. At a pre-arranged time, RAAF aircraft strafed and bombed the Japanese positions. On the appearance of aircraft, the enemy promptly went into the jungle and sat under a bush, waiting for the aircraft to leave. On the aircraft departing, our guerrillas would rise from the next bush and decapitate the Japanese before they could reoccupy their defensive positions. To counter this, the Japanese dug slit trenches on the edge of the jungle to which they would retire. Unfortunately, they carried out the current drill for concealment from the air, and from chance bullets, by building roofs on the trenches. The Dyaks took to sitting on the roof during the raid and removing the heads of the Japanese as they stuck them out when the raid was over. The taking of heads was for ritual purposes but had been strictly suppressed by the Government of Sarawak pre-war. It had been resumed with enthusiasm by local tribesmen when they realized that it was open season on Japanese. Jap-hunting was risky, so Sea Dyaks (Ibans) would sometimes cheat and chop the head off some unfortunate Chinaman; it was hard to tell the difference after the head was smoked – at least to the untrained eye.

Following the landings of the Australian 1st Corps at Tarakan on the east coast of Borneo and on Labuan on the west, direct physical contact between us at Headquarters and Semut parties in the field became of great importance. It was provided by 1 TAF RAAF in the shape of two-seater Auster biplanes and Catalina flying-boats.

Tom Harrisson found a site for an airstrip in the Bawang Valley of central Borneo, and local labour built a runway out of thousands of giant bamboos, each thirty-five feet long. Each bamboo was split longitudinally and laid out with the inside upward. The internode sections along the bamboos' length served as long lines of little sprockets or pegs which helped to slow the aircraft incoming. Outgoing aircraft kept their wheels between these lines. On 7 June 1945 two Austers landed from Tarakan, but the first plane to take off on the return journey, and carrying Harrisson, ended up on its nose in the mud. The strip was hurriedly lengthened by another eighty yards and thereafter regular flights were made to and from Tarakan and Labuan.

The photographs reproduced in this book show the strip quite clearly as well as Tom Harrisson and some of the Semut I party. His guerrillas were armed mainly with rifles but, as can be seen, there was also a blow-pipe platoon with poisoned darts. On ceremonial occasions there would be a march-past and the firing of a *feu-de-joie*. This was safe enough for the riflemen but less so for the blow-pipe platoon because what goes up must come down.

Early in June 1945 the first ground contact with Semut II was made when an RAAF Catalina landed on a rather dangerous short stretch of the Baram River. Thereafter Catalina sorties to the Headquarters of Semut II and III became frequent as they progressed down the rivers into the broader and straighter stretches. It was quite an experience to visit Semut party leaders for a conference by this method. The rivers were fast and dark brown in colour, and the Catalina would slip down between the trees onto the water without quite knowing whether there was a heavy log just under the surface to rip out its bottom. We would be greeted by dug-out canoes manned by muscular brown tribesmen armed with *parangs* (sword-knives) who would help to secure us against the bank, nose to the current. Ashore we would be honoured by an invitation to enter the long-house up a notched log, at the top of which one was beaten over the head with a live cockerel to discourage evil spirits from entering as well. I was never quite sure that this was not an elaborate leg-pull laid on by the party leader for the gullible visitors, rather like a sheep's eye pressed upon the foreigner by Bedouin during an Arabian 'mutton-grab'. The take-off from the river valley on the return journey was always tricky, with the heavy Catalina clawing its way up the mountainside so as to clear the top, and sometimes banking steeply at the last moment for another try when we could not make it.

We had the pleasure on one occasion of bringing in Captain W.R. 'Tiny' Fell, of the Royal Navy, to meet Major Sochon of Semut III at headquarters in an Iban long-house on the Rejang River. Captain Fell had brought HMS *Bonaventure* to Labuan to prepare for the ultimate phase of Operation Crocodile, mentioned earlier. *Bonaventure* was the Depot ship for X Craft miniature submarines and similar craft. At the time his submariners were under-employed and he was keen to co-operate with Semut and to send some of his junior officers in to work with the guerrillas. We were interested in a plan to arrange naval support for an attack on the small town of Sibu, then held by the Japanese. Both projects failed to materialize with the Japanese surrender in mid August. His reactions to the outing are told in *The Sea Our Shield* by Captain W.R. Fell, CMG, CBE, DSC, RN.

'On our return we found Colonel Courtney of cloak and dagger fame waiting for us. He had a series of intensely interesting plans for discussion, all of which involved aid from *Bonaventure*. Two of these seemed feasible and a tentative programme was drawn up for carrying them out. Near Kuching, the capital of Sarawak, there were known to be living many prisoners and internees, mostly British, who had been held since Japan invaded Borneo. In Borneo there were estimated to be five thousand Japanese who, even after the fighting had nearly ended, were still active in areas round the oilfields of Brunei, Sarawak, and North Borneo. The operation was designed to cut off and capture the main body of the Japanese forces and separate them from the area where the prisoners and internees were held and then to effect the release of the prisoners before the Japs had time to kill and starve them.

'Nearly two years earlier, small parties of British soldiers had been dropped into the jungles of Central Borneo where, after incredible adventures, they had organized the head-hunting Dyaks of the jungles and rivers into formidable and efficient guerrillas. These guerrillas were now to harass the flanks of the Japs, landings were to take place near the Seria oilfields, the Army in Labuan was to surround the enemy, the Navy was to effect the escape of the internees and prisoners and the Air Force was to assist with reconnaissance and air drops.

'With all this in view Colonel Courtney suggested to me that I might like to fly into Central Borneo and meet the leader of the Dyak guerrillas to discuss their part in the operation . . . I took off from near Brunei in a Catalina flying-boat with Courtney and a few others, and flew over the impenetrable jungle in the wildest country I have ever seen. For hour after hour we did not see a break in the forest, but on three occasions some light tracer fire came climbing up slowly towards us. Each time it looked so harmless, but each time the old Catalina zigzagged and bucketed about and the force of Spitfire escorts with us – I think we had eight of them – swooped and opened up with cannon fire into the green jungle below us.

'At last I saw a foaming yellow strip of river far below. It seemed impossible that we should be going to land in this between its arching banks of huge trees, but down we came, circling lower, till we could clearly see the rocks and rapids and foaming water. To my horror it appeared to be full of logs, floating tree islets, tree stumps and snags – none of which knew the rule of the road. Choosing the only possible spot between snags, where the water was not actually boiling, our pilot made a perfect landing and dropped his anchor. At the same time two dug-out canoes shot out from the jungle and came racing towards us, manned by the wildest looking crews imaginable.

'While they were still three hundred yards from us our anchor dragged and in an instant we were spinning round and rushing downstream towards a cataract. The men in the canoes were waving and gesticulating towards a tiny backwater, overhung with huge trees and into this our pilot taxied us.

'Here we found a space scarcely wider than our wing span, with a tiny bamboo jetty. Our pilot brought our fuselage alongside this jetty with one wing over its top, whereupon a yelling swarming mob of Dyaks rushed down onto the jetty, firing fusillades of poisoned darts from blow-pipes over us, while the canoeists yelled and fired from the other side.

'We stepped out of the Catalina onto the flimsy jetty as the Dyaks were trying to form into some semblance of a guard of honour, but our combined weights were too much for the jetty and we all descended quite slowly into primaeval mud up to our armpits. As I went down I saw Colonel Courtney, already over waist deep, with his arm rigidly at the salute.'

Who am I to spoil a good story?

After the official surrender of the Japanese Government, the Major-General commanding 9th Australian Division ordered that no Australian lives were further to be risked and that all units were to stand fast in their positions. Unfortunately, the Japanese troops inland either did not know or did not choose to believe that the War was over and continued to rampage through the interior. This meant that defence of the civil population, persuasion of the Japanese to surrender, and the preparation for the entry of the British Borneo Civil Affairs Unit (BBCAU) devolved entirely on SRD parties in the field. This inevitably led to friction and misunderstanding with HQ 9th Australian Division, and my role as meat in the sandwich became ever more demanding. After a short interlude in Melbourne for consultations, I returned to Labuan and sent the following signal: 'To all parties from Courtney. DO NOT REPEAT NOT HARASS KILL SNUB SPIT ON OR LOOT ANY JAPS WITH WHOM YOU COME INTO CONTACT WHO ARE NOT HOSTILE. ANY TIME ANY SRD PERSONNEL HURT JAP FEELINGS IN ANY WAY JAPS COMPLAIN TO 9 DIV WHO THEN MAKE LIFE DIFFICULT FOR YOUR POOR OLD COLONEL WHO HAS NOW RESUMED COMMAND GROUP A. LET US DEPART IN PEACE.' Which I did.

As a postscript to these recollections of service with the

Australian Armed Forces, I can do no better than to quote from Tom Harrisson's *The World Within* where he is giving his opinion of the Australian fighting man.

'It is perhaps appropriate that a British officer . . . should make a few general observations about the Australian soldiers who formed the main body of Semut personnel and did much the larger part of the toughest work . . . for their fundamental approach to military service was almost diametrically opposed to that of the ordinary English training . . . where acceptance ruled in the latter, initiative and independence played a much greater part among the Aussies. In particular, the conception of the officers as a separate class barely existed, whereas this was the fundamental assumption . . . in Britain at least up to 1944 when I left. This related partly to the less differentiated class structure of Australian society. But it goes deeper than that. Much of it has to do with the Australian's estimate of himself as a man. And to the outsider, this estimate seems to be almost as dramatized as when American children dress up as Davy Crockett and patrol the frontiers of the Yank mind. There is really a sort of exaggerated masculinity and virility among the better type of Australian men, which at times can be fairly insufferable, but which is absolutely invaluable under active service military conditions. . .

'Thus many Australians were delighted to have the chance to be soldiers; and even delighted to have the chance to fight. Such an attitude was consciously rare among the British, and almost neurotic. To the Australians there was nothing neurotic about it. In fact, the neurotic soldier . . . was a great rarity. So for that matter was the intellectual soldier, the sort of chap I had got to know as an officer and in cloak and dagger training, who had all sorts of philosophies and principles and determinations of a mental kind connected with fighting. Without over-generalizing, or over-simplifying, I think it would be true to say that the great majority of Australian soldiers who were any good at the job, and by definition all those who volunteered for our kind of operation, had a really good, gutsy, personal, proud, determined, individual, sensible yet passionate approach to the business of fighting Japanese.'

14
'A' Group SBS in Burma,
1944–5

'A' and 'B' Groups[1] of the Special Boat Section under Major M.R.B. Kealy disembarked in Bombay from the troopship ss *Otranto* in May 1944 and found that nobody knew what to do with them. Corporal Sid Longhurst recalls that they slept for a few days on top of their stores on the quayside until they were moved into barracks. They were then taken to a place about forty miles east of Poona for acclimatization, where they played cricket and football and swam in the water-tanks. They then travelled in an ancient, leaky, ant-ridden railway carriage down to the south coast and then by ferry to establish a camp among palm trees on a sand-pit about ten miles from Jaffna on the north end of Ceylon. There was an old Dutch fort called Fort Hammanhiel on an island in the strait, and this was turned into a stores depot. The camp itself was at a place called Hyatt's Ferry, which Longhurst described as a sailor's delight, full of old square-riggers, said to be ex-Japanese pearl-fishers, and the building of local wooden boats.

In June the Royal Marines, with COPP and a detachment of the SRU (Sea Reconnaissance Unit), arrived to establish the headquarters of the Small Operations Group (SOG), and a properly designed camp was constructed. SBS acquired three of the new Mark VI rigid canoe catamarans, and when not on training, these were used to sail round the shallow coral lagoons or for fishing:

---

[1] Nominal rolls will be found at Appendix H.

the best bait was held to be the Mills 36 Grenade. SBS made and fitted lee-boards to the canoes, which helped when trying to sail into the wind.

The Mark VI canoe was 1×8 inch 'aircraft' plywood covered in fabric and treated with sealer (dope). A lining of heavy rubber-proofed stockinette kept the hull watertight if the wooden skin was fractured. The outriggers were of fabric-covered wood on alloy arms. The load was two men and 350 pounds, or three men and 150 pounds. Equipment included mast and sails, double paddles and a fabric sea anchor. It was built in three sections by bolting together. The No. 1 crewman in front had a Vickers 'K' machine-gun with one-hundred-round magazines. The gun was fitted to an improvised traversing mount designed and fitted by SBS members. In front of the No. 2 crewman in the rear section was an aluminium 'sleeve' into which clamped a 2½ h.p. 'Middi' engine. By rotating the sleeve, the engine could be lowered so that the propeller protruded through a sort of bottomless bucket in the bilge of the canoe to turn in the water below. The engine was fitted with a home-made silencer which was so effective that it was extremely difficult to locate in the dark even when close up.

Attached to SBS as operational fitter was Craftsman Geoffrey Wood (known as 'Little Timber') of REME (Royal Electrical and Mechanical Engineers). His most important work was to keep the 'Middi' engines starting promptly and running smoothly, under the most adverse operational conditions. He was a superb mechanic and a perfectionist and insisted that every spot of fuel must be filtered before being put in the tank and that water-filters must be kept scrupulously clean. As a result of his strict instructions, no member of SBS was killed or captured as a direct result of engine failure during the campaigns that followed. He was eventually Mentioned in Dispatches for his work and many years later received a letter of gratitude from one of his old comrades on behalf of the children and grandchildren of happy wives now living because of his war-time skill and dedication.

'C' Group, under Major R.P. Livingstone MBE, arrived later in the month, and all three groups settled down to prepare for operations of a very different nature from those they had been used to in Europe, and in a much more exacting climate.

After a period of training with the other SBS groups in Ceylon, which included a canoe safari down the Mahaweli Gunga River for about 180 miles, from a point just north-east of Kandy to Trincomalee, 'A' Group left in September 1944 for an airfield near Rawalpindi for training as parachutists. They were thereafter allowed to wear their 'wings', of which they were very proud, on the left breast. Many of 'C' Group had already qualified in England in December 1943.

In early October 1944 'A' Group left for the Arakan front for attachment to 15 Indian Corps from 16 October until 14 December 1944. All their operations in the Arakan were carried out from motor launches (MLS) using the paddled Mark I** canoe, the long-standing maid-of-all-work of SBS and COPP. (It was not until the river crossings and patrols on the Rivers Chindwin and Irrawaddy during the first half of 1945 that the motorized Mark VI plywood catamaran canoes were employed instead, mainly to cope with the current.) A graphic eyewitness account of their operations on the Arakan front has been written by Corporal W.H. ('Bill') Merryweather:

'By 3 October news came that operations were in the offing, and the group left Kankesanturai in the north of

Ceylon by Dakotas to fly up the east coast of India to Calcutta. Here they met Captain Barnes whose advance party had been held up for lack of aircraft. The usual Commando enterprise produced two Dakotas for the following day, and the group moved to Chittagong where the men stayed at No. 47 rest camp; with the stores housed with NSO Coastal Forces. From here Major Holden-White accompanied Commander Nicholls DSO, RN down the coast to Bawli Bazaar, where he met Major Eastwood of 15th Indian Corps and Major Drysdale RM Brigade, Major of 3 SS Brigade. Details were worked out for a raid on the Japanese-occupied island of Ramree just off the Arakan coast; and the following day he returned to Chittagong to pass on the good tidings. The canvas two-man folboats were assembled, grenades primed and tommy-gun magazines loaded, tides and moon phases worked out, and on 15 October 1944 the landing party consisting of Major Holden-White and Corporal Merryweather, Sergeant Hawkins and Corporal Westow, Sergeant Roberts and Lance-Corporal Edwards of the Burmese Intelligence Corps, set off on ML 412 to carry out a reconnaissance of Uga Chaung on the west coast of Ramree Island (Operation Gregory). Aerial photographs showed jungle on the left bank of the river as it swept into the sea, with a long sandy beach backed by scrub and cultivated land on the right. The ML was commanded by Lieutenant John Kent RINVR and on the way down the coast two planes that approached the vessel were fired on when they failed to flash any recognition signals, and were thought to be Japanese reconnaissance jobs. About dusk, the ML cruised in between Cheduba Island and Ramree, and a tropical storm blew up accompanied by thunder and lightning – however it soon died down and the canoes were slipped over the side and loaded about 1½ miles off shore.

'The sea was reasonably calm, and the canoes went in line astern towards the sound of heavy surf on the landing beach. The OC's canoe stopped about 150 yards off shore, and the signal was passed back for the others to hold off while he tried the beach. This was the normal drill, after which a torch signal would bring in the remainder of the party. Paddling slowly forward toward what appeared to be the entrance to the Uga Chaung, the canoe rose and fell in three-to-four-foot swells – then without any warning, a breaker picked it up and carried it in a flurry of foam and at considerable speed between two huge rocks which were about ten feet apart. While the No. 2 was still laying on his paddle to steer it straight, the canoe scraped hard up onto a beach where jungle came right down to the water, and the pair quickly nipped out and dragged it up a slope under the over-hanging trees. Signals were flashed out to sea for nearly ten minutes, but no other canoes arrived, so Major Holden-White and Corporal Merryweather decided to carry out the recce on their own.

'Following the left-hand bank of the river, they went inland about 600 yards and were halted by a mangrove swamp. It was obvious there was habitation on the right-hand bank, for glowing fire embers could be seen fifty yards away, and the smell of curry and burning coconut wood pervaded the night atmosphere. Retracing their steps, they decided to cut across the final bend of the Chaung to where their canoe would be under the trees. They were stopped short by the sight of very fresh-cut branches laying in a clearing with lots of wood chippings. As they stepped forward, a dark "hole" in the ground turned out on inspection to be the start of the defence system. It comprised a five-foot-deep trench some sixty yards long neatly revetted with timber along which were five rounded machine-gun pits covering the beach approaches. Above in the trees appeared to be a rope ladder leading to a tree-top platform, and at the seaward end above ground level was a coconut palm-leaved lean-to hut. This was shaken violently by the OC, but it was unoccupied. Climbing out over the front of the trench, they discovered that they had actually parked their canoe upside down on the Panjis[2] stuck in the front slope of the defence system.

'Figures doubled up and hurrying along the beach where the Chaung ran into the sea turned out to be the rest of the party, so moving the OC's canoe along the beach to the others, they all set off up the right-hand side of the Chaung where the fire had been seen. Corporal Merryweather crept forward to recce a hut in the dark shadows among the trees, and after hearing some creaking sounds a figure shot off across a gap in the bushes. Reporting back to Sergeant Harry Roberts, the party dashed through the trees to the nearest hut, where the Burmese Intelligence Lance-Corporal acquired a young Burman to lead them to a house some way inland along a track, where the Japanese-appointed head man lived.

'Crossing a vast paddy field in the twilight made the party feel a bit "naked", but they eventually entered a bamboo compound where they surrounded a large wooden house on stilts. While the interpreter tried to coax the occupants to let him in, Sergeant Hawkins caught a woman escaping through a back door. This caused the occupant to let the party in, and it was discovered that the Jap administrator who lived there had been called to his HQ on the other side of the island that very day for briefing. Information was disclosed that a four-man

---

[2] Panjis: Sharpened bamboo spears facing 45 degrees at groin height as defences against invaders.

Japanese police post was established about a mile along the track, but the time factor ruled out a snatch that night. While the inhabitants were being questioned, two men crept in to the compound and were captured. The building contained Japanese posters and propaganda leaflets, and a vast amount of information was obtained about enemy strength and positions.

'Due to the length of time the interrogations took, Corporal Merryweather was sent back with the young Burman to the landing place to prepare the canoes for a quick get-away. Approaching the village in the trees from where the lad had been abducted, dogs were barking and the villagers were all up and shouting, in the shadows, so he indicated to go well away to the south to avoid contact. Nearing the beach, he seemed to get very scared, so lying in some tall lily-like leaves, he was paid 150 silver rupees and after a lot of salaams and hands in the praying position took off into the night. Between the "paying-out" spot and the beach, a huge and recently dug anti-tank ditch had been dug, and along the sandy beach itself were five fifteen-foot-high timber towers which looked like observation posts as they had what appeared to be cables running from them back inland.

'Doubling along the beach until he found the upturned canoes, Merryweather called out softly for Corporal Westow, who had been left behind to guard them, and although the surf must have made it difficult to hear, Westow eventually appeared from the water's edge to announce that a Jap patrol had found the canoes and had bolted "over there", pointing to the first defence trenches that Holden-White had discovered. Dragging the canoes into the sea and up to their necks in the waves, the two waited for the remainder of the party to return, and they paddled furiously out to find the ML. It was much to the credit of the crew that they had waited more than half an hour over their allotted time, and with engines roaring and gun crews on the alert, another successful recce had been carried out.

'The party returned to Chittagong safely and prepared to move down to form a base at Tek Naf on the peninsula opposite Maungdaw.

'On 23 October the group under Major Holden-White set off on ML's 437 and 391 and proceeded down the Arakan coast to the estuary of the river Naf, where they arrived the following day. At this time the village of Tek Naf was the most forward coastal base, and it was from here that a succession of very interesting operations were carried out.

'Due to the fact that the nearest civilization was 120 miles away, all supplies were brought in by naval coastal forces, while Captain Peter Tripp, Camp Commandant, 3 SS Brigade HQ organized accommodation etc.

'On the night of 3/4 November No. 42 RM Commando carried out a small-scale raid on Elizabeth Island, and unfortunately one of their party got left behind. Holden-White was asked if he could lay on a rescue party to recover the marine, and this task was allotted to Captain Barnes, Sergeant Tough and Corporals Longhurst and Hanna. It so happened that Major Mike Kealy of SBS arrived just in time to book himself in for a trip on this one, so he accompanied the ML on this dodgy mission. That night the party slipped their canoes off Elizabeth Island but, although they patrolled just off the beach for about three hours, they saw no signals, nor did they hear any reply to their calling of the man's name. It was presumed at the time he was either dead or lost, but months later when the war ended he was discovered in Rangoon jail, having been betrayed and captured the day after the raid.

'Following the safe return of the party to Tek Naf, a fortnight of feverish activity ensued, preparing for an ambitious follow-up of the Uga Chaung raid on Ramree Island.

'This raid (Operation Profit) was timed hoping the Japs would have finished their defence system, and the idea was that, as before, SBS would do the landing and carry out a search and recce. If all was well, they would signal out to sea, where another vessel carrying a contingent of No. 5 Commando would come ashore and under the guidance of the SBS lay a host of mines and delayed booby-traps in the defences and make off quietly like the proverbial "cat that crept into the crypt, crapped and crept out again". They would then kick up a shindig hoping the Japs would race into their positions and do an assisted Hari Kari.

'The raiding force consisted of 2 MLs nos 412 and 413, 2 LCPs and a detachment of 4 Troop No. 5 Commando along with the following members of SBS, Major Holden-White, Corporal 'Bill' Merryweather, Lieutenant Rodney and Corporal Les Bell, Sergeant Freddie Hawkins and Corporal Eddie Griffiths, Sergeant Harry Roberts and Sergeant Barney of BIC (Burma Intelligence Corps).

'The force set sail from Tek Naf on 13 November but had to wait thirty-six hours off St Martin's Island while one of the LCPs had some mechanical repairs carried out. At 0700 hours on 15 November they set off, arriving off Ramree at 2130 hours. The night was dark, and the SBS party quietly off-loaded their canoes and, having packed their tools of the trade handy, set off towards the mouth of the Chaung. Although the canoeists paddled very silently, the dipping of the blades sent large fluorescent "moons" swirling back behind each canoe, due to the high phosphorus content of the sea water. This was a rather disturbing factor when watching eyes could easily pick up eight such uniform patterns.

'About a hundred yards from the beach, the OC and his No. 2 discussed moving a bit to the left of the original landing spot mainly to avoid being caught in the gap in the rock's situation they had encountered on the first raid. Signalling with raised perpendicular paddle that they were going in, the lead canoe rowed through thirty to forty yards of gently rolling surf into a pitch-black spot under the trees on the shore and bumped against the rocks. Holden-White grabbed the bow rope and stepped out to belay the canoe, while Merryweather scrambled up a large, smooth rock in his canvas gym-shoes to cover the spot where they knew the end of the Jap machine-gun trench was, with his tommy-gun and grenades. Just as the other canoes were about to beach, a sharp "DONG" sounded a few yards away, and a couple of seconds later a huge parachute flare burst right overhead, lighting up the whole party. It would have been the easiest thing in the world to have lobbed grenades into the Jap trench, but as the first flare was falling into the sea, another one burst farther away where the sandy beach to the south of Chaung began. It was very obvious that the Japs knew the drill, for on the previous raid, with a dropping tide and the thunderstorm that had smoothed the sand out, they would have been able to follow every footprint left on the beach and in their trenches by the raiders. Major Holden-White gave the order to re-embark, and as soon as the lead canoe had been turned round, thrashing paddles sent the party out to sea. At this time beacon fires were set alight on tree-top platforms, and the sea was lit up like daylight. Further along the coast two other beacons were lit – a simple but very effective warning system. The canoes were well out to sea on no particular bearing when the fires faded and darkness gave the paddlers a breathing space. After careful consideration, it was decided that the MLs were somewhere south and in-shore from the group, and after a very lucky break the party came up against the vessel carrying No. 5 Commando. The ML skippers in conjunction with SBS decided to have a shoot-up, but first of all they loaded a Carley float with a "Mock Battle" (a series of detonators and explosives on a long fuse which when lit gives a good impression of rifle fire and grenade explosions for several minutes) and launched it to float down between Ramree and Cheduba Island to create a diversion.

'As the two MLs with all the commandos and SBS lining the decks cruised very close to the beach, the lead ML fired a three-inch mortar parachute flare which burst right over the entrance to Uga Chaung. Immediately every gun and weapon on the vessels opened up on targets designated by SBS who had them pin-pointed.

'The ship's crews had their twin Lewis guns, Bofors and three-inch mortar (deck-mounted for close Chaung bombardment), while the commandos and SBS hosepiped the shore positions with Bren-gun and rifle fire – the tracers and incendiary bullets creating a continuous stream into the look-out posts and trenches. The Japs replied with spasmodic rifle and LMG fire, but no hits were recorded. The crews on the three-inch mortar lobbed HE bombs right onto the beach and really livened up the positions there. A time-expired Quartermaster who had pleaded to come on this raid as an observer had the time of his life firing off magazines of Bren-gun ammo until even the spare barrel was red-hot, and the SBS member who was doing the clearing and loading for him had to grab a spare Bren-gun to have a go himself at a known observation tower in the trees. When the firing ceased and the boats were cruising up the coast of Ramree Island, a lone tree beacon was lit, so a long burst of Bofor shells was fired at it as a farewell gesture. The force returned to Tek Naf the following day.

'On 20/21 November the following group left Tek Naf on ML 437 (on Operation Fitting) under the command of Lieutenant Matthews RINVR (Burma): Captain Barnes, Lieutenant Ryan, Sergeant Tough, and Corporals Longhurst and Hanna, with Corporal Kiernan as spare man, and Sergeant Barney of BIC. Their job was to land and obtain information of Jap strength and positions south of Donbaik. Very heavy surf was encountered on landing, and all three canoes capsized. The party recced a Jap-occupied bunker manned by at least two Japs but, due to the state of the canoes being un-seaworthy, reluctantly avoided conflict, as the secrecy of the information they acquired was far more important than a couple of dead Japs. With great difficulty the party launched their canoes through the surf and after a hazardous journey reached the MLs.

'While they were away, Holden-White was preparing for a raid in the Alethangyaw area, and acquired the services of one Bhadur Mia of the British "V" force as a guide and contact with the Japanese "V" force. These latter chaps seemed to operate in both directions and, knowing which side their bread was buttered on, gave valuable information to what now seemed to them was a return to British domination. The object of the raid was to find out the state of occupying forces, to identify units by capturing a prisoner or uniforms, or by questioning the Jap "V" force. On 23 November the raiding party, consisting of Major Holden-White and Corporal Merryweather, Lieutenant Rodney and Sergeant Roberts, Sergeant Hawkins and Corporal Griffiths, Corporals Bell and Westow and Captain Knight of BIC, and Bhadur Mia of "V" force embarked on an LCP at Tek Naf, and eight miles down the coast behind the Jap lines launched their canoes and headed in-shore to the entrance of Ton Chaung some three-quarters of a mile away. The sea was dead calm, and the usual off-shore smells of cooking and fires drifted out to meet them. As the line of canoes nosed up the mouth of the Chaung from which the tide was receding, they slid repeatedly on to wet sand and mud banks which blended in the dark with the surface of the river.

'Each stroke of the paddles produced glaring pools of fluorescence, and suddenly the canvas canoes were spattered with tiny flapping fish which had been herded up the river in front of the canoes until deciding to make a break down river, each tiddler having its own fluorescent "light". Finally, striking water 1½ miles up river too shallow to paddle the canoes in, the party took their bow ropes and walked two to three hundred yards to the southern bank and hid their canoes under coarse grasses. Voices were heard on the east bank but not identified. To save weight, and deciding that it was not likely to be used on this patrol Corporal Merryweather's "cosh" (a heavy lead-filled piece of metal tube with a leather thong) and a water-proofed walkie-talkie set were left under the canoe.

'The party waded the Chaung and proceeded across salt marsh, and paddy fields, often floundering in drying out creeks with the inevitable two to three feet of mud at the bottom. About a mile west of Alethangyaw they contacted two Jap "V" Force agents who swore they were for the British. In a village three more Jap "V" Force joined the patrol, and even mounted sentry on the Jap track used by their patrols, while the other two went into Alethangyaw to see if the enemy were in occupation. On returning, they reported that, two nights before, a patrol had spent the night there. Other information gained was the names of the local Jap commanders, the position of a very large supply dump, enemy strength and habits, and the times and routes of standing Japanese patrols.

'As the Chaungs were now filling fast with the making tide, Holden-White decided to withdraw with this useful information. This was done successfully, but the main Chaung fifty yards wide had 5½ feet of water in it by this time, and although most of the party were able to wade across, the smaller members, Corporals Westow and Merryweather, being weighted down with ammo and grenades, were completely submerged, the only parts visible being their forearms bearing aloft their tommy-guns. On their returning to the canoes, the walkie-talkie radio set and the cosh were found to be missing. The patrol made out to sea and after being picked up on the LCP returned to base at dawn.

'While they had been away, Captain Barnes, Lieutenant Ryan, Sergeant Tough, Corporals Longhurst and Hanna and Sergeant Barney BIC did a very successful recce on Indin (named Operation Concert). On the night of 25/26 November the canoes were slipped from ML 416 skippered by Lieutenant-Commander Howard and having negotiated heavy surf all crews landed safely. The usual tactics of rearing unsuspecting civilians out of bed in the middle of the night was repeated, and much valuable information about the Japs was gained. In actual fact, an enemy platoon was in garrison at Indin, and at any time a local could have given the game away. Captain Barnes recced a road to see if any Jap MT had used it, and eventually the party returned to the ML through bad surf.

'A couple of days after this a strange thing happened, namely the return of Corporal Merryweather's cosh and walkie-talkie which had disappeared on the Alethangyaw raid. Apparently a Burmese villager had found them some hundreds of yards away from the landing point. The water-proof bag containing the walkie-talkie had been badly chewed, and it was assumed that the articles had been dragged away by a dog or a jackal. The villagers handed them over to a British "V" Force agent who brought them back to our lines and was rewarded with 100 rupees.

'On 2 December a raiding party (Operation Hurry) consisting of Major Holden-White and Corporal Merryweather, Sergeant Hawkins and Captain Knight of BIC, Lieutenant Sherwood and Corporal Westow, and Corporals Bell and Griffiths, set off on ML 829 to do a recce-prisoner-snatch a mile west of Kyaukpanduywama. Canoes were slipped a mile offshore and were making for the beach when a fire was started at the exact spot the party intended to land. It was decided to land a hundred yards south of this, and as the canoes crept towards the heavy surf bursting on the sandy beach, figures could be seen around the fire. When Holden-White's canoe touched shore, the occupants quickly dragged the canoe just clear of the water and took up defensive positions. As the other crews landed, all the canoes were dragged well up into some two-feet-high spiky grass which stretched inland for about two hundred yards. From the direction of the fire a thin wailing voice singing in some unintelligible language approached the party, who were lying in a semi-circle ready for a shoot-up. As the figure entered the trap, Corporal Griffiths grabbed the intruder, pulled him to the ground and stifled his cries. From the fire came an enquiring call which obviously asked, "What's up mate, are you all right?" Immediately the BIC member, Captain Knight, who had slid alongside Griffiths, told the captive

to say, "Come here," and after a few murmurings in the
distance, four very tall individuals in white attire walked
into the SBS ambush.

'A few questions were put to them by Captain Knight,
who then asked, "Are there any Japs about?"
Simultaneously, the first captive, a young Burman about
fifteen years old, said, "Yes" as his elderly friends said
"No". Separating them, the lad said there was one Jap in a
hut a quarter of a mile behind the beach, so leaving two
SBS members to guard the other four prisoners, the party
set out to get the Jap. As no Jap prisoner had been taken
alive by any unit in Burma for nearly two years, a "cosh"
job was laid on. As the party were led into the darkness of
the trees onto a track going north, Holden-White
arranged for the lad to go into the Jap hut and say that he
had seen suspected British soldiers landing down the
coast, whereupon it was hoped he would come out and
subsequently be captured. The boy warned the SBS party
when it was about fifty yards from the Japs' hut, and as the
main party took up ambush positions on the track in a
dark "tunnel" of trees, Corporal Merryweather went forward to a position ten yards from a hut which lay behind a
clump of bushes on a bank to the left.

'As the lad walked around these, Merryweather could
see a figure by the light of a tiny oil lamp sitting cross-
legged on a charpoy, and two or three other voices were in
conversation. The figure of the lad temporarily shut off
the view as he stood in the gap that was the doorway, and
presently the light was extinguished. Although it was
comparatively dark under the trees, the moonlight coming
over the hills inland provided reasonable visibility as it
filtered through. Crouched three feet above the track with
his cosh in his right hand and a Colt .45 automatic in the
left, Merryweather was surprised to see not only the lad

leading one tall man, but three other individuals behind them. As the party walked a few paces towards the cosh position, and the lad was almost level, he stopped, turned round and, as the followers shunted together, pointed to a short stocky figure in the middle, and cried *"Japani – Japani."* As the group tried to scatter, all getting in each other's way, Merryweather threw his cosh to the ground, swapped the Colt .45 into his right hand and charged after the *"Japani"*, who fled a few yards back along the track and was in the act of bolting over a high bank out into the open on the right. Unfortunately he wasn't quite fast enough, and as the .45 pistol shot rang out a few inches behind him, the dull flash seemed to light up the baggy white shirt in the middle of his back. As he fell and grunted, Merryweather tripped over his legs, as one of the tall members of the entourage was legging it out towards the open paddy fields. The chase now concentrated on this individual, and as the hunter and the hunted cut through the last of the trees, a short burst of tommy-gun rounds from one of the raiding party ripped through the under-growth between them.

'Three rounds from the .45 and a bit of shouted Urdu eventually brought the terrified individual to a halt with his hands in the air, and he was guided back to the main section with a Colt rammed in his ribs. While this was going on, the main party had failed to locate the fallen Jap, and it was assumed he had crawled or been helped under cover by one of his attendants who now stood in the shadows with their hands in the air. As there had been shots fired (which were even heard on the ML far out to sea), it had obviously been heard by any other Japanese close handy, so the hut was searched.

'British mortar bomb boxes used for storing documents contained maps of the defence systems down the whole of the Arakan coast – unit positions, a mixed collection of military documents, medicines, grenades, anti-VD pills and personal possessions, obviously looted from a British source.

'Round the back of the hut was a British Lee Enfield rifle with five rounds in the magazine. Clothing with identification badges and items of equipment were carried back to the beach, and when firing started from down the coast, the party withdrew through very heavy surf with two of the ambushed prisoners to the ML.

'On interrogation back at base, it was discovered that all the individuals caught on the raid were employed by the Japs as coast-watchers, the three in the hut with the Jap being Sikhs who had "gone over" to the Japanese when captured earlier in the war. The post had only been established three days (in all probability due to the raids carried out by SBS) and on their third night had all been captured.

'On 20 December Major Livingstone MBE arrived at Tek Naf, with "C" group SBS to take over.'

In Major Holden-White's appraisal of the various services, he wrote, 'The highest possible praise is due to the MLs of Arakan Coastal Forces for their part in the group's operations. SOACF never failed to produce boats when they were required, and the skippers always found the right spot for slipping canoes. Officers and crew were most kind in their treatment of the raiding parties on their journeys to and from the objectives. It was due to their care that no canoes or stores were damaged whilst being carried in the MLs, or when being slipped by them. Thanks are also due to the "Q" side of 3 SS Bde for the way in which they made up for the losses of kit on operations and to the signal troop for their maintenance of the group's wireless sets.'

During the Arakan campaign, as in Scotland and the Mediterranean, SBS again experienced the lack of confidence sometimes shown by Planners in the accuracy of their beach reconnaissance information. Hilary St George Saunders, in *The Green Beret* (1949), describes the Myebou Peninsula as follows: 'By then the tide was low and their landing craft touched down some 400 yards short of the beach. It took the disembarking Commandos three hours to cover that distance. The Special Boat Section had reconnoitred the beach and reported that, before firm ground could be reached, a wide stretch of mud covered with a foot of water would have to be traversed. The scientific advisers at General Headquarters, from an examination of photographs, had deduced that the beach was firm all through.' Luckily, they met no enemy fire from that beach while they were struggling through mud towards it.

'A' Group then returned to Hammanhiel Camp in Ceylon for local leave and re-equipment.

15
'B' and 'C' Groups SBS: Sumatra Sabotage, 1944

In early September 1944 'B' Group SBS, under the operational command of Major D.H. Sidders, was sent to the Depot ship HMS *Adamant* of the 4th Submarine Flotilla. They were ordered to destroy a bridge in northern Sumatra over the Peudada River. This was a combined road and rail bridge with a single track for both road and rail and was assumed to be the sole connection along the coast of Sumatra for all movement between the aerodromes to the west and the towns to the east.

The party planned to operate in four Mark I** canoes from HMS/s *Trenchant* commanded by Lieutenant-Commander A.R. Hezlet DSC, RN, and were divided into pairs. Major D.H. Sidders and Sergeant T. Williams in Boat 1, Lieutenant E.A.W. Wesley and Corporal B. Hickman in Boat 2, Sergeant D. Dawkins and Corporal Wells in Boat 3, and Corporals J. Watt and A. Shearston in Boat 4. Private F. Hillinshead was carried as a reserve. The operation was named 'Spratt Baker'.

As personal weapons, each canoe pair carried one .45 automatic pistol and one Thompson submachine-gun, and the party was equipped with 250 pounds of plastic high explosive (PHE), 150 pounds of gelignite and an appropriate amount of cordtex, primers, detonators, safety fuse, orange line, pull switches and time fuse pencils.

'Spratt Baker' party embarked in *Trenchant* on 5 September 1944 and reached the target area five days later, when the moon was in the last quarter.

I have received from Captain 'Teddy' Wesley MC a copy of his personal account of the operation, written in diary form. This gives an excellent account of the two attempts to destroy the bridge – the first a near disaster, and the second a complete success. His account is substantially confirmed by the official report on 'Spratt Baker' handed in afterwards by Major 'Doug' Sidders.

'*Sunday 10 September 1944*
'I have just seen the coast of Sumatra through the periscope! It's almost uncanny, that after five days of continuous sailing one pops up to see exactly the outline of hills that we expected to see! (A COPP party on a previous trip did a panorama drawing of this point.)

'Being thirty miles off yet there are only the shapes of the mountains to see, but by this afternoon we will be close enough to scan the beaches and take photographs through the periscope. The Engineer Lieutenant does this. Tomorrow night we land – all being well.

'*Monday 11 September 1944*
'Tonight's the night, but so far things aren't particularly favourable. Yesterday, as light failed, we approached land. It was too late to carry out a proper periscope recce but from four miles out we were able to see the bridge, painted a pale grey and looming very large indeed on the horizon. Then dusk set in and we dived to fifty feet to hold a church service! I never imagined that they held services on S/Ms, but I suppose danger makes all the men devout! It was very strange, only four miles from the enemy coast, in the tomb-like silence of the submerged sub, the men gathered together in the cramped space of the Control Room singing hymns to the tune of a mouth-organ. Being RC I didn't attend, but the men seemed to enjoy their

singing and I rather envied them their simple service. On the second hymn the organist (not an expert) forgot the tune, so the Captain had to strike up alone! No sooner was it finished than "diving stations" were sounded and we surfaced – very thankful for the fresh air as we'd been underneath for fifteen hours and the air was pretty foul.

'At night we went up on the bridge and had a look through the binoculars at the outline of the hills and a few winking lights which we imagined to be from the little village near the bridge. Last night I slept well, though I woke a little earlier than usual.

'This morning we've had bad luck. The officer of the watch stuck up his periscope to find a zero (Japanese fighter plane) flying not far off. He immediately ducked down again, but half an hour later when the Captain went to have a look, he saw another plane, so we dived to one hundred feet and have stayed there for two hours. This is interfering with our periscope recce of the beach, as if there are planes about we can't go in close in the shallow water.

'*Friday 15 September*
'The diary still goes on, though there were moments when I thought it wouldn't! Going back to where I left off on the 11th – about midday we spent a couple of tense hours in the Control Room. The Captain, Douglas (Sidders) and myself taking peeps through the periscope. We were within 2½ miles of the shore and daren't go in any closer as the Japs are reported to keep a very sharp look-out, and should the periscope be sighted the whole operation would be jeopardized. What we did see was rather disturbing. There were a number of large tents in the trees by the beach not half a mile from the river mouth. There seemed to be a lot of activity. Two fires could be seen, and

there were square shapes that might be huts, pillboxes or watch-shelters on the river mouth itself. We weren't close enough to be able to tell whether there were wire defences and bunker positions. It was all very disturbing at first, as we knew that the Japs have been carrying out extensive shore defence works recently. However, we reasoned that if the Japs were really defending that spot, they wouldn't show their tents, so we decided to go and find out.

'The bridge itself showed up clearly – a magnificent girder construction nearly as tall as the trees.

'The 'scope could remain up for only about thirty seconds at a time, and half that time was spent doing a sweep around the horizon and the sky for hostile ships or aircraft, so that one only got very hasty and unsatisfactory glimpses.

'However, we decided to go in and make the best of it and set about making our preparations. The Chief's (Engineer's) photographs failed miserably – much to everyone's amusement.

'At 1900 hours we surfaced about six miles from shore, opened the torpedo hatch and got our four canoes on the casing. Then we started running quietly in towards land. In the meantime we were dressing, loading pistols and tommy-guns, crimping on detonators to fuses, and making all the 101 last-minute adjustments. Then we sat round the wardroom table and had a last cup of tea while the sweat from our exertions ran down our faces, mingling with the grease paint. The red bulbs cast an eerie light on our features.

'2020 hours. The Captain's voice came down the pipe calling for No. 4 Boat Crew and I started forward and scrambled up the conning-tower hatch, encouraged by a friendly "Good Luck" and pat on the back from unseen hands. Once out and over the bridge I scrambled along the casing picking my way over the other canoes to the bows, filling my lungs with the sweet damp air. The canoe was swung over and lowered, and the two heavy packs followed. Hickman already seated in the stern seat, I climbed down. A whispered "cast off" and we were afloat on our own, drifting slowly away from the dark outline of the submarine, with its silhouetted boat party already stooping to lower the next canoe. The night was beautifully calm. The overcast sky pitch black with the oil-like surface of the sea casting a faint luminosity so that the other canoes appeared like dark shapes floating not on but in a pale ether. The night was so dark that distances were difficult to judge so that while trying to keep in sight of the submarine one would suddenly be startled at finding its bows looming almost overhead while the gentle swell running over its ballast tanks and through the casing made a noise like a gigantic sea shell.

'2040 hours. We were all afloat gathered before the s/m's bows in arrowhead formation. Douglas Sidders leading on a course of 180 degrees.

'The mechanical process of paddling leaves one's mind free to think! And during that hour's paddling towards the enemy shore my mind was very active. I felt happy, scared, brave and amused, in turn. The physical pleasure of being out of the stuffy submarine, together with the conscious enjoyment of paddling a canoe on a warm night, with every dip of the paddle making a million twinkling lights in the dark water, and each canoe leaving a faint, luminous trail, was my first reaction. For a while I just paddled on, contented.

'Then I began to think of what lay ahead, and the unwelcome thought of machine-guns suddenly shattering the stillness as they fired point-blank at us over the beach, came into my mind. I tried to think out the best action to take, so as to store it in my mind and not be caught unawares if that happened, and from there my thoughts went to home, and the fact that they might never know of this. I thought of them all in turn, Mother, Father, Andy in Canada, Lalita and her kids. I thought of Father and knew that, if he was told what I was doing, he would expect me to behave as a man should. That knowledge and my resolve not to let him down gave me a great deal of comfort and a resolve to face whatever came my way without flinching.

'My mind at rest on that point, I was suddenly amused. We seemed so puny. Sailing against the Japanese, not in a steel tank or battleship, with guns and armour as protection, but in a frail canvas-sided folding boat! It seemed so ludicrous that I grinned in the darkness.

'Then I was brought back to reality when I looked at my compass. What the hell was Douglas steering south-east for? He kept stopping every five or ten minutes steering south-east, then changed his mind, thinking he had gone too far and went south-west, then south again. Naturally, when we were near the coast, rising and falling just beyond the surf line, we didn't know whether we were east or west of the river mouth. We paddled first one way, then the other, without being able to see the river, so decided to make a landing.

'Lightning was playing in the east, showing us up for brief seconds. The surf's booming was alarming but when we went through it, it turned out to be only about two feet high and we all got through safely with no more than a few splashes. We lay on the beach in a semi-circle while Douglas and his partner made a recce. The sand was damp and even I had nothing better to do than feel for shells with my hands, while I kept my eyes on the skyline. It was already 2230 hours.

'Soon Douglas returned, saying that they had found a wired-in bunker position and that something was moving about – might be a Jap, might be a cow. At any rate, we were in the wrong place so we re-embarked and paddled through the surf again.

'A little further up the coast we spied what looked like the river mouth and turned in again. Sure enough, we went over the surf on the sand bar and found ourselves in the still water beyond. The boats had got slightly separated in coming in (we do this backwards – facing the surf) and when I landed with the others I found Douglas was missing. While I was questioning the others, we saw his canoe coming in, only to discover that Sergeant Williams was alone in the rear seat. He said that Major Sidders had jumped out of the canoe to do a recce and not moored it, so that the swift current had swept him off the bank and he had been unable to hold the boat in on his own. I took Williams and walked to the river mouth to look for him, finally spotting him, with the aid of my night glasses, wandering up and down the sand spit looking for his canoe.

'It was 2350 by the time we were all together again. At 2350 we set out on foot for the bridge, leaving our canoes unguarded on the beach, camouflaged with sand.

'We tried to walk up by the river bank but soon came to impenetrable undergrowth growing down to the water's edge. There was a large sampan moored a few yards from the shore, and Douglas had the crazy idea of going up stream in it! I objected strongly as we could no more pole a sampan than fly a plane. Finally we agreed to go back again and try the original plan of paddling up the river. The current at the mouth was too swift for us and we pulled in to the opposite bank and landed again for another try at walking up. It was now 0100 hours, and we were supposed to be off the beach by 0200 hours when the moon rose. The river banks again proved to be an imposs-ible path and we struck inland. We walked within touching distance of a large shelter in which we could hear breathing. This was obviously a shelter used by the men constructing the beach defences that we had found – whether native or Jap labour we never found out. We ploughed inland through difficult undergrowth for half a mile but had to give up to return as it was nearly 0200 hours, and we were still a good half a mile from the bridge.

'Back on the beach we stood, in a foiled angry bunch. We had been entirely unsuccessful. The bridge was still intact, and we were powerless to do anything about it now. No longer afraid of the defenders, we argued in loud tones and suggested wild schemes. However, we knew that nothing could be done about it and at 0215 we embarked in our canoes and steered due north signalling out to sea once we were about a mile from the shore. At 0300 hours the s/m was sighted and dead on our course, and we were soon aboard her – a frustrated, shamefaced bunch! We felt that by our failure we had let the SBS down, and also everyone who had co-operated in getting this job put on the face of the opposition.

'*Tuesday 12 September 1944:*
'We hadn't heard "C" Group's bang, and we thought that if they hadn't been able to reach their objective either we might repeat the operation. It seemed a faint hope. We started travelling towards our rendezvous trying to contact *Terrapin* by Asdic. Something went wrong and we weren't able to exchange messages till 1600 hours. They reported: "Unable to land because of surf – believed undetected." Thereupon we spun round and headed back for our bridge again.

'We pulled on our wet clothes and hurriedly made ready all over again.

'2045 hours. I was in my canoe again floating on a surface as smooth as a sheet of ice, watching the dim form of the submarine and hearing the peculiar noise of the water running over its semi-submerged hull and casing, with a noise like the drag of a wave on a shingle beach.

'I had told Douglas that his compass was out so he readily agreed that I should lead.

'2050. We started paddling for shore. I kept my eyes on the compass and the faint outline of the hill and never slowed down till we could recognize the river mouth straight ahead and had come level with the fishing huts on poles way out at sea that had given us a scare on the previous night.

'2200 hours. We landed at a spot about a quarter of a mile west of the river mouth. Douglas and his partner were doing a recce of the beach when a very agitated Corporal came up and whispered that there were two men coming down the beach. Through my glasses I could see what looked like two men bending over a canoe.

'Organizing the men into a semi-circle, we did a pincer attack – only to find it was a washed-up log with two thick branches!

'2230 hours we set out. We walked a couple of hundred yards down the beach to get clear of the trees and then struck inland. On coming off the beach we ran into two rows of new "double-apron" wiring. I cut a path through. Behind this lay a zigzag trench four feet deep, camouflaged with palm leaves – we seemed to be in a well-defended area and we went carefully. Our direction lay over a dry paddy field (grass growing) which luckily made no sound. We were very keyed up at this stage and rustlings in the trees on our left, and some unknown night bird or frog with a peculiar call repeatedly brought us to a breathless stop. One could almost feel the eight fingers slipping round the triggers! Just when we were getting used to these night sounds, there was a rush of heavy footsteps from behind – we found a herd of cattle following us!

'We struck the railway line at Culvert. It was 2330 hours and we removed our heavy packs for a rest. Ten minutes later we resumed the march along the side of the embankment. Dogs barked on either side of us as we passed near houses, but we ignored them and kept going.

'I was leading when we came to a little bridge over a stream. I picked my way carefully and had just reached the far side when there was a clatter behind me – then a long pause – then an enormous splash. I thought, "There's one of our men lost" for the bridge was about fifteen feet high and with a fifty-pound pack on his back a man didn't stand much chance. As soon as the rest of the men were over, I was going back to see if the fellow could be rescued, but he was already crossing the bridge again on his own, with his pack on his back and tommy-gun under his arm as if nothing had happened! It was Corporal Wells, a massive fellow – our biggest man, which accounted for the gigantic splash! He had been walking on the *side* of the line and hadn't even noticed we were on a bridge till he walked into space and hit the water flat on his back. Luckily it was only waist deep.

'This night seemed to be full of incidents. Next time we paused to listen (the night was ominously silent, without a breath of wind) there came a shattering crash on our left flank, only a few yards away. Again all muzzles pointed in that direction, but on investigation it proved to be a ripe coconut which had fallen on dry underbrush! Nature couldn't have timed a booby-trap better for us!

'A little further on we saw the pale grey form of the bridge ahead of us, whilst on our right the road came alongside the line. Here we all removed our packs, leaving them hidden in the shadow of the embankment, and moved as a patrol across the gravelly road towards the bridge. We could see no sentries through our glasses, but there was no means of telling whether there were any or not as the shadows were too deep and the bridge too far away being separated by the ramp leading on to it.

'So we decided that boldness was the safest policy, and Douglas and myself set out down the middle of the road trying to look as much like a pair of natives as possible. We reached the ramp unchallenged, crossed the bridge and went fifty yards the other way to make sure. All was well so we hastily examined the girders and construction and hurried back to our waiting men. At this stage we heard a train approaching from the west. We crouched down to let it pass. It carried no lights but threw out showers of sparks. It was a long, heavily laden train and I prayed that it might be the last ever to cross that bridge. My prayer wasn't fulfilled – not quite.

'No sooner had it passed than we crossed over, shouldered our packs and were just about to start crossing the road again when there came a faint crunching on the macadam road. We froze instantly in our tracks, most of us not having time even to crouch down. It was a bicycle patrol. They swept by us, not more than three or four yards away, in silence and without lights. We were able to count five or six of them, their weapons slung on their backs. It was a close shave.

'We carried on then, crossing over the bridge by the road and, while the men took up positions on the far end and concealed the packs that weren't needed yet, I got to work laying my charges on the huge girders. I had no sooner started work when I heard a train approaching. I crouched down at the base of the girders, getting my binoculars focused on the spot where the engine would pass as I wanted to see if the engine driver was a Jap. The train puffed nearer, going very slow and obviously heavily loaded while I waited impatiently with my glasses to my eyes pointing almost vertically in the air, as my head was no more than a yard from the rails. Again I was disappointed though, as the cylinder outlet blew such a load of steam in my face that I was unable to see anything at all! Singing could be heard in one of the carriages as it passed. After this interruption I had just hoisted the two large Bergen rucksacks with fifty pounds of high explosive each onto the girders when I was warned of a light approaching from the other direction. They were the headlights of a car. Its powerful unshaded lamps seemed to illuminate everything with the brilliance of day. Again I crouched, hiding behind the rucksacks, thinking surely that these must be seen as the headlights were playing full on them. The car crawled by, a big American-looking staff car. I expected it to stop once it cleared the bridge but it went over the line and seemed to stop in the village where someone seemed to shout orders. Obviously the bridge was an unhealthy place so we worked feverishly.

'The main girders of the arch and the span met on top of the supporting concrete pillars, making a steel box of about 1½ feet wide by two feet deep by two feet long. Into this box I stuffed both packs, fixing a cutting charge of ten pounds onto the lower span just to make sure of the cut. Douglas was working just across the road on the other pillar. I heard one of our men walk up and tell him in a hoarse audible whisper: "I've got five of them, sir" – "Five what?" says Douglas. "Five wogs, sir!" This made us all chuckle silently and somehow relieved the tension so that

we were able to work better. When that side of the bridge
had been completed, we all crossed back again, herding
our five prisoners with us. They weren't the slightest bit
alarmed; in fact they hardly seemed to find anything unusual in the proceedings and sat in the bushes quite quietly
under the guard of one of the Sergeants.

'The other side of the bridge could hardly be said to
have been done quietly. People seemed to stamp about,
bang weapons against the girders, drop tools and mutter
and curse at each other! To add to this seeming noise,
some natives came and started a fire in a three-walled
shelter not twenty yards from the far end of the bridge
where we had been working! Once we saw they were
natives we carried on with our work, ignoring them completely, but every now and again they would pile
brushwood on the fire so that the flames leaped up,
illuminating the whole scene, throwing the shadow of the
girders onto the line of trees beyond.

'By this time I had finished my side and was waiting for
Douglas to finish, so that I was able to look around and
take in the whole fantastic scene. Douglas took ages.

'It's much more trying on the nerves waiting for other
people to do their work and hearing them make all manner of noises that may bring out a patrol or sentry to
investigate it, and our sentries during that hour must have
felt decidedly uncomfortable. I went and spoke to Corporal Wells as he crouched tommy-gun in hand and he
voiced his thoughts – and mine too – by saying: "I wish I
was in my f. . .ing bed!" We consoled each other by
saying that the s/M would feel like home. At last Douglas
had finished. We pressed the time pencils which were
taped onto the instantaneous fuse which linked all the
charges. The time was 0205 hours.

'We collected our prisoners and started down the line

the way we had come – happy and relieved to be leaving the bridge without incident. We gave them some money to show our goodwill and that we weren't going to ill-treat them, as I was afraid they might become doubtful as to our intentions and call out. This at least was a language that they understood! Immediately they brightened up and came with us willingly.

'On approaching we had crept along the side of the embankment with bated breath, but now we strode along the top of the railway line, as boldness seemed to be the best policy and we had to hurry away (the time pencils were "white" – 1½ hours). I felt my spirits soaring. The little Malay I was leading timidly caught my arm, as I was walking fast. I held his hand as we crossed the bridge Wells had fallen from, and this reassured him, and from then on we walked hand in hand like a couple of schoolchildren.

'On two forms on the line we made a converging attack but found them to be a couple of natives with baskets of vegetables having a rest. They didn't even bother to get up, just remained squatting, so I patted them on the head, said: "OK Johnny" and carried on. My little Malay kept on talking to me but of course I understood not a word, except when he said "Nippon", pointing to the beach over to our left. I said "Nippon" and made throat-cutting signs which seemed to amuse him. He seemed to share the sentiment. We crossed the paddy field, the trench, through the gap in the wire and onto the beach. I prayed fervently that our canoes might be still there – and they were. We kept the prisoners some way from our canoes so that they shouldn't see what sort of craft we used. We had been told before leaving *Adamant* (Submarine Depot ship) that a prisoner would be of the greatest value – particularly a native, as they know much more about the local defences, disposition of troops and administration than does the average Jap soldier.

'Accordingly we decided to take one along with us. We picked a young fellow from the five and led him to the boats. Here the difficulty started. As soon as he saw the boats and realized what was on, he sat back and started pleading to be left. We tried to reassure him and lead him on quietly, but he naturally understood nothing except the fact that we were trying to take him away from his native land. He started struggling and calling out. I felt really sorry for the boy, and I realized his feelings at being whisked away by strange whitemen but now he was blubbering and making a hell of a noise, so I decided to knock him out. It's the rottenest thing I've had to do to hit an unsuspecting man but I couldn't help seeing the funny side of it as Williams said to him, "Look up there, Johnny" and pushed his head round so that I could get a swipe at his chin! It was like a comic film in earnest. However, knocking a black man out on a dark night is a more difficult proposition than we thought. I loosed my treacherous swipe but missed his chin, hitting him too far under. He collapsed in a struggling, howling heap. The men holding him – thoroughly alarmed by the noise he was making – took it into their own hands to "put him out", but at each blow the poor wretch howled the louder! I drew my luger, and while they tried to hold him down, I seized it by the barrel and brought it down with terrific force on the top of his head. The result was surprising. There was a metallic clang, the magazine flew out of the butt, one of the wooden butt grips splintered – and the man let out a wail louder and longer than the rest! I couldn't club him again as, without the magazine in, the sharp metal would have only cut open his head. Then we tried carrying him bodily into the waiting canoe, while I tried to stifle his yells by holding my hands over his mouth. He struggled so that we fell in a heap in the water. I held on to him alone, forcing him under to try and drown some of the life out of him, but each wave rolled us over and then drew away letting him get air enough to breathe – and yell. I told the men to get a paddle to hit him with. They tried unsuccessfully to "break" one while I was left struggling with the little fellow in the water. He got my fingers in his mouth and bit hard, holding them there. I was feeling exhausted by this time with all the night's events. They couldn't "break" the paddle, being jammed by sea water, and we decided to abandon the idea of a prisoner. I let him go and patted him on the back – a poor atonement for all that bullying! The poor devil was at the end of his tether too. He crawled up the beach and lay there moaning. He had been yelling intermittently for more than five minutes so we launched in great haste in case someone should come to investigate. From what we could make out from the natives there was a Jap machine-gun post about two hundred yards up the beach.

'This was probably correct, as no sooner were we afloat than we saw a torch shining from that direction, the owner apparently running along the beach towards us. We paddled like mad, expecting a burst of fire at any minute, but once we were through the waves they obviously couldn't see us from the shore, and a Jap machine-gunner would be too well trained to open up on an invisible target. We drew away further and further from the danger area. Douglas had ordered the other two boats away while we were struggling on the beach, so there were only two of us now. The time was 0245 hours.

'We continued paddling in silence hoping and praying that the charges wouldn't be discovered. At 0335 hours I already had a sinking feeling that we had failed, that all this night's work and hazards had been in vain. All the danger, work, planning and hopes had come to nothing.

'Suddenly there was a flash like lightning. We spun our heads round, and there more than a mile distant we were able to see distinctly the two ends of the bridge heated to a glowing red by the explosion. We cheered, and as we did so, we heard the booming roar of the four hundred pounds of PHE (Plastic High Explosive). There followed a pause, and then a low continuous rumble like distant thunder. The bridge had crashed down!

'We turned on to our course again, flashing our Z signal and paddling on contentedly, in spite of our tiredness. The moon was high and strong in the sky. Half an hour later we were beginning to get worried. We reasoned that perhaps the submarine had gone out further on account of the moon. We paddled on. No sign of the other boats either. By 0400 hours we knew that it was no use thinking up excuses for the submarine not being there. Something definitely had gone wrong. We searched the clear night to seaward with our glasses, without success. There was only half an hour left before dawn and we decided to push on a little further so as to be out of sight of land when day broke. It was with dismal thoughts that we paddled on. It seemed such irony that after all the night's escapes we should fall into the Japs' hands in this way. I tried to visualize what would happen if their planes spotted us. Would they machine-gun us? If so, well and good, we could die happily, firing back with pistol and tommy-gun. Much more likely though they would signal back for a launch to come out and capture us. To this of course we would give the same reception – but what if they came on and rammed us and fished us out of the water like a couple of half-drowned rats? These were the thoughts that passed through my mind. We didn't speak at all, as to have made

cheerful remarks would have just been bravado too trans-
parent to the other, and to tell the truth, and our fears,
was unnecessary.

'Of course I knew that if the s/m was there looking for
us, the best time to spot us would be with the first light of
day. I prepared to stick up my shirt on a paddle. The
Captain had said that he would surface in daylight if he
saw us, provided we were four or five miles from shore.
But after all, if the submarine was there, why hadn't she
seen us? We had been signalling for 1½ hours. Had she
been sunk or perhaps chased away by surface craft?

'Hickman had been looking back towards the outline of
the hills, clearer now as the sky began to lighten in shade.
"There she is!" his shout brought all our heads round, and
there, coming up behind us was the dark shape of the
bows and conning-tower. A few seconds joyfully paddling
at full speed, a scramble up the ballast tanks, and the
canoes were being tossed down the open hatch. Five minutes from being sighted we were safely inside, talking our
heads off, while the klaxon sounded diving stations. The
time was 0505 hours 13 September.

'What had happened was that the submarine had gone
to pick up our first two boats which were slightly off
course, and while they were at it we had passed them and
gone out to sea. The Captain had ordered diving stations
in four minutes' time, just before sighting us!

'We changed, washed and had breakfast, and then came
a tense moment in the control room as we sailed back to
2½ miles from the shore to see what effect we had had on
the bridge. The Captain was at the periscope as we sailed
parallel with the coast and level with the river mouth.
Douglas, myself and the other officers stood expectantly.
"There it is", "Yes, there's the bridge" and our hearts
sank . . . "but it's down", and we cheered. After that, we

all had a look, and sure enough, the great white pillars were seen and below them the tops of what had been the girders of the arch. We went to sleep contented men.'

This was the last of a long list of railway sabotage operations carried out by SBS during World War II, and its complete success was a tribute to the skill and tenacity of Major Sidders and his party. He was awarded the Military Cross and his Sergeant Toc Williams the Military Medal.

On the way back to Trincomalee *Trenchant* torpedoed a *German* submarine sighted on the surface off the entrance to Malacca harbour on the west coast of Malaya and in full view of the Japanese garrison. Believe it or not, Lieutenant-Commander Hezlet immediately surfaced and picked up sixteen survivors before the Japanese counter-attack began. They were carried back to Trincomalee and he was subsequently awarded the DSO.

During November and December 1944 'B' Group acted in support of the 21st (East African) Brigade on the Chindwin River crossings (Operation Sandbank) and from 21 January 1945 was allotted to 33 Corps for recon- naissance work on the Irrawaddy River crossings. During an offensive patrol with Corporal Black and Bombardier Harding on 8 February Lieutenant R.J.M. Peters was missing and later confirmed killed in the village of Nyaungo during exchange of fire with a JIFC (Pro-Japanese Indian), he was given a decent burial.

During the period of the Chindwin River, Major Sidders and Sergeant Williams, and Lieutenant Wesley and Sergeant Hickman captured a motor boat containing one dead Japanese officer complete with ceremonial sword, nine dead Japanese soldiers and one still alive. A live Japanese prisoner was a rare boon for Intelligence, and they were able to deliver him upstream in his own motorboat against a current of about seven knots, an impossible task in their own canoes. For his work during this period Wesley was awarded the MC.

Escaping down the river, the Japanese took all available Burmese boats but could only use them by night owing to Allied air activity by day. During the day they sank them in the river by pulling out the wooden plugs and would have to bail them out again that evening. SBS canoe patrols used to start off silently at nightfall in pairs and drift down the river on the current, listening for the sound of bailing. They would lie up in dead water close to the banks, or using a kedge anchor on one canoe with the other facing the opposite direction holding on alongside ready for immediate action. In emergency the kedge rope would be cut.

At the same time that 'B' Group sailed in HMS *Trenchant* to destroy the rail and road bridge over the Peudada River, 'C' Group sailed in HMS/M *Terrapin*, commanded by Lieutenant R.H.H. Brunner RN, on Operation 'Spratt Able'. Their mission was to destroy the bridge over the river at Pente Radja, also on the north coast of Sumatra. The party consisted of Major R.P. Livingstone MBE, who had experience in railway sabotage in the Mediterranean, Lieutenant J.B. Sherwood MM, Sergeants Roberts and Smith and Corporals Toogood, Somers, Smithson, Burns and Palmer. The operation was abandoned because of bad surf, and they returned in the submarine to Ceylon.

'C' Group then flew to Burma and relieved 'A' Group on the Arakan coast from 21 December 1944 attached to the 15th Indian Corps. They carried out several reconnaissances and offensive patrols at Kyaukpyu and Ramree Town. On one of these, in early February 1945, named Operation 'Corona', Corporal E.C. Palmer was fatally wounded when an RN motor launch mistook the SBS party for Japanese. Corporal J. Summers of the SBS was wounded by enemy action during the same operation but in another sector.

Their experiences on the Arakan would have been similar to those described in some detail previously by Corporal 'Bill' Merryweather, who has also provided some interesting sidelights on the campaign:

'The type of work was mainly reconnaissance to gather information ready for the final sweep down the Arakan coast. Up to that time absolutely nothing was known of Jap strength, fortifications, arms and equipment, or positions. The Japanese chose to keep their main forces in tunnels on the jungle-covered Arakan Yomas about 1½ miles in from the coastal plain, sending foraging parties to the villages along the coast for supplies. This was paid for by printing useless occupation money on the spot, and each note was stamped by the issuing officer. They had little or no aircraft at that time, and any shipping which moved had to do so by night, creeping around coastal mangrove swamps. No radio equipment was discovered in the area, so it was assumed that everything was done by messenger. When they discovered that raids were being carried out behind their lines, coastal watch parties of one Jap and three or four JIFFS (Japanese sponsored Indian National Army) were posted at intervals along the shores, sometimes using local Arakanese to assist. Civilians encountered on our raids changed sides according to who approached them, and one couldn't really blame them. This posed quite a problem, for rewards were offered by both sides, and treachery was always at the back of one's mind. This aroused an extra-sensitive awareness in the raiders, which can't have been a bad thing. One realized early on from stories of Japanese atrocities when they overran Burma that there was no future for anyone getting captured, and unlike the European theatre, white skins and fair hair in a "black" country cannot be camouflaged for escape purposes. There were a few exceptions.

'Japanese weaponry was pretty poor, with old-fashioned rifles and grenades, but their machine-guns and mortars were highly effective when used by fanatical troops. Artillery was meagre, the odd field-gun here and there, but these were moved around to give the effect of many. Propaganda leaflets and posters discovered on raids proved that dirty work had been going on long before the War, under the heading "South East Asia Co-Prosperity Sphere".

'Japanese propaganda directed at British troops had its funny side: "HOME, HOME, SWEET, SWEET HOME. London Bridge – Boats flying here and there . . . Streets lit dimly yet invitingly seen . . . all the family except one is sitting by the fireside softly singing 'There's no place like Home'. Listen closely . . . I wonder who it is that is singing . . . Could it be your loving wife . . ."

'On the leaflet some Tommy had written, "If that lousy old trout is waiting at home for me, then let's stay here".'

16
Irrawaddy Crossings (Burma) and the End

From February to May 1945, 'A' and 'B' Groups were engaged in reconnoitring river crossings and carrying out fighting patrols on the lower reaches of the Irrawaddy River in support of 33 Corps. Major Harry Holden-White had become unfit for operational duty because of ill-health and was posted to the headquarters of South East Asia Command in Kandy as SOG Liaison Officer. Major E.J.A. Lunn MC took over command of 'A' Group from him in January 1945. 'A' Group were reinforced with swimmers from the Sea Reconnaissance Unit (SRU), namely Sergeant Cave and Leading Aircraftsman Cobb of the RAF, Able Seaman Robson RN and Corporal Holding, Gunner Cridland and Marine White.

Corporal 'Bill' Merryweather has given the following account of operations on the Irrawaddy carried out by 'A' Group.

'On 31 March 1945 the unit left Ceylon by air on a second series of ops against the Japs. The journey by air, road, rail and sea, was via Vizagapatam, Calcutta, Combo Ghat and Chandpur to Comilla. The final stage was movement by two Dakotas on 10 April to the most forward airstrip at that time, a converted paddy field at Mytche in the central plain of Burma. Pagan, the city of temples and pagodas, lay just across the river, and having loaded and unloaded stores and kit from one conveyance to another numerous times, we were glad to leave that busy beach to the Pioneers, who worked wonders with improvised rafts powered with very obstinate outboard motors.

'The unit was now complete, and with two three-tonners loaded with the gear, the men tried to make themselves comfortable anywhere where there was a foot or handhold on top of the vehicles. The four-hour journey to Ywatha (our forward operational base to be) was along a very narrow sandy track, through parched country which seemed lifeless, but here and there villagers were seen foraging in still smoking villages fired by the retreating enemy and our own attacking aircraft.

'About a mile north of Ywatha, the convoy was halted by a bush-hatted figure whose first words were, "where the bloody hell have you lot been, I've been here three weeks and got a dixie of stew waiting for you." It was none other than Major "Sally" Lunn, our new OC, and true to his word he had got a stew waiting; he'd probably had it cooking since he arrived there by the taste of it, but it really was welcome after the very dusty journey. The first four days were spent preparing the motor-powered canoes. These were three-sectional plywood jobs with out-riggers carrying a Vickers "K" machine-gun mounted on a transversible fitting on the bows and powered by a two-stroke silenced engine. After studying maps, loading magazines, priming grenades and organizing canoe pairs in operational sections, it was decided that the most convenient method was having three parties, one operating every night, two resting and carrying out maintenance. The object of these raids was to harass Jap boats, using the river at night.

'On the night of 14 April Major Lunn with Corporal Merryweather, and Sergeant Tough with Corporal Westow, pushed off at dusk to drift downstream on a 3½ knot current to the oil fields of Chauk and Seikpyu, where it was anticipated the Japs were crossing.

'Both oil fields were heavily defended, but it was known the enemy were about to pull out, and our own troops, mostly Ghurkas, Sikhs and Indians were massing on the banks of a dry river bed just north of Chauk, ready for an attack.

'The night was very dark so the 2½ miles to the target area called for expert navigation, because the main stream ran "S" fashion from east to west bank, with sandbanks extending accordingly. On the east bank it was flat country, which necessitated keeping to the west, where the silhouette of a ridge of hills was good company for straining eyes. Spirits rose high when oil derricks were spotted at Seikpyu, some eighty yards to starboard, and by gentle exertions on the paddles, the canoes were man-oeuvred out of the main current into a dead water some thirty yards from the west bank.

'As the canoes drew together and parked, one facing upstream and the other down, voices were heard on the bank, against the night sky figures were seen moving about. On the opposite bank at Chauk there was also activity, with the Nips dashing about in a vehicle which sported full headlamps.

'For over an hour, loud noises were heard on the west bank, and a vehicle with sidelights pulled right to the edge of the river. Oil drums could be heard being man-handled then the vehicle left. All eyes were strained on the west bank just a few yards away, then after a few splashes, the creak of oars could be heard and a large boat suddenly appeared. At the angle it approached, the canoes were liable to be rammed, but the oars dipped a few feet astern, and someone in it called across to the party enquiringly, whereupon the OC gave orders to start the engines. Try as they might, neither engines responded to No. 2's efforts, and on hearing the spluttering of an engine, the crew of

the challenging boat shot off into the darkness at a speed
that would not disgrace an Oxford eight.

'This was no place for the party to hang about after
being challenged, so, long after the rowers had got home
and told their tale, the inboard motors were eventually got
going and a tedious journey upstream to Ywatha began.
Twice the party ran up on sandbanks, and they eventually
arrived back at base all thoroughly browned off with the
motors' behaviour. Two nights later, on 16/17 April,
Lieutenant "Buck" Ryan with Corporal Kierman,
Sergeant Wood and Corporal Kilkenny, went over the
same territory with great success. After patrolling down
the Chauk area for some hours, they became separated.
As the canoe farthest down the river was about to return
to base, a party of Japs pushed off from the bank at Chauk
in a large boat loaded with ammunition and a 75mm gun.
This was just what the doctor ordered. Sergeant Wood
and Corporal Kilkenny had a great time circling the
vessel, blasting away with their Vickers "K" MG. Their
efforts soon produced a fireworks display as ammunition
was detonated with the stream of tracer and incendiaries –
the boat burst into flames and revealed a 75mm field gun.
As the canoes made off, the whole issue blew sky high.
Slight opposition was encountered from the enemy on the
river banks but the party returned highly delighted from
the night's work well overdue because of their evasive
tactics after the shoot.

'A similar raid took place the following night when a
party headed by Lieutenant Rodney with Sergeant
Roberts and Corporals Griffiths and Bell blasted a smaller
boat carrying Japs and live cows.

'On 19 April the Japs left Chauk in a hurry, and the SBS
found good quarters there within the hour, also the result
of Wood's and Kilkenny's shoot. Four large-calibre guns

and ammunition stores had been abandoned intact, for with their "ferry" blown up, the Nips had no means of removing them.

'Shells and gun limbers had been dumped in the river and dead bodies were floating in the slack water.

'After a night at Chauk, the race was on out along the desolate road inland to Gwegyo, the Japs were in disorder, and so hot on their heels were our troops that Jap reinforcements were rolling in broken-down vehicles right into our forward road blocks. During the night of 21 April SBS and a company of Gurkhas did a nightmare ride across to Kyaukee, where the Japs were purported to be. Dawn found SBS surrounded by villagers who indicated the Japs were in full flight. The first to approach the SBS defences was an Anglo-Burman by the name of Henry Ellis, ex-employee of the Burmah Oil Company. He gave valuable information about the Japanese defences at Yenanyaung oil field and was duly attached to the group. Under "house arrest" by the Japs, he had been badly treated but, feigning sickness and knowing the British would return, had regularly visited the fortified oil field and taken mental notes for future reference.

'These great oil fields of Yenanyaung were the next objective, and as the SBS entered from the north, they saw what a party the Gurkhas, "Queens" and Indian troops had just had. Japs lay everywhere, and their tunnels and defences brought gasps of amazement from everyone. The road cuts inland from the river at this point as SBS formed an operational base here.

'Three operations were made from Yenanyaung, all reconnaissance, and were very successful. During the first one, Major Lunn and his party, consisting of his No. 2 Corporal Merryweather, Sergeant Tough and Corporal Longhurst went down river at night to recce a powerhouse cum pumping station under Jap control. Landing on the opposite side of the river to shelter from a tropical storm, they ran into a Jap patrol of four men in flat territory, both parties dropping to the ground for cover.

'Avoiding contact so as not to be deterred from their planned operation, SBS got back to their canoes and battled across a wave-tossed river with their paddles to the target area. Having beached their canoes, they actually sheltered in Jap dug-outs until the storm abated. Having approached the pump house and ascertained it was working, they returned to their base with the information. On 29 April the unit moved on to Magwe where the Nips had just hightailed it. It was here that information was received that two "German generals" were operating with the Japs, and some sort of confirmation of this was found on a dead Jap in the form of a 1,000 Reich banknote. (After the war a book was published about three German POWs who escaped from a camp in northern India, and two of them, Rolf Magener and Heinz von Have travelled through the British forces across Burma and gave themselves up to the Japs in this area. They were eventually sent to Japan, and after many experiences were not sent home until 17 August 1947.)

'The following morning an early riser in the party reported that the canoes had disappeared from their moorings and after some rapid scouting found them being literally pulled apart by Burmese villagers who no doubt took them to be abandoned Japanese equipment.

'Within forty-eight hours the unit was on the move again, this time to Migyaunge, where once again they acquired ex-Jap billets in the form of a civilian police barracks. The situation here became very sticky, for owing to torrential monsoon rain, several Chaungs were impassable between the unit and GHQ. Food had to be parachuted in, and all the time the possibility of Japs crossing from the west bank of the Irrawaddy behind the extended lines could not be ignored. Some recce work was carried out from this base but was very limited owing to the Positions held.

'The move on 11 May took them to Allanmyo, but the Japs were fast movers too, so off they went on the 12th for Prome. Hardly had the unit left Allanmyo when they stopped. The road to Prome was blocked. This was to be a showdown.

'The Japs had been driven down from the north, from the Arakan in the west and from Rangoon in the south, and here, in the scrub jungle that flanks the river for three miles south of Kama, they were keeping open a bridge-head to escape to the east.

'SBS quarters were in Kamagelle, a small village opposite Kama. Between the unit and the Japs two hundred yards away were the finest fighters in the world, the Gurkhas, and these were dug in covering the north of the bridgehead. Across the river at Kama the villagers were being beaten up almost every day by retreating Japs who wanted food. Arrangements were made for a flag to be flown when the Japs came there, and on several occasions the six-pounder field gun team attached to SBS were able to do firing over open sights, when warnings were given. One night the Gurkhas picked off a suicide party of Nips trying to pole-charge the guns which were actually in the same compound as sleeping SBS members.

'Operations were being laid on to ascertain how the Japs were crossing the river, for no boats had been reported in that area. Night after night patrols of SBS returned without firing a shot, although on one occasion a party consisting of Major Lunn, Merryweather, Tough and his No. 2 watched fires on both banks and Japs smoking and drying their clothes. It had been arranged with long-range artillery that, if any Japs were spotted on either bank, SBS would fire up green Very lights, so that the AOP (Artillery Observation Post) up river could direct a barrage onto the designation target. In the early hours of the morning and before any signals had been fired, a large explosion (thought by the SBS to be a ranging shell from the impatient artillery) went off on the east bank among the Japs. Within seconds the enemy on both sides of the shellburst started firing rifles and machine-guns, and as the tracers flew between them the canoeists were delighted to watch them annihilating themselves.

'For sheer audacity a raid on the Jap bridgehead on 18 May 1945 takes some beating. At approximately 1300 hours Major Lunn returned in haste from BHQ with the news that a company of Dogras had patrolled inland to the centre of the Jap bridgehead on the east bank of the river where the Japs, strongly resenting this intrusion, had them surrounded on the river bank and were wiping them out slowly but surely. These Dogras had sent a radio signal that they were almost out of ammunition and asked could anything be done to help them.

'"Sally" Lunn got a unanimous reply to his call for volunteers, for cruising into Jap territory in the afternoon with a load of explosives was no job to be detailed for. A Burmese country boat was loaded with boxes of grenades and all kinds of ammunition for mortars, rifles etc; and with best wishes from those remaining, the flotilla pushed off. With "Sally" Lunn and Corporal Merryweather in one motorized canoe as tug to the country boat, and Corporal Harry Roberts manning the latter's sweep, Sergeant Tough and Corporal Westow manned the other canoe as escort. As the trio passed down river beyond the last

Churkha positions, Jap dug-outs with reed shelters were easily detected high up on the left bank overlooking the river, but no activity was noted. The current was very swift and about three miles downstream shacks were seen on the port side. This was Zolan, the very heart of the bridgehead. Keen eyes detected a white vest being waved on the bank, and with the aid of binoculars the Dogras were spotted. As the country boat came alongside the bank, eager hands swung the cargo ashore and warnings were given regarding snipers in the vicinity. From his covering position Merryweather spotted one inquisitive Jap some thirty yards from the relief party but he soon disappeared when everyone swung in his direction.

'After the boat was emptied, ten badly wounded men were carried down the bank and placed aboard, and last but not least their English Captain, severely wounded in the abdomen. He was placed on an improvised stretcher and made as comfortable as possible. It was intended that Sandy Tough and his partner Ron Westow should push off first, start their engine and wait out in midstream ready to hitch a line aboard after "Sally" Lunn's canoe had towed it out in the river. Unfortunately their engine failed to start and drifted downstream with its occupants farther into the Jap lines. "Sally's" canoe struggled out in the stream with a load far in excess of the capabilities of a two-stroke engine but once in midriver made a gallant half knot against the current. Suddenly a spout of water on the right of the canoe drew attention, and Corporal Merryweather saw a Jap leap down the bank at the same place as the previous one had been spotted. Two or three more shots clipped close to the boat, so "Sally" returned the compliment with a well-aimed drum from the Vickers "K" MG on the bows which blasted the ground around the offender and made him keep his head down. As the canoe faced upstream again, three American Mitchell bombers appeared from the north flying at about five hundred feet, but the cheers that were on the lips of the canoeists froze when the front plane nosed down to come roaring overhead with all guns blazing. Rounds thundered all around the party as the plane's multiple MGs hosepiped the boats. As the tail gunner of the first plane was emptying his guns, the front gunner of the next one came in range, belching black smoke from his turrets, and so it continued.

'In the short lull as they circled for another run, a Jap LMG opened up from the west bank, rippling the water about six feet off the port side. A mile up river the planes began their run in again, and it was just there that Corporal "Eddie" Griffiths had chosen to stooge around on his own in a buckshee canoe until the raiding party returned. He became No. 1 target; then came the OC's canoe, while farther down "Sandy" Tough's canoe could be seen floating apparently with no one aboard and no sign of the engine working. The second plane of this run dropped a bomb on a Jap anti-aircraft post which had fired the first time they had flown over, but, nothing daunted, the Japs kept up a tracer barrage, ignoring the canoes. During the previous goings-on, Harry Roberts stuck to his unenviable job of steering the country boat, while the wounded sat mumbling in front of him; Corporal Merryweather was sat up on the back of the canoe waving like mad to the planes to lay off, while at one time "Sally" Lunn calmly turned round and asked, "Are they shooting at us, Merry? If so, they're bloody rotten shots." Downstream "Sandy" Tough and Westow had sheltered near the jungle-covered Jap-occupied bank. For the third time the planes banked round and came in for the kill. The phrase "The persistent bastards" from the Noël

Coward film *In Which We Serve* seemed a fitting remark for the occasion.

'As the last plane went over, a .5 incendiary bullet from the rear gunner passed right through a two-gallon can of petrol under Corporal Merryweather's seat, ripped a hole along the canoe locker and expended itself on the engine. The blazing petrol can was quickly snatched out of the locker and dumped overboard, the fire in the canoe put out, and the next run in awaited. Only one plane came down the next time, and banked on her side to have a look, waggled her wings and made off. By this time the Japs must have been thoroughly confused for they ceased fire, and the OC's partner was able to remove the engine and free the propeller of weeds which were clogging it, while the Nips were still trying to figure things out. The rest of the journey was uneventful, but to make the last three hundred yards the petrol tank had to be rocked to keep the towing canoe going as all the reserve petrol had gone overboard on fire. All Members of the SBS returned without casualties, Tough and Westow arriving shortly afterwards, and they too had collected a hit from the planes. Captain Andrews of the 1st Dogras died *en route*.

'Major Lunn shot off to Brigade HQ to pass his opinion about American air crews.

'On 22 May, 89 Brigade occupied Kama, airstrikes were put in on the Jap positions in the bridgehead, and it was decided to bypass them and move further south. After a short stay in Prome, the unit moved to Shwedaung, where a most ambitious plan was hatched. SBS and COPP were to tow rubber dinghies and rafts full of Gurkhas' kit down the Irrawaddy during the day, allowing the men to march down the banks and congregate at night at a given point. The ultimate objective was Bassein, where by devious routes it was hoped to do a "Wingate" through Jap

country and link up with our own troops in the south at
Rangoon. The first night was spent at Kyangin, after
Major Lunn almost drowned when the canoe capsized
when overrun by one of the rafts and he was trapped
underneath. The next day's trip was to Thalidan, where
the motley collection of craft was concealed in a narrow
Chaung, a hundred yards from a track used regularly by
the Japs. The whole outfit got bogged down here, for it
was reported, from good authority, that two thousand
Japs were congregated at Tonbo, just south of the unit's
position. After several days, SBS were withdrawn to
Shwedaung, and thence to Allanmyo, where from an improvised air strip they were flown to India.'

Merryweather writes that:

'In Burma working on the Irrawaddy was much
different than in the Arakan. Here the Japs could be
anywhere on either bank, in front or behind one. They
were being driven down from the north, pushed in from
the Arakan in the west, and later on up from the south.
Communications between their units were virtually non-
existent, and their sole object was to congregate in the
central plain and get away to the east. This was where the
SBS were to operate. The Japs carried the minimum
amount of arms and equipment, were well shod and with
good clothing. Each man wore a tag on his left lapel with
his name, rank and unit on it. Equipment was made of
good solid leather, as were the boots. Some units wore
canvas and rubber-soled shoes with the big toe separate,
which left easily identifiable prints. (Some SBS members
on finding stores containing these shoes preferred to wear
them in lieu of their own issued jungle-boots.) Around
their necks and hanging down to their waists they carried a
three-inch diameter canvas "sausage" containing weevil-
infested rice for rations. Their waists were bound with a

wide cloth belt of a thousand stitches, adorned with coins etc from friends and relatives, which was supposed to bring them good luck. With this went a neck sachet hung on a string containing rice paper "good luck charms", and their hand imprints with zodiac signs probably from a fortune-teller.

'Forays into the Jap lines down river were made by drifting two canoes down at nightfall to the proposed area and lying up in dead water close to the banks, or using a kedge anchor on one canoe with the other facing the opposite direction holding on alongside ready for immediate action. In emergency the kedge rope would be cut. The dress for night ops was usually jungle green slacks and jacket, bush hat or cap comforter, gym shoes or jungle boots. No. 1 had the Vickers "K" and a .45 Colt and any other death-dealing accoutrements he chose to add with his American fighting knife and toggle rope. Several spare mags for the Vickers were fitted on either side of No. 1's position, and usually some Mills 36 grenades. No. 2 had the engines to look after, and had a one-gallon "kidney" petrol tank on either side as reserve. Behind his seat in a circular hatched locker was another two-gallon petrol tank. His weapons were a Thompson sub-machine gun, a .45 Colt and as many grenades as could comfortably be stowed, eight single thirty-round magazines of .45 ammo in pouches on his body, with two mags taped together side by side fitted on the tommy-gun for quick changing in emergencies. Spare magazines hung in pouches on the inside of the canoe. He also carried an American fighting knife and a toggle rope around his waist. Deflated life-belts were worn by both men and escape kits carried on their person. Water-bottles were stowed handy in the canoe and could contain anything from cold tea to the hard stuff, "purely for medicinal purposes" of course. The steering rods on the canoe could be operated by either man. To complete their kit they had a torch fitted with a blue filter and made waterproof by using outsize rubber sheaths. A handy conversion to the tommy-gun was used by some No. 2s, the butt being discarded and one of the spotlights taped to the barrel with the signalling press button in a position so that it could be switched on with the left hand while the right hand fired the gun. This meant that wherever the spotlight was pointed, the rounds were bound to strike the target.'

Following a few days leave in Calcutta, "A' Group was sent south by train to the ferry for Ceylon, carrying their operational gear and two pet monkeys adopted in Burma. On the quayside in Ceylon strenuous objections were raised by Customs Officers to the admission of the monkeys. One was small and well-behaved and easily concealed, but the other, named 'Sally' after 'A' Group's Commanding Officer, was very large and fierce and bit everyone. 'Sally' was suspended on a string under the lid of the water-tender of the locomotive which was to take 'A' Group on to Hammanhiel Camp. She was not discovered, despite a lengthy search.

'A' Group, reinforced from 'B' and 'C' Groups, was then sent to Madras to train with 3 Special Service Brigade (Commandos) for Operation 'Zipper', the invasion of Malaya. Shortly after they had completed their preparations for reconnaissance duties with the Commando Brigade and were ready to sail, atomic bombs were dropped on Hiroshima and Nagasaki, and on 14 August 1945 the Japanese nation surrendered unconditionally.

'A' Group was recalled to Ceylon and, on its return to Hammanhiel Camp, found that the COPP and SBU contingents had already left for the United Kingdom and demobilization. SBS had officially been disbanded with effect from 27 October 1945, but no arrangemente for their disposal; they were told to fend for themselves. Major Lunn succeeded after considerable efforts in fixing up his men with good jobs in Ceylon until their release was due. He himself finished up as Registrar of the 35th British General Hospital near Colombo and moved with it to Singapore.

Relations between SBS and the Royal Marines within the Small Operations Group had always been reasonably cordial, though never close, as the groups trained and operated separately because of their differing roles. Also their different conceptions of discipline would have made any closer integration uncomfortable. SBS men were often stirred to happy laughter by the sight of Royal Marines sitting in ranks in their canoes on dry land learning to paddle by numbers. However, SOG Commander's Progress Report on 11 June 1945, covering the period January 1944 to May 1945, stated: 'It is considered that praise is due to the OC SBS and to the three Group Commanders for the energy and resourcefulness they have shown, throughout the period covered by this report, in their planning and execution of operations, the training of their units, and the overcoming of administrative difficulties.'

It was therefore a pity that the association should end on a sour note through a piece of insensitivity on the part of SEAC Headquarters in Kandy. Not only were SBS no longer to be looked after by SOG, or anyone else for that matter, but they were forbidden by order of the Chief of Staff to wear the commando green beret, which was to be worn henceforth only by Royal Marine Commandos. This order caused great resentment as SBS had worn the green beret since 1942, long before Royal Marine Commandos were formed, and it was a tremendous source of pride to individual officers and men. In effect the instruction was quietly ignored. During the same period it seems that recommendations for gallantry awards put forward in 1945 by SBS Group Commanders for operations in Burma got side-tracked and lost in SOC or SEAC Headquarters in the confusion. A pity, as the decorations would have been well earned.

As each man's demob group came up, old comrades disappeared to the four corners of the earth. But it was not the end. For two years a small group held a purely SBS reunion in Manchester and London under the inspiration of Major R.P. Livingstone; many ex-SBS members formed a boating squadron in the 21st Regiment SAS TA, and this was a highly successful post-war unit, some of whom re-enlisted in 1949 and joined 'Mad' Mike Calvert's 'Malayan Scouts'.

Of course, it was a logical decision that the Royal Marines should assume the role of the amphibious Special Forces at the end of World War II, and they have carried on the SBS tradition with skill and dedication, as was amply proved during the operations on the Falkland Islands in 1982.

17
Conclusion

From January 1941 until October 1945 the officers and
men of Nos 1 and 2 Special Boat Sections of the Army
Commandos took part in forty-eight separate planned
operations from submarines, thirty-one from surface craft
and three by other means of transport. In addition, a considerable number of minor reconnaissance and fighting
patrols were carried out on the Chindwin and Irrawaddy
rivers in Burma in late 1944 and early 1945 in close
support of the British 14th Army.

During major campaigns between 1941 and 1945, when
SBS were allowed to operate in the specialized roles for
which they had been carefully chosen and trained, their
casualties in killed and missing were only four officers and
seven other ranks, and in prisoners of war only one officer
and three other ranks.

In 1942, after the departure of Roger Courtney from
the Middle East, No. 1 SBS was mainly employed in *coup
de main* raiding on inland enemy airfields, more properly
the province of the Special Air Service. They lost five officers and ten other ranks taken prisoner.

The prime function of SBS was to do maximum damage
to the Axis war effort with a minimum outlay of men and
stores, by small-scale operations on hostile shores where
the use of conventional means, such as aircraft or naval
vessels, would have risked losses uneconomic in a long
war of attrition. SBS was cost-effective.

Their regular employment was on railway sabotage,
minor beach reconnaissance and pilotage, enemy de-

ception, ferrying of agents and stores, limpet raids on enemy shipping in harbour, and close support of advancing troops. Weigh the possible loss of two men in a canoe against one or more bomber aircraft in an attack on a railway bridge and you have an example of cost-efficiency.

Field Marshal Lord Slim has written that any single operation in which more than a handful of men are to be engaged should be regarded as normal and should be carried out by any well-trained standard military unit without the need for a specially equipped *corps d'élite* of super-soldiers. This judgement may or may not be valid when applied to the Special Service Brigades after mid-1943, when the number of commando units had been much increased and the volunteer principle partly abandoned. I am not really qualified to express an opinion. However, at no time did SBS exceed a hundred officers and men. If one sets the number of operations successfully completed against the costs of administration and the casualties sustained, the Section was a credit to those who had the faith to form, nurture and support it through five gruelling and dangerous years.

Not that SBS was a *corps d'élite* of super-soldiers. The officers and men were volunteers from the commandos, which itself was a volunteer force, and were perhaps initially attracted by the freedom with self-discipline of life in the SBS.

It was Roger Courtney's great strength as a leader that he was able thereafter to fan the spark of imagination that exists in most men and inspired them with his own enthusiasm and sense of adventure. During his years of nomad existence in Africa as a white hunter and gold prospector, he had become a shrewd judge of men and was able to recognize the potential poacher under the veneer of military discipline. The aptitude for calculated risk was as important in the business of tip-and-run raids on enemy coasts as it was in raiding the squire's pheasants. There was nothing extraordinary about the officers and men who served in SBS. They were ordinary Britons drawn from a wide range of routine peacetime occupations and, with few exceptions, had no exotic background. Nor were they undisciplined misfits and trouble-makers, for neither could exist in a unit where the most rigid self-discipline and loyalty were required for survival. Their motivation was as mixed as one would expect – the normal measure of undemonstrative patriotism, youthful adventure, self-reliance, independence of mind, and a liking for responsibility. Generally speaking, they were individualists, loners and survivors. A psychologist might have detected in some a masochistic urge to take risks as part of a hidden death-wish or to escape some ghost from the past. This urge, however, never seemed to survive the actual shock of danger, when the animal instinct for self-preservation could be expected to reassert itself with its usual force.

They were full of spirit but were quiet fellows, intent on getting on with the job. They were not boastful or belligerent and certainly not the bloodthirsty thugs that commandos were made out to be by some irresponsible sections of the British Press. In fact, the taking of human life played little direct part in the type of operation carried out by the SBS until the later stages of the war against the Japanese in the Arakan and Burma. Rather to the contrary: beach reconnaissance and pilotage were designed to save life, as was amply proved in North Africa, Italy and Burma by SBS as well as its friend and companion COPP.

Lord Slim has also written that, 'There is one kind of special unit which should be retained – that designed to be employed in small parties, usually behind the enemy, on tasks beyond the normal scope of warfare in the field.' SBS and COPP were small and very specialized, and their retention since the end of 1945 under the mantle of the Royal Marines has, during the Falklands campaign, shown the wisdom of his words.

Brother Roger and his old friend Nigel Clogstoun-Willmott had every reason to be proud of the healthy offspring they fathered on the beaches of Rhodes in March 1941.

Appendix A:

Report by Captain R. ('Tug') Wilson on operation carried out from HMS/M P42 Unbroken, 5/6 September 1942 in the harbour of Crotone, Italy
(from Public Record Office, Kew)
(See Chapter 2)

Personnel.

Captain R. Wilson.
Bombardier Brittlebank.

Intention.

To enter the enemy harbour of Crotone, approach a pre-selected target, i.e. a merchant vessel of 2–3000 tons, and release four aimed baby torpedoes in direction of target, thence to return to submarine.

Information.

Crotone was chosen for the scene of the operation on the advice of Captain G.W.G. Simpson CBE, RN, Commanding Officer of the 10th Submarine Flotilla, after the close study of aerial photographs of several harbours in Sicily and Italy for the following reasons:

(a) Since the operation was in the nature of an experiment on the use of the baby torpedo, it was considered of great importance that the harbour selected should afford the maximum chances of success and particularly escape after the attack, in order to assure authorities of a report on the effectiveness and running of the torpedo.

(b) The non-existence of a minefield outside the harbour permitted a close approach by the submarine to the harbour entrance, i.e. 2–3000 yards.

(c) The harbour was small and any worthy target would necessarily, owing to its size, lie alongside the mole in the deepest water not far from the harbour entrance, thus affording a quick departure for safer and open waters after the attack.

(d) The harbour was not a busy one.

(e) Had sustained only one RAF raid during the war, otherwise had not been molested or threatened in any way.

(f) During this raid, the southern mole had received a direct hit by a bomb and had been breached in one place down to sea level.

(g) Numerous aerial photographs of the harbour were available, the latest having been taken the day *P.42* left Malta (31 August 1942), the boom across the entrance being clearly discernible.

(h) Vessels up to 4000 tons could be accommodated in the harbour.

OPERATION.

5 September 1942.

Periscope reconnaissance of harbour was carried out during afternoon from a distance of about four miles. The target, a merchant vessel of 2–3000 tons was located in anticipated position lying alongside the northern mole.

The chart of the harbour and the aerial photographs

were closely studied. It was estimated that the operation, from leaving the submarine to the return, would occupy about one and a half to two hours.

The Commanding Officer of the submarine proposed that I should be launched about 2330 hours owing to the phase of the moon, which would rise about 0300 hours the following day, and since he expressly desired the operation to be completed and under way from the vicinity of the harbour by that time.

On the return I was to flash a pre-arranged signal with a blue torch to seaward, at a point approximately three-quarters of the way along the course back to the submarine if the craft had not already been sighted.

In the event of circumstances arising preventing my return at the anticipated hour, an alternative rendezvous was fixed at a point five miles off the harbour on the same bearing at dawn, where the submarine would remain on the surface for a period of one hour in accordance with *P.42*'s orders.

At 2340 hours canoe was launched approximately 2000 yards off the harbour with personnel, necessary stores and equipment. I proceeded on compass bearing for harbour entrance. There was a slight breeze and a faint swell, otherwise it was flat calm. A clear sky with visibility excellent.

At about 250 yards I sighted the seaward end of the south mole. After splitting paddles, I cautiously approached harbour entrance square on so as to present minimum silhouette. The boom on closer approach looked rather formidable, but certainly not insurmountable. I knew that the distance across the entrance was very short but from my position, now some 200 yards, each individual boom-float support, from end to end, was clearly visible. I considered that if look-outs were posted at the end of each mole, a craft even smaller than a canoe would most certainly be spotted whilst approaching from seaward. I decided, therefore, to turn about, make a wide circle southward to approach and investigate the bomb-damaged south mole and see if the breach would afford a possible means of penetration into the harbour.

I made the approach at a discreet distance from and parallel to the beach, taking advantage of the excellent cover of the dark background of the land. Having arrived at the breach and no sentry being apparent, I investigated the possibilities. At one point the gap was down to sea level. Barbed wire and rabbit wire had been erected but not very efficiently, for it was possible without much difficulty to fold this upwards very conveniently over a large piece of masonry which was luckily just awash with three or four inches of water.

Having made the gap sufficiently large, it was then simple to ease the canoe through into the harbour proper by hand.

Inside the harbour the stillness was intense and the sky clearly reflected on the water.

The target was distinctly visible lying alongside the northern mole, the funnel, bridge and mast silhouetted against the sky. A large schooner was lying in the middle of the harbour in a line parallel with the target and away towards the boom. The breach in the mole was almost directly opposite the target, in other words, the target formed the horizontal stroke in the letter 'T'.

Considering the target to be 100 yards in length, the ideal position of attack would be at a point where the target length would subtend an angle of between 46 degrees and 50 degrees, affording a good angle of error and necessitating only 25 per cent of the torpedo's maximum effective range (i.e. 400 yards) whilst the chances of being observed at that distance would not be great.

To reach this ideal position I decided to take a course, as indicated in sketch, in order to keep the maximum distance between canoe and schooner until absolutely necessary, when it could be approached bow on until the final turn to deliver the attack from the desired position. It will be noticed that in this position of attack, the canoe is considerably nearer to the schooner than the target, hence the necessary caution of the indirect approach.

Bombardier Brittlebank sat forward using single split paddle, myself aft with torpedoes ready for immediate action, excepting that the nose caps were still in the 'safe' screwed-on position. The final approach was made at absolute minimum speed owing to the extreme stillness of the water and the amount of phosphorescence stirred up when paddle was used with other than the smallest effort. The too perfect visibility also warranted additional caution.

Having just arrived in the attacking position and in the process of checking the angle subtended by the target, the stillness was exploded by a challenge from the schooner. This was followed immediately by a shout from the target, then by the noise of people running about and shouting in a manner unmistakably Italian.

Although the Italians were aware that the British operated special service personnel from submarines and I knew that the coastal defences had been warned in the form of a pamphlet to expect attacks from the sea, I decided that it would be some moments before they would recover themselves sufficiently and do something reasonable in the way of counter-attack or counter-measures.

I removed the nose cap of one torpedo, made certain that the split collar fell from its groove in the striker head, placed it in the water and pressed the starter button. It was necessary to make the customary quarter turn of the propeller and press the button a second time. The starter functioned and the motor started, sounding extremely healthy. I ordered Brittlebank to stand by with double-ended paddle in readiness for departure. With torpedo just submerged, I took careful aim at the target (the canoe being stationary) and with a gentle push to overcome the initial resistance of the water, released it. Almost simultaneously I ordered Brittlebank to proceed in accordance with previous order.

Having quickly found my own paddle, I stole a last glance at the torpedo. The white line painted fore and aft along her back was pointing directly at the centre of the target's length. Her depth was about five feet and appeared to be running steadily, with no suggestion of a 'porpoising' motion, during the few brief moments I was able to follow her.

There was now plenty of commotion and lights were beginning to appear, but as yet no shots were fired. With both double-ended paddles now in use, our point of exit, the breach, was soon reached. No very definite explosion was heard or noticed during the retreat – I could therefore not guarantee a hit.

The retreat was made bearing in mind my instructions and the main point of the operation, and I rather regretted at the time not having withdrawn with a full complement of torpedoes for a further attempt in another, or the same harbour later on in the patrol, under more favourable conditions, but, as it was, I still had a formidable salvo of three of them left and I was in safe waters outside what had become something of a hornets' nest, with my parent craft in waiting at the rendezvous only some 2000 yards away.

Having set the back-bearing on the compass, I proceeded towards submarine's position. When in vicinity of rendezvous I carried out the customary procedure of signalling in accordance with instructions, the submarine not having already been sighted. This procedure was only used after a most intensive scanning of the horizon, both from a few inches above the water and from the sitting up position. On only one other occasion in an operation of a similar nature had I resorted to the use of the torch. The swell was increasing very noticeably now and the horizon becoming gradually less and less distinct. I proceeded a little further along the course signalling at specified intervals.

About half an hour after reading first signalling position, I located the familiar looking blob of a submarine off my port bow and turned towards it. A moment later I discerned a similar object some short distance to port of the first. It was soon apparent that this was no submarine, but two surface craft approaching line abreast. I remained turned towards with the intention of passing between them since time would not permit taking a course at right angles, apart from the fact that in so doing I would have crossed their bows and presented a maximum silhouette. Crouching low in the canoe as the craft bore down on us, I estimated that enemy's speed to be about ten knots, the bow waves now being very marked and about sixty yards apart.

On the spur of the moment I quickly made ready and launched one of the torpedoes over the port side.

A few moments later the knife edge bows and low waist of the dark and light grey camouflaged craft now very close and on my port beam suggested a light destroyer. Now between the two vessels and at such close quarters, I expected some form of challenge so held the remaining two torpedoes in readiness to be jettisoned. This was not necessary, however, as it appeared that the canoe had not been observed by the enemy.

I proceeded at a steady speed in a direction opposite to that of the enemy and as he altered course, presumably zigzagging, so I did the same until he was no longer in sight.

A few unhappy moments were experienced in passing through the immediate wake of the two vessels but the canoe withstood the test without capsizing.

I considered that owing to the now prevailing swell it would have been difficult to sight a canoe, which under such conditions must have melted very favourably into insignificance, and further, that in any patrol vessel, the look-outs would be searching well ahead and towards the horizon and not down under their noses for any possible enemy.

I realized that the submarine would certainly have picked up H.E. (Hydrophonic effects) with her Asdic and would have taken evasive action. Also I was quite certain that the submarine had not been spotted by the enemy since any action would have been most audible.

Having assumed that the enemy vessels were patrolling the harbour area, I dismissed from my mind any hope of contacting *P.42* that night.

It was now approximately 0145 hours. The alternative rendezvous was to be at dawn. The weather was gradually worsening unfortunately. A considerable swell with occasionally white horses running diagonally across my harbour rendezvous course, conditions most unfavourable for maintaining an accurate course and position in an open canoe.

If the minimum amount of water was to be shipped, it would be necessary to patrol up and down, square into the weather up, and with and slightly faster than the weather down. This course was adopted throughout the night. The avoidance of capsizing required such concentrated attention that the accuracy of my position for the rendez-vous at dawn could be no other than a little doubtful. The canoe was heavy with water and did not feel too stable after her recent buffeting.

Everything in the canoe was drenched, thus it was im-possible to wipe the compass and binoculars effectively, but Crotone could be seen however, roughly in the right direction some six miles distance. The sea had quietened appreciably with the dawn.

Having remained in that position for about two hours keeping a sharp look-out, without having sighted a surface craft of any description, I decided to try to attract the attention of *P.42* in the event of her being dived in the vicinity, by creating under water explosions.

Two four-second hand grenades were thrown astern after maximum speed had been attained to avoid possible damage to canoe by fragmentation. No periscope was observed. I concluded that the canoe was not accurately in position or that *P.42*'s captain had not considered it advisable to remain on the surface in daylight for very good reasons unknown to myself.

Conditions now demanded that the canoe should be beached as soon as possible for maintenance, so I aban-doned the area rather than run the risk of sinking.

I proposed to make a bid for Malta some two hundred and fifty miles away. The conditions of the canoe, how-ever, and the equipment in our possession and the absolute necessity of frequent landings tended to force our admission that the odds of success of such a venture might be a little in the Italians' favour.

I proceeded SSE, towards Capo Calonne. Having

rounded the Cape, reconnoitred that part of the coast now visible for a suitable point of landing. A beach was selected, approachable only from the sea, being hemmed in by sheer cliffs. Before landing the remaining two torpedoes were flooded and sunk some two miles offshore.

On inspection the canoe was found to be in a not very stable condition. After some twenty minutes work on her, we pushed off. It was now about midday.

I set a course to cross the Golfo Di Squillace. We passed a few fishing craft but by this time there was no indication of military uniform visible. We were hailed, I replied with a wave of the hand. By six o'clock the same evening I was forced to beach by conditions then prevailing in the canoe. This time it was not possible to select a suitable beach. We had been observed landing. Some twenty minutes later we found ourselves surrounded by a large number of Italians. Throughout the operation Bombardier Brittlebank's conduct and reactions to the varying circumstances left nothing to be desired and also during the subsequent interrogations after capture. He proved to be the model soldier. When told by the Italian General at Catanzaro, where we were interrogated, that he was to be shot at dawn he merely requested permission to write a letter to his next-of-kin.

Bombardier Brittlebank took an active part in the Rommel raid, in which he did splendid work, and succeeded in finding his way back to Egypt after enduring forty days in the desert behind the enemy's line.

Appendix B:
Ferry Party Report – Carpenter 1
by Captain W.G. Davis
(see Chapter 13)

5 October

We surfaced at 1945 hours and the order was given to open forward hatch. This proved difficult and the clips required lots of hammering before finally surrendering to brute force. The order was received 'Away Landing Party'. This had been rehearsed on two previous occasions. The Landing Party including Major Martin, took position near the conning-tower to await their boats. Next H.P. air operators followed by Ferry Party whose duty it was to inflate and launch the boats and fit the engines. The boats were then sent up in reverse sequence of loading.

Galloway and Preece inflated seats, floor and Mae Wests by hand pump and I operated the H.P. air. As each boat was ready and launched I jumped onto the ballast tanks and assisted the Landing Party, who were heavily equipped, into their respective boats. Seamen towed boats forward to a position near forward hatch for loading from an improvised loading stage. As each boat was loaded it was towed right forward by Hydroplanes, a non-engined made aft of an engined boat. When loading was complete the boats were four abreast and made fast together. Ferry Party got into their boats last and the Bongle was handed down to me by Lieutenant Pope No. 1 of the Submarine.

I had to do the navigating with Galloway running my engine. We cast off at 2055 hours and paddled away from the submarine. When some fifty yards away the submarine headed to sea. We got two engines running satisfactorily after twenty minutes, Galloway's and Preece's. The others started and petered out. I gave orders for my boats to take Major Martin's in tow and Preece to take Captain Sime. We got under way at 2130 hours and set course to two hundred and fifty degrees heading for a high point which I recognized as Balau. The sea was glassy calm with a slight ground swell, set was south, visibility seven hundred yards. There were three lights, which appeared to be shore lights off to port. These later turned out to be lights on fish traps approximately one and a half miles offshore.

As the moon rose, 2200 hours, we sighted a large sailing vessel approximately 2000 yards to port with sails set. As there was little wind this was not disturbing. We felt conspicuous in the bright moonlight.

2215 hours Captain Sime reported enemy following. Looking back I discovered that one of Preece's boats had slipped its tow this being the 'enemy'. I ordered Preece to return for this boat whilst we circled them. As we circled one of the Chinese reported enemy to starboard. This proved to be the lights on Kelongs, (fish traps) which appeared to starboard as we circled. I passed back the order that only vessels closing astern must be reported. After taking the stray boat in tow Preece's engine 'cut out' and refused to start. We, Galloway and I, returned with our boats to take Preece in tow, thus making one engine pull eight boats.

We proceeded towards land and at 2230 hours sighted what appeared to be a large three masted vessel, sails furled and a smaller one moored across the bay which was our objective. We altered course to port and our engine 'cut out'. We then heard an engine from shoreward and noticed that it came from the larger vessel which was towing the smaller and heading North. I altered to our original course to give as small a silhouette as possible to these vessels.

We were coming out of the moon and the ships to shoreward were difficult to see with a background of land. These ships were only three hundred yards away and must have seen us had they been keeping proper 'look-out'.

Major Martin clambered over the boats at 2245 and came forward to me to query my course and saying that the lights to port would be the village North of Balau and that we should go south of these lights. I informed him that I considered we were still three miles from shore and that the point to which I was heading was Balau which I had seen through the periscope in daylight.

We then sighted two ships moored across the Bay North of Balau; these were three hundred yards off the starboard bow. Shortly after we sighted a sailing vessel eight hundred yards off the port bow and heading, probably with auxiliary motor, North. I changed course slightly to starboard, ordered all personnel to paddle and raced this vessel crossing its bows and getting landward of it with only two hundred yards to spare.

Two other vessels appeared immediately ahead and heading North. This was getting monotonous, so I decided that as the engine was unreliable and might 'cut out' at any moment, I should make direct to the point, Balau, without further alteration of course; all personnel still paddling. We made the point without further incident and, when six hundred yards off I altered course South and headed diagonally across the Bay. As we rounded the point we saw a light in the South of the Bay. Major Martin said that this must be the fisherman's hut. It turned out to be a fire and, as Major Martin had said, was the fisherman's hut.

About five hundred yards from shore I decided to continue at three-quarters engine speed and ran in until almost in the surf which was not heavy. I ordered all boats to slip their tow and proceed independently. We landed without incident excepting three tins falling from one boat. These were retrieved. Two of the boats had leaked air – not very serious.

The time of landing was 0300 hours 6 October.

The tide was full and we only had sixty yards to carry the stores to the Casuarina trees. The boats were concealed later. Beach was cleared of boats and stores by 0230 hours; no sign of activity on beach other than fire at hut. The beach at our landing point was of soft sand to H.W. line and firm sand from H.W. line to Casuarina trees. We covered our tracks on beach and rested until daylight.

The Ferry Party took upon itself the duty of Boats guard, resting in the boats. All were very wet and cold whilst the Landing Party guarded stores.

0630 hours three men and one woman appeared near the hut and stretched fish nets. This was some four hundred yards North of our position. Major Martin decided to make a temporary camp two hundred yards south of fisherman's hut with a view to observing their (the fishermen's) activities during the day. The day was spent in Landing Party moving stores inland and Ferry Party overhauling engines and cleaning boats. Two engines only started under shore test.

It was decided that two engined boats, Galloway and Preece, would tow two boats each making a total of six. As the greater part of the stores were brought ashore the previous night six boats were considered sufficient. Major Martin, Lieutenant Browning, Allen, and two Chinese would remain ashore. We left the shore at 1945 hours and were assisted through heavy surf by Major Martin and shore party, who stripped and waded out as far as possible towing the boats. When clear of the surf, which incidentally swamped all boats and engines, the engines were started by Galloway and Preece. Neither engines started properly and Preece's only ran for a few minutes. After twenty minutes Galloway's engine, which had been running very badly, cleared itself and we circled and took Preece's boats in tow. We now had six boats being driven by one engine.

We steered diagonally across the Bay until Balau appeared two hundred and fifty degrees off our Port beam. I altered course to fifty five degrees allowing for a flowing tide, current running South and kept Balau astern. This should take us to the position from which we disembarked from the submarine. Visibility two hundred yards, sea flat calm, heavy ground swell. The latter made binocular look-out very difficult, in fact almost impossible.

At 2230 hours when on or near the position from which we left the submarine I saw a dark object to starboard which I presumed to be the submarine and altered course to close same. When one hundred and fifty yards from this dark object I noticed I had been mistaken and that there were three small vessels in line abreast and facing in our direction. They appeared to be stationary so I altered course slightly to starboard intending to keep to shoreward and hoping to pass unnoticed. When some seventy-five yards away we were challenged by lamp flashes from the nearest vessel. They appeared to be of the small patrol type of boat. I ordered Galloway to hard about. We went around so quickly that we hit the stern of the last boat on our tow, not serious. I had previously detailed one Chinese that, should we be challenged, he was to reply in

Malay that we were fishing. Not very convincing but just a chance. The best and only thing to do was to run for it and be prepared to shoot if necessary.

I ordered all personnel to paddle which they did, including Galloway who fixed the steering heading for Balau the nearest point. The three boats gave chase, still in line abreast and closing slowly. The boat to port was smaller than the other two and closed much nearer. When some fifty yards from our stern boat, in which Reddish was paddling and which he says the bow of the leading patrol was over the stern of his boat, for some unknown reason, these vessels opened astern of us and turned to starboard. This was after the chase had been on ten minutes.

I assumed that our submarine might have been detected especially later as when we were near the shore aircraft flew low overhead heading to sea. After a further ten minutes running towards the shore, I decided to make a circuit well off to port and try again. We altered course for this purpose and the engine stopped. The engine would not start so I decided to abandon the effort for that night. The moon rose at 2300 hours. We paddled towards land heading for Balau and making full use of the flowing tide. When in the Bay I passed word back to slip all tows and proceed independently. We finally beached at 0230 hours. As we landed several aircraft flew low overhead heading to sea. They were showing navigation lights. Major Martin was on the beach to meet us.

7 October
After breakfast, we, the officers, discussed the position and after a check up of stores ashore, four tons of the most essential having been brought in on the first night, Major Martin decided that it would be unwise to make a further

attempt with only one engine so I suggested that I leave with the Ferry Party in one boat, and, if we contacted the submarine and the Commander was prepared to wait, we, the Ferry Party, would inflate the yellow dinghy which was in the submarine and bring as much as possible of the remainder of the stores ashore. Major Martin agreed to this but said that, if I would take three Chinese with me leaving a total of eleven Europeans and Chinese ashore, and if not feasible to return with stores, those already ashore would be sufficient to last six months. The three Chinese would return with Ferry Party.

Ferry Party spent the day overhauling the engine and preparing one boat for sea.

At 1945 hours we left the beach under very much the same surf conditions as the previous night. When clear of surf the sea was flat calm with a ground swell. Visibility good. We, Preece, three Chinese and I paddled until Galloway got the engine started. The engine would only run at half speed. At 2045 hours we passed a stationary fishing boat two hundred yards to starboard. We got on our course of the previous night and headed to sea, all paddling to assist the engine. At 2200 hours we were some one thousand yards south of where the submarine should have been. We stopped the engine and I started to 'Bongle' in groups of four pause two seconds for period of five minutes during which time the remainder of the party paddled North to keep position against the current. Interval of five minutes then carried out the same procedure. This we continued to do until 0010 hours when the moon rose and visibility almost unlimited. There was no sign of shipping of any description. Galloway endeavoured to start the engine but it refused to spark. We all started to paddle and I set course for Balau. We landed at South end of beach at 0310 hours. This was an extremely tiring journey and being the third night at sea without sleep none of the party had much reserve of strength to carry the boat up the beach. However we finally got it up and concealed.

8 October

After breakfast Major Martin suggested that if I would make the attempt again that I need not take the Chinese. I said I would do this considering we could get an engine running. After Galloway had worked all that morning on the engines and none of them would even spark I suggested to Major Martin that we endeavour to call the submarine up on the Walkie-Talkie at the pre-arranged times and that if they answered me, the Ferry Party would go out to contact. We couldn't paddle ten miles or more, out and back, in our present condition. Major Martin fully agreed and that night we went to the beach and Major Martin called up on W/T from 0737 hours and each seven minutes after the hour and half hours until 2207. All we could get was music from Singapore.

The success of the original landing was largely due to Galloway's careful and untiring efforts with his engine. Without an engine it would have been very difficult to make land with such heavily loaded boats and a one to a one and a half knot cross current. We disembarked from the submarine some five to six miles from shore which I consider excessive. Probably, due to the amount of shipping, this was unavoidable. The current was in our favour being dropped north-east of Balau and setting course for the point.

Appendix C:

Operation Barbarism
by Captain G. Barnes MM,
Commanding 'A' Group, No. 2
Sub-section
(see Chapter 14)

On the night of 15/16 December 44, at 2210 hours, 3 canoes slipped from M.L.438 which was under the command of Commander MacDonald, from a position about 2½ miles off the North of Kalayaung village, and proceeded in line astern on a course of 47 degrees. Progress was rather hard as the tide was ebbing strongly in a South-West direction. Captain Barnes drew ahead as the beach was in sight, landed first, the other 2 canoes coming in on getting the 'all clear' sign; all canoes were beached safely without any surf, at 2345 hours, and the M.L. contacted Walkie-Talkie to report landing.

The Group took up defensive positions on the beach and Captain Barnes went ahead to recce inland to the scrub, and returned. Leaving Cpl Longhurst as guard on the canoes, the remainder advanced in file towards the village across a narrow belt of sand-dunes, a narrow strip of paddy, and into the trees where a basha (hut) was found about 400 yards from High Water mark. At 2358 hours, Lt Ryan and Cpl Kiernan were posted as sentries to stop anyone approaching or leaving the basha. Captain Barnes, Sgt Barney (Burma Intelligence Corps), and Sgt Tough entered the door of the basha, awakened the native and his family. On questioning the native, it was found that he was rather dull, with little knowledge of the enemy, but he said the fishermen of the village knew much more than he did and supplied the Japs at Taungup with fish. Captain Barnes persuaded him to guide them to the fishermen's basha which he did readily. The Group crossed small paddy fields for about 300 yards inland, and the fisherman proved to be a very old man, but he had quite a lot of knowledge about the enemy, and he called a younger man about 20 years of age who knew still more than himself, so it was decided to bring him back. The simple native and the old man were both given a small amount of money and warned not to say anything of the visit to which they readily agreed. The young man came down to the beach willingly and got into the canoe of his own accord.

The time was now 0110 hours, and all 3 canoes put out to sea on a course of 230 degrees, without getting contact on the Walkie-Talkie to the M.L. After about 20 minutes on the course, Captain Barnes flashed a torch to sea, as arranged by the M.L. which was to light a mast head-lamp. A light was seen South-West of the original position of the M.L. and it was believed that the craft had moved out to sea on the ebb-tide to avoid grounding. Course was then changed and the mast-light approached. After about 25 minutes paddling, the light turned shorewards, and Captain Barnes decided that it was a native boat, as the M.L. could not get into that depth of water; through the night-glasses, it was visible as a large sailing boat either fishing, or a Jap patrol. A new course was worked out to rectify the mistake, and after paddling for 15 minutes, Captain Barnes tried Walkie-Talkie and got contact with the M.L. As it was impossible to see the signal light, Captain Barnes asked for a Very light which was instantly seen directly ahead. From this time on, both canoes and

M.L. exchanged signals on lamp, and all canoes were aboard at 0345 hours.

The anchor was weighed and, going slow ahead, at 0355 hours the M.L.s engaged with their guns the vessel with the mast-head light, which went out immediately as did the lights ashore. Owing to the distance between the M.L.s and the unknown craft, it was impossible to say whether the shoot was successful or not. At 0405 hours a course was set for the base, and all except the duty watch turned in.

The native who had been brought aboard seemed quite happy and content and enjoyed a good meal with the Indian seamen.

Field,
17 December 1944

Appendix D:
101 Troop at Dover (HMS Lynx), 1941

Captain K. Smith	(Prisoner of War Operation Sunstar 23.11.41)
Captain G.C.S. Montanaro	(Royal Engineers)
Sergeant J. Embelin	(Royal Engineers)
L/Sgt D. Craig	(Royal Engineers)
L/Sgt S.T. Weatherall	(Duke of Wellington's Regiment)
Corporal Ingram	
L/Cpl C. Woodhouse	(Prisoner of War Operation Sunstar 23.11.41)
L/Cpl N. Thompson	(Royal Engineers)
L/Bdr J. Galloway	(Royal Artillery)
L/Cpl R. Kirk	
Guardsman R. Sidlow	(Genadier Guards)
Trooper F. Preece	(Royal Tank Regiment)
Private J. Allander	(Duke of Wellington's Regiment) later Corporal 'Charioteer'
Private Palmer	
Private A. Le M. Salisbury	
Trooper J. Newsome	
Private J. Hutchinson	
Private T. Lewis	
Private T. Milne	

Private D. Ellis   (King's Shropshire Light Infantry)

Private Gilmour   (Argyll & Sutherland Highlanders)

Private L. Bates   (Welch Regiment)
Private C. Blewitt
Private Skeggs
Sapper A. Harrison   (Royal Engineers)

Appendix E:
No. 1 Special Boat Section (Eastern Mediterranean) 1941 and 1942

Captain R.J.A. Courtney (King's Royal Rifle Corps) later Major MC

Captain M.R.B. Kealy (Devonshire Regt) later Lt/Colonel

Captain R. Grant-Watson (Scots Guards)

Captain G.I.A. Duncan (Black Watch) MC and Bar

Captain R.K.B. Allott (Middlesex Regiment)

Captain Montgomerie

Captain H.A.D. Buchanan MC (Grenadier Guards)

Lieutenant T.R. Langton (Irish Guards) later Major MC

Lieutenant Ingles

Lieutenant D.G.R. Sutherland (Black Watch) later Lt/Colonel

Lieutenant Eric Newby (Black Watch) MC

Lieutenant M. Alexander

Lieutenant R. Wilson (Royal Artillery) later Lt/Colonel DSO (Bar)

L/Sergeant Warburton

Sergeant Allan (Royal Marines)

Sergeant G. Barnes (Grenadier Guards) later Captain MM

Sergeant W. Dunbar (Argyll & Sutherland Highlanders)

Sergeant Moss (Devonshire Regiment)

Sergeant R. Mallaby

Corporal J.B. Sherwood (Royal Army Service Corps) later Captain MM

Corporal G.C. Bremner (London Scottish) later Sergeant
DCM

Corporal I. Booth DCM

Corporal Severn

Corporal C. Feeberry, later Sergeant, DCM

Corporal E. Barr (Highland Light Infantry) later MM

Corporal Riley (Irish Guards)

Corporal Gurney

Corporal MacKenzie (Highland Light Infantry)

Corporal D. Pomford

Corporal D'Arcy

Corporal Duffy (Coldstream Guards)

Corporal Durand

Corporal H.H. Butler (South Lancashire Regiment) MM

Bombardier Brittlebank (Royal Artillery)

Marine W.G. Hughes

Marine Miles

Marine Barrow

Marine Harris

Marine Duggan

Marine Bick

Private G. Blake (Hampshire Regiment)

Private T. Watson

Private Edsall

Corporal Childs

Corporal J. White

(Errors and omissions regretted)

Appendix F:

No. 2 SBS at Ardrossan-Saltcoats, 1942

Major R.J.A. Courtney MC	(King's Royal Rifle Corps)
*Captain G.C.S. Montanaro DSO	(Royal Engineers) later Brigadier
Captain G.B. Courtney	(Royal West Kent Regiment) later Lt/Colonel MBE, MC
Lieut R.P. Livingstone	(Royal Ulster Rifles) later Major MBE
Lieut J. Kerr	(Highland Light Infantry) 'Charioteer' killed December. 1942
Lieut B.N. Eckhard	(The Buffs) later Captain
Lieut E.J.A. Lunn	(Royal Artillery) later Major MC and Bar
Lieut N.G. Kennard	(Gordon Highlanders) later Captain
Lieut D. Sidders	(Royal Welch Fusiliers) later Major MC
Lieut J.C.C. Pagnam	(Gordon Highlanders) later Captain
2nd/Lieut D. Smee	(Royal Artillery) later Lieutenant
2nd/Lieut H.V. Holden-White	(Royal Sussex Regiment) later Major MC
2nd/Lieut J.P. Foot	(Dorsetshire Regiment) later Captain MBE
2nd/Lieut P.A. Avton	(Argyll & Sutherland Highlanders) later Captain, Croix de Guerre
*Sergeant J. Embelin	(Royal Engineers) later WO II

*Sergeant D. Craig	(Royal Engineers) 'Charioteer'
*Sergeant S.T. Weatherall	(Duke of Wellington's Regiment) later Lieutenant
Corporal A.R. McClair	(Essex Regiment) later Captain
Corporal H. Quigley	later Lieutenant (Admin)
Corporal H.H. Austin	later Sergeant (Admin)
*Corporal L. Bates	(Welch Regiment) later Sergeant
Corporal G. Harrod	later Sergeant (Transport)
*L/Cpl N. Thompson	(Royal Engineers) later WO II MM
*L/Bdr J. Galloway	(Royal Artillery) later WO II
*Guardsman R. Sidlow	(Grenadier Guards) later Sergeant
*Trooper F. Preece DCM	(Royal Tank Regiment) later Sergeant
*Trooper J. Newsome	later Corporal
*Private A. Le M. Salisbury	later Sergeant
*Private J. Hutchinson	later Sergeant
*Private A. Milne	later Sergeant
*Private J. Gilmour	(Argyll & Sutherland Highlanders) later Sergeant
*Private D. Ellis	(King's Shropshire Light Infantry) later Sergeant MM
*Private G. Blewitt	later Sergeant
Private F. Hawkins	later Sergeant

*Denotes ex 101 Troop absorbed into No. 2 SBS 1.3.42.

Appendix G:
No. 2 SBS Reinforcements joined at Hillhead, 1943–4

Major M.R.B. Kealy   (Devonshire Regiment) Later
                          Lt/Colonel

Captain W.G. Davis   (Royal Artillery)
Captain W.   (Instructor in seamanship)
  Armstrong
Captain R. Davy   (Royal Artillery) Attached for
                          canoe training
Captain A. Colville   Attached for canoe training

Lieut R.J.M. Peters   Killed Burma
Lieut A. Sandford   (King's Own Scottish Borderers)
Lieut J. Rodney   (22nd Armoured Car Regiment
                          Canadian Army)

CSM G. Barnes MM
CSM J. Jones

Sergeant J.B.   (Royal Ulster Rifles) Later
  Sherwood MM   Captain
Sergeant E.A.W.   (Gordon Highlanders) Later
  Wesley   Captain MC

Corporal I. Booth   Later Sergeant
  DCM
Corporal J. Parkes

Corporal Loasby	Later Sergeant
Corporal E. Barr MM	(Highland Light Infantry)
Corporal H.H. Penn	(Bedfordshire & Hertfordshire Regiment) Later Sergeant
Corporal French	
L/Cpl A. Tough	Later Sergeant
L/Cpl G. Hanna	Later Corporal
Private Scruton	
Private F. Swain	Later Corporal
Private J. McKenzie	Later L/Cpl
Private R.W. Moore	(Welch Regiment) Later Corporal
Private B. Moores	
Private T. Wells	Later Corporal
Private C. Holding	Later Corporal
Private A. Harding	Later Bombardier
Private W. Merryweather	Later Corporal
Private H. Roberts	Later Sergeant
Private R. Boyes	
Private S.K. Gimlinge	Later Corporal
Private S. Longhurst	Later Corporal
Private J. Gains	Later Corporal
Private C. Dawkins	Later Sergeant
Gunner J. Morrison	Later Bombardier
Private R. Didcot	Later Corporal
Private C. King	Later Corporal
Private Miles	

Private R.E. Lovell	(Royal Artillery) Later Corporal
Private P. Hickman	Later Corporal
Private D.C. Toogood	(Hampshire Regiment) Later Corporal
Private R. Westow	(Royal Engineers) Later Corporal
Private F. Vick	
Private D.L. Roberts	(Royal Armoured Corps) Later Sergeant
Private J. Kilkenny	Later Corporal
Private D. Burns	(Royal Scots) Later Corporal
Private J. Summers	(King's Own Scottish Borderers)
Guardsman I. Lawson	(Coldstream Guards)
Private J. Carver	
Private H. Wright	
Private M. Smithson	(Royal Tank Regiment)
Private E. Palmer	(London Irish)
Private T. Williams	
Private S. Smith	(Bedfordshire & Hertfordshire Regiment) Later Sergeant
Private C. Kiernan	Later Corporal
Private E. Griffiths	Later Corporal
Private J. Watts	Later Corporal
Private A. Shearston	Later Corporal
Private L.J. Bell	Later Corporal
Private J. Black	Later Corporal
Private Buckley	
Private Hook	
Private Williams	
Private Tarbox	

Appendix H:
SBS with Small Operations Group (SOG) Ceylon and Burma, 1944–5

'A' GROUP SBS

Major H. V. Holden-White MC

Captain E. J. A. Lunn MC (later Major)
Captain D. W. Ryan

A/Captain G. Barnes MM

Lieut J. Rodney

Sergeant F. Hawkins
Sergeant H. A. Roberts
Sergeant A. Tough
Sergeant H. Wood

Corporal W. Merryweather
Corporal R. A. Westow
Corporal E. Griffiths
Corporal S. Longhurst
Corporal G. Hanna
Corporal G. Kiernan
Corporal L. J. Bell
Corporal J. Kilkenny
Corporal C. Holding
Corporal J. Morrison (storeman)
L/Corporal A. Edwards

Craftsman G. Wood
(Royal Electrical and Mechanical Engineers)

'B' GROUP SBS

Major M.R.B. Kealy
Major D.H. Sidders MC

Lieut R.J.M. Peters
Lieut E.A.W. Wesley MC

Sergeant A. Salisbury
Sergeant T. Williams MM
Sergeant C. Dawkins
Sergeant C. King

Corporal T. Wells
Corporal P. Hickman
Corporal J. Watt
Corporal K. Gimlinge
Corporal J. Black
Corporal A. Shearston

Bombardier A. Harding
Private F. Hollinshead

'C' GROUP SBS

Major R.P. Livingstone MBE

Captain J.B. Sherwood MM

Lieut S.T. Weatherall

Corporal R.W. Moore
Corporal R.E. Lovell
Corporal E.C. Palmer
Corporal J. Summers
Corporal H. Smithson

Lieut F.N. Best

Sergeant L. Bates
Sergeant S.R. Smith
Sergeant H.H.V. Penn
Sergeant D.L. Roberts

Corporal I. Lawson
Corporal D.C. Toogood
Corporal D.S. Burns
Corporal M. Smithson
Corporal F. Swain (storeman)
Corporal H. Wright (clerk)
L/Cpl McKenzie (storeman/driver)
Private R. Bridges
Private A. Britain

'Z' SBS (Far East) 1944–5
FORCE 136 (CEYLON)

Captain A.R. McClair
Captain J.P. Foot MBE

Sergeant R. Sidlow
Sergeant C. Blewett
Sergeant D. Ellis MM
Sergeant J. Gilmour

Private B. Moores

SO (AUSTRALIA)

Major G.B. Courtney MBE, MC
Captain N.G. Kennard

Captain W.G. Davis

WO II N. Thompson MM
WO II J. Galloway MM and Bar

Sergeant R. Preece DCM

November 1941	HMS/M *Triumph*	Agents to Greece
December 1941	HMS/M *Torbay*	Limpet raid – Navarino
January 1942	HMS/M *Triumph*	Objective unknown

1 SBS IN THE MEDITERRANEAN, 1942

January 1942	HMS/M *Triumph*	Objective unknown
January 1942	MTB	Pilot recovery near Gazala
January 1942	With 1 SAS overland	Raid on Bureat Harbour
January 1942	HMS/M *Urge*	Agent ferry to N. Africa
April 1942	HMS/M *Upholder*	Agent ferry to Tunisia
May 1942	MTB	Coastal reconnaissance
June 1942	Overland motor transport	Reconnaissance of Syrian coast
June 1942	With 1 SAS (s/m unknown)	Raid on Cretan airfields
August 1942	HMS/M *Una*	Raid on Sicilian airfields
August 1942	MTB	Raid on transport dump – Daba
September 1942	s/M *Papanikolis*	Raid on airfields – Rhodes
September 1942	HMS/M *Unbroken*	Mini torpedo raid – Crotone

Appendix I:
SBS Operations 1941–5

1 SBS IN THE MEDITERRANEAN, 1941

March 1941	HMS/M *Triumph*	Op. Cordite Beach Recce on Rhodes
April 1941	HMS/M *Triumph*	Commando raid on Bardia
April 1941	HMS/M *Triumph*	Offensive Patrol
June 1941	HMS/M *Taku*	Raid on Mersa Brega
June 1941	HMS/M *Urge*	Railway sabotage – Sicily
July 1941	HMS/M *Taku*	Limpet raid – Benghazi
July 1941	HMS/M *Utmost*	Railway sabotage – Italy
July 1941	HMS/M *Torbay*	Evacuation from Crete
August 1941	HMS/M *Utmost*	Railway sabotage – Italy
August 1941	HMS/M *Thrasher*	Evacuation from Crete
September 1941	HMS/M *Osiris*	Agent pick-up – Scutari
September 1941	HMS/M *Thunderbolt*	Agent ferry to Crete
September 1941	HMS/M *Utmost*	Railway sabotage – Italy
September 1941	HMS/M *Triumph*	Agents to Greece
October 1941	HMS/M *Truant*	Railway sabotage – Italy
November 1941	HMS/MS *Torbay/Talisman*	Raid on Rommel HQ

2 SBS IN EUROPE AND MEDITERRANEAN 1942–3

April 1942	Motor Launch	Limpet raid – Boulogne Harbour
October 1942	HMS/M *Seraph*	Secret visit to Algeria
November 1942	HMS/M *Seraph*	Evacuation of General Giraud
November 1942	5 submarines	North African landings
November 1942	HMS *Hartland* *Walney*	Assault on Oran
	Op. J.V.	
	Op. FLAGPOLE	
	Op. KINGPIN	
	Op. TORCH	
	Op. RESERVIST	
November 1942	HMS/M *Ursula*	Railway sabotage – Italy
		Beach recce –Channel Islands
March 1943	MTB	Op. FORFAR LOVE	Snatch raid – Dunkirk
July 1943	MGB		
December 1943	*Dory*	Op. HARDTACK 28	Deception raid – Channel Islands
December 1943	*Dory*	Op. HARDTACK 2	Deception raid – Gravelines

'Z' SBS (MEDITERRANEAN AND FAR EAST)
1943–5

April 1943	HMS/M *Trident*	Op. ETNA	Agent ferry to Corsica
May 1943	HMS/M *Trident*		Agent/stores ferry – Corsica
June 1943	HMS/M *Safari*	Op. MARIGOLD	Deception raid – Sardinia

June 1943	HMS/M *Sportsman*	Agent ferry to Italy
June 1943	HMS/M *Severn*	Boat duty – 1 SAS Sardinia
June 1943	MTB	Raid with 1 SAS Lampedusa
July 1943	HMS/M *Severn*	Hawthorn pick-up with SAS Op. HAWTHORN
August 1943	HMS/M *Shakespeare*	Beach recce – Salerno
August 1943	HMS/M *Seraph*	Agent ferry to N. Italy
September 1943	HMS/M *Sickle*	Agent ferry to N. Italy
October 1943	S/M *Curie*	Railway sabotage (aborted)
November 1943	MAS boat	Beach recce – Anzio
November 1943	MAS boat	Beach recce – Anzio
March 1943	US/PT boat	Beach recce – Anzio
March 1944	HMS/M *Unruly*	Deception – Greek Islands
March 1944	HMS/M *Sybil*	Deception – Greek Islands
August 1944	HMS/M *Sybil*	Deception – Greek Islands
October 1944	HMS/M *Severn*	Agent ferry – Malaya
October 1944	Catalina Flying-Boat (PBY)	Agent ferry – Thailand
February 1945	HMS/M *Telemachus* Op. CARPENTER	Agent ferry – Malaya
February 1945	HMS/M *Thule*	Agent ferry – Malaya
February 1945	HMS/M *Telemachus*	Agent ferry – Malaya

SBS IN THE INDIAN OCEAN, 1944–5

September 1944 HMS/M *Trenchant* Op. SPRATT BAKER
Railway sabotage – Sumatra
September 1944 HMS/M *Terrapin* Op. SPRATT ABLE
Railway sabotage – Sumatra

From September 1944 to early February 1945, 'A', 'B' and 'C' Groups carried out between them some eighteen operations on the Arakan coast from MTBs. From February to June 1945, 'A' and 'B' Groups carried out many reconnaissances and fighting patrols on the River Irrawaddy.

The official Combined Operations historian has credited SBS in the Burma campaign with more than eighty sorties in all.

Appendix J:
Submarines which carried SBS

March 1941	HMS/M *Triumph*	Lt/Cmdr W.J.W. Woods
April 1941	HMS/M *Triumph*	Lt/Cmdr W.J.W. Woods
April 1941	HMS/M *Triumph*	Lt/Cmdr W.J.W. Woods
June 1941	HMS/M *Taku*	Lt/Cmdr E.C.F. Nicolay
June 1941	HMS/M *Urge*	Lt E.P. Tompkinson
July 1941	HMS/M *Taku*	Lt/Cmdr E.C.F. Nicolay
July 1941	HMS/M *Utmost*	Lt/Cmdr R.D. Cayley
August 1941	HMS/M *Torbay*	Lt/Cmdr A.C.C. Miers
August 1941	HMS/M *Utmost*	Lt/Cmdr R.D. Cayley
September 1941	HMS/M *Osiris*	Lt R.S. Brookes
September 1941	HMS/M *Thunderbolt*	Lt/Cmdr C.B. Crouch
September 1941	HMS/M *Utmost*	Lt/Cmdr R.D. Cayley
October 1941	HMS/M *Truant*	Lt/Cmdr H.A. Haggard
November 1941	HMS/M *Torbay/Talisman*	Lt/Cmdr W. Willmott
December 1941	HMS/M *Torbay*	Cmdr A.C.C. Miers

January 1942	HMS/M *Triumph*	Lt J.S. Huddart
January 1942	HMS/M *Urge*	Lt E.P. Tompkinson
April 1942	HMS/M *Upholder*	Lt/Cmdr M.D. Wanklyn
August 1942	HMS/M *Una*	Lt C.P. Norman
September 1942	S/M *Papanikolis*	Lt H. Roussen RHW
September 1942	HMS/M *Unbroken*	Lt A.C.G. Mars
September 1942	HMS/M *Traveller*	Lt M.B. St John
October 1942	HMS/M *Seraph*	Lt N.L.A. Jewell
November 1942	HMS/M *Seraph*	Lt N.L.A. Jewell
November 1942	HMS/M *Ursula*	*P.54, P.221, P.48, P.45.*
November 1942	HMS/M *Ursula*	Lt R.B. Lakin
January 1943	HMS/M *P.311*	Cmdr R.D. Cayley
April 1943	HMS/M *Trident*	Lt P.E. Newstead
May 1943	HMS/M *Trident*	Lt P.E. Newstead
June 1943	HMS/M *Safari*	Lt R.B. Lakin
June 1943	HMS/M *Sportsman*	Lt R. Gatehouse
June 1943	HMS/M *Severn*	Lt/Cmdr A.N.G. Campbell
August 1943	HMS/M *Shakespeare*	Lt M.F.R. Ainslie
August 1943	HMS/M *Seraph*	Lt N.L.A. Jewell

September 1943	HMS/M *Sickle*	Lt J.R. Drummond
October 1943	S/M *Curie*	Lt de Vaisseau P.M. Sonneville
March 1944	HMS/M *Unruly*	Lt/Cmdr A.C.G. Mars
March 1944	HMS/M *Sybil*	Lt E.J.D. Turner
August 1944	HMS/M *Severn*	Lt R.H. Bull
August 1944	HMS/M *Clyde*	Lt/Cmdr R.S. Brookes
September 1944	HMS/M *Trenchant*	Lt/Cmdr D.R. Hezlet
September 1944	HMS/M *Terrapin*	Lt R.H. Brunner
October 1944	HMS/M *Telemachus*	Cmdr W.D.A. King
February 1945	HMS/M *Thule*	Lt/Cmdr A.C.G. Mars
February 1945	HMS/M *Telemachus*	Cmdr W.D.A. King

Appendix K:
SBS Casualties 1941–5

No. 1 SBS

Captain Grant-Watson (Scots Guards)	Drowned December 1941
Captain H.A.D. Buchanan (Grenadier Guards)	POW August 1942
Captain G.I.A. Duncan (Black Watch)	POW August 1942
Captain R.K.B. Allott (Middlesex Regiment)	POW September 1942
Captain R. Wilson DSO (Royal Artillery)	POW September 1942
Lieutenant M. Alexander	POW August 1942
Lieutenant E. Newby (Black Watch)	POW August 1942
Sergeant Allan (Royal Marines)	POW July 1941
Sergeant Dunbar	POW August 1942
Sergeant Moss (Devonshire Regiment)	POW September 1942
Corporal I. Booth DCM	POW August 1942
Corporal Duffy (Coldstream Guards)	POW August 1942
Corporal Gurney	POW August 1942
Corporal Severn	Killed January 1942

Corporal MacKenzie (Highland Light Infantry)   POW September 1942

Corporal Childs   Killed January 1942
Corporal Butler   POW August 1942
Bombardier Brittlebank (Royal Artillery)   POW September 1942
Marine Miles (Royal Marines)   POW July 1941
Marine Barrow (Royal Marines)   POW September 1942
Marine Harris (Royal Marines)   POW September 1942
Private Blake (Hampshire Regiment) POW September 1942

No.2 SBS

Captain P. A. Ayton (Argyll & Sutherland Highlanders)   Died of wounds December 1943
Lieutenant J. Kerr (Highland Light Infantry) 'Charioteer'   Killed December 1942
Lieutenant R. J. M. Peters   Killed, Burma, February 1945
WO II J. Embelin (Royal Engineers)   Killed, Oran, November 1942
Sergeant A. Milne   Missing believed killed June 1943
Sergeant Loasby   Missing believed killed June 1943
Corporal J. Parkes   Killed, France, December 1943
Corporal E. C. Palmer   Died of wounds, Burma, January 1945

(With apologies for errors and omissions)

Appendix L:

COPP Army Personnel – as at 1 April 1944
Taken from the COPP Nominal Roll of that date. Listed
alphabetically

Name	Rank	Regiment	COPP No	Remarks
Adamson, R.	Sapper	R.E.	4	
Blackmore, H.	Sgt	R.E.	2	
Booth, G.F.	Spr	R.E.	6	
Bromfield, D.G.	L/Cpl	R.E.	2	
Cockram, R.P.	Spr	R.E.	3	
Colson, A.F.L.	Capt.	R.E.	8	MBE.
Cumberland, J.	Cpl	Royal Scots	8	
Davidson, T.	L/Sgt	R.E.	4	
Duffy, J.	Spr	R.E.	8	
Edgeley, F.	Spr	R.E.	5	
Foley, D.M.	Spr	R.E.	Depot	
Francis J.H.	Spr	R.E.	6	
Freeman D.R.	Capt.	R.E.	2	
Gale, D.S.	Cpl	R.E.	9	
Gammidge, F.	Cpl	R.E.	3	Killed Far East
Gates, R.H.C.	Lieut.	R.E.	5	
Gray, E.A.	Cpl	Hampshires.	6	
Griffith, J.B.	Capt.	R.E.	4	

Name	Rank	Regiment	COPP No	Remarks
Hawkin, J.	Spr	R.E.	1	
Hinkley, J.B.	Spr	R.E.	9	
Johns, W.E.F.	Capt.	R.E.	3	Killed Far East
Kedge, R.W.M.	L/Cpl	R.E.	1	
Lamb, J.C.	Capt.	R.E.	10	
Lamont, P.	Cpl	Royal Scots	10	
Lewis, G.B.	Capt.	R.E.	9	
Lloyd Jones, G.R.	Spr	R.E.	2	
Lucas, P.W.T.	Capt.	R.E.	7	
McCarey, H.	Spr	R.E.	10	
Mackenzie, I.C.C.	Capt.	R.E.	6	
McNally, F.	WO II	R.E.	Depot	
Morrison, A.A.	Spr	R.E.	7	
Ogden-Smith, B.W.	Sgt	East Surreys	1	DCM, MM
Owen, D.J.	Cpl	Beds & Herts	7	
Plummer, J. W.	L/Cpl	R.E.	Depot	
Poole, G.J.H.	Spr	R.E.	9	
Powell, J.	Cpl	R.E.	5	MBE, MM Ret'd Major
Salter, A.C.	Spr	R.E.	Depot	
Scott-Bowden, L.	Major	R.E.	1	DSO, MC
Smith, J.R.	L/Cpl	R.E.	5	
Tanner, R.R.	Spr	R.E.	4	
Young, C.G.	Spr	R.E.	3	

Additional personnel held on strength before 1.4.44.

Name	Rank	Regiment	COPP No	Remarks
Burbridge, G.N.	Capt.	R.C.E.	3	Drowned Sicily 1943
Cooke, E.	Sgt	R.E.	1	
Crane, J.	Capt	R.E.	6	
Eckhard, B.N.	Capt.	Buffs.	1	
Hunter,	Capt.	R.E.	6	
Kingston,	Lieut	R.E.		
Lomas, J.	Sgt	R.E.	3	
Matterson, P.D.	Capt.	R.E.	5	MC
Mills,	Capt.	R.E.		
Page, E.	Sgt	R.E.		
Parsons,	Capt.	R.E.	4	
Rice,	Capt.	R.E.	6	
Williamson, R.A.	Cpl	Royal Scots.	5	

[With apologies for errors and omissions]

Bibliography

ANSCOMBE, Charles, *Submariner* (Kimber, 1957)

BAXTER, R., *Stand by to Surface* (Cassel, 1944)

BULL, Peter, *To Sea in a Sieve* (Peter Davies, 1956)

CHURCHILL, Winston, *The Second World War*, VOL IV (Cassell, 1951)

COOK, Graeme, *Silent Marauders* (Hart-Davis, 1976)

COPE, H.P. & KARIG W., *Battle Submerged* (W.W. Norton, N.Y., 1951)

COWLES, V.S., *The Phantom Major* (Collins, 1958)

FELL, W.R., *The Sea our Shield* (Cassell, 1956)

FERGUSSON, Bernard, *The Watery Maze* (Collins, 1961)

GLEESON, James and WALDRON, Tom, *Now It Can Be Told* (Elek, 1951)

HARRISSON, Tom, *The World Within* (Crescent Press, 1959)

HART, S., *Discharged Dead* (Odhams, 1956)

HART, S., *H.M. Submarine Upholder* (Oldbourne, 1960)

HOWARTH, P.J.F., *Special Operations* (Routledge & Keegan Paul, 1955)

JEWELL, N.L.A., *Secret Mission Submarine* (Ziff-Davis, N.Y., 1944)

KEMP, P.K., *H.M. Submarines* (Herbert Jenkins, 1952)

KING, W.D.A.E., *The Stick and the Stars* (Hutchinson, 1958)

LADD, J.A., *Commandos and Rangers of World War II* (Jane's, 1978)

LADD, J.A., *The Royal Marines 1919–1980* (Jane's, 1980)

LAPOTIER, H.A.M., *Raiders from the Sea* (Kimber, 1954)

LOCKHART, R.B., *The Marines were there* (Putnam, 1950)

LODWICK, John, *The Filibusters* (Methuen, 1947)

MARS, Alastair, *HMS Thule Intercepts* (Elek, 1956)

MARS, Alastair, *Unbroken* (in *Three Great Sea Stories*) (Collins, 1958)

MASKELYNE, Jasper, *Magic – Top Secret* (Stanley Paul, 1945)

MASTERS, D., *Up Periscope* (Eyre & Spottiswoode, 1942)

MAUND, L.E.H., *Assault from the Sea* (Methuen, 1949)

NEVILLE, R., *Survey by Starlight* (Hodder, 1949)

NEWBY, E., *Love and War in the Apennines* (Hodder, 1971)

ROBERTSON, Terence, *The Ship with Two Captains* (Evans, 1957)

SIMPSON, G.W.G., *Periscope View* (Macmillan, 1972)

SAUNDERS, H. St G, *The Green Beret* (Michael Joseph, 1949)

SLIM, F/M Sir William, *Defeat into Victory* (Cassell, 1956)

STRUTTON, Bill and PEARSON, Michael, *The Secret Invaders* (Hodder, 1958)

Time-Life Books, *The Commandos* (Time-Life Books, 1981)

VERNEY, John, *Going to the Wars* (Collins, 1966)

WARNER, Philip, *The Special Air Service* (Kimber, 1971)

WARREN, C.E.T. and BENSON, James, *Above us the Waves* (White Lion, 1971)

WHITEHOUSE, Arch, *Subs and Submarines* (Frederick Muller, 1963)

WILKINSON, J.B., *By Sea and by Stealth* (Coward-McCann, 1956)
YOUNG, Edward, *One of our Submarines* (Hart-Davis, 1952)

Index

Compiled by I. D. Crane